Southern GUI
California
Backroads &
4-Wheel Drive
Trails

By CHARLES A. WELLS

Easy • Moderate • Difficult
Backcountry Driving Adventures

FunTreks, Inc.

Published by FunTreks, Inc.
P.O. Box 3127, Monument, CO 80132-3127
Phone: Toll free 877-222-7623, Fax: (719) 277-7411
E-mail: books@funtreks.com
Web site: www.funtreks.com

Edited by Shelley Mayer

Cover design, photography, maps, and production by Charles A. Wells

First Edition

Library of Congress Control Number 2002117630
ISBN 0-9664976-4-3

Printed in the United States of America

To order additional books, call toll-free 1-877-222-7623 or use order form in back
of this book. You may also order online at www.funtreks.com.

TRAIL UPDATES:
For latest trail updates and changes, check the Trail Updates page on our Web site
at www.funtreks.com.

GUARANTEE OF SATISFACTION:
If you are dissatisfied with this book in any way, regardless of where you bought it,
please call our toll-free number during business hours at 1-877-222-7623. We
promise to do whatever it takes to make you happy.

DISCLAIMER

Travel in California's backcountry is, by its very nature, potentially
dangerous and could result in property damage, injury, or even death.
The scope of this book cannot predict every possible hazard you may
encounter. If you drive any of the trails in this book, you acknowledge
these risks and assume full responsibility. You are the final judge as to
whether a trail is safe to drive on any given day, whether your vehicle is
capable of the journey, and what supplies you should carry. The information contained herein cannot replace good judgment and proper prep-
aration on your part. The publisher and author of this book disclaim any
and all liability for bodily injury, death, or property damage that could
occur to you or any of your passengers.

ACKNOWLEDGMENTS

I am very much indebted to the following individuals and organizations who helped with this book:

U.S. Forest Service, Bureau of Land Management, California State Parks, Anza-Borrego Desert State Park, Death Valley National Park and Joshua Tree National Park. I worked with a long list of hard-working staffers who provided courteous and professional advice. Special thanks to Mike Ahrens of the BLM in Barstow, Bill Cook, a BLM volunteer and expert on the Calico Mountains, Greg Hoffman, OHV Coordinator with the San Bernardino National Forest and Mike Rizzo, a volunteer ranger with the San Bernardino National Forest who guided me on Cucamonga Mountain.

Gene McKenney, a long-time, former member of the Riverside 4-Wheelers who spent many days showing me his favorite trails in California including the Mojave Road and the Panamint Mountains. He introduced me to Steve Allison, an active Riverside 4-Wheeler who along with Carl Williams, Gary Karp and Dale Smith, took me on many more runs.

Jim Cowling and Roy Peace of the San Diego 4-Wheelers. After wheeling with them in Arizona, I joined them on runs at Superstition Mountain where they introduced me to Ed Webster, club expert on the mountain. He gave me a first-class tour and some good route-finding tips. Others who helped included: Liz Cowling, Dustin Webster, David & Julie Grimmes, Dave & Dorys Prentice, Jody Everding, Kelly Marquis, Roger Baggett, Mark Sutton and Dom Sandoval.

Chuck Shaner and Jim Atkins of the Victor Valley 4-Wheelers who took me through Sledgehammer without a scratch. A big thanks to all club members who helped build the *Hammers* trails. Thanks also to Fuzzy Winters and Joe Likins for their advice.

Frenchie La Chance of Western Adventures 4x4 Driving School and Guide Service. He graciously shared his decades of southern California driving experience and sat down with me for hours plotting trails on maps.

Joe and Rachel Branch of the Tierra Del Sol Club for guiding me through Truckhaven. Also, John Stewart and Ken Osborne for providing pictures of the popular Tierra Del Sol Desert Safari. I'd also like to thank Rob Estes and Mark Dunham for guiding me through Doran Canyon, Sam Cochran, Jr. for his help with Smugglers Cave/ Elliot Mine and Bill Evans on Mortero Wash. Thanks to countless others who participated in trail runs and allowed me to take their photographs.

My own club, the Colorado Four-Wheelers in Colorado Springs, who first introduced me to four-wheeling and have supported me over the years.

Shelley Mayer, a respected editor and writer in Colorado Springs, for her thorough editing of this book.

Last but not least, my wife, Beverly, and daughter, Marcia Levault, for their encouragement and assistance.

Easy portion of Goler Wash (Trail #7) below difficult side trip to Lotus Mine.

Contents

Page *Topic*

6   Trails Listed by Area (& ATV trails specified)

7   Trail Locator Map

8   Trails Listed by Difficulty, Ratings Defined

10   Trails Listed Alphabetically, Author's Favorites

11   INTRODUCTION

12   Keeping It Simple

13   Selecting the Right Trail for Your Vehicle

13   California Laws, Licensing and Fees

14   ATVs and Dirt Bikes

15   OHV Areas and SVRAs

15   National Parks and Forests

16   Anza-Borrego Desert State Park, Mojave National Preserve

17   Safety Tips

18   Desert Survival

20   Checklist

21   Your Responsibilities as a Backcountry Driver

23   Backcountry Driving Lessons

29   Final Comments

30   Map Legend

31   THE TRAILS (Individual trails listed on next page)

32   Area 1-   Death Valley National Park, Panamint Mountains

58   Area 2-   Santa Barbara, North of Los Angeles, Hungry Valley

82   Area 3-   Barstow, Calico Mountains

104   Area 4-   The Mojave Road

118   Area 5-   Inland Empire, San Bernardino

132   Area 6-   Big Bear, Lake Arrowhead

164   Area 7-   Anza-Borrego Desert, Ocotillo Wells, Truckhaven

186   Area 8-   Anza-Borrego Desert, Corral Canyon, Ocotillo

224   Area 9-   Superstition Mountain, Imperial Sand Dunes

238   Area 10-   Other Trails

259   APPENDIX

260   GPS Basics

264   GPS Waypoint Coordinates

277   Glossary

278   References & Reading

279   Addresses & Phone Numbers

282   Index

286   The Author & His Vehicles

Trails Listed by Area

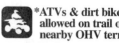

*ATVs & dirt bikes allowed on trail or nearby OHV terrain.

Pg. No./ Trail, Rating (Easy, Mod., Diff.)

32 AREA 1
Death Valley National Park,
Panamint Mountains

34 1. Titus Canyon (**E**)
36 2. Chloride City (**M**)
38 3. Cottonwood/ Marble Cyn.(**M**)
40 4. Echo Pass/ Inyo Mine (**D**)
44 5. Jail Canyon (**M**)
46 6. Pleasant Cyn./ South Park (**D**)
50 7. Goler Wash/ Mengel Pass (**D**)
54 8. Butte Valley (**E**)
56 9. Fish Canyon Escape Trail (**E**)

58 AREA 2
Santa Barbara, North of
Los Angeles, Hungry Valley

60 10. Santa Ynez Peak (**E**)
62 11. Agua Caliente Springs (**E**)*
64 12. Lockwood/Miller Jeep Trail (**D**)*
68 13. Alamo Mountain Loop (**E**)*
70 14. Pronghorn Trail (**M**)*
72 15. Liebre Mountain (**E**)
74 16. Rowher Trail (**D**)*
78 17. Sierra Pelona Road (**E**)*

82 AREA 3
Barstow, Calico Mountains

84 18. Wall St. Canyon Overlook (**E**)*
88 19. Doran Loop (**D**)*
92 20. Odessa Canyon (**D**)*
96 21. Phillips Loop (**M**)*
98 22. Mule Canyon Road (**E**)*
100 23. Achy-Breaky (**D**)*

104 AREA 4
The Mojave Road

106 24. Mojave Road East (**M**)*
110 25. Mojave Road Central (**M**)
114 26. Mojave Road West (**M**)*

118 AREA 5
Inland Empire, San Bernadino

120 27. Rincon-Shortcut Road (**E**)*
122 28. Cucamonga Big Tree Trail (**M**)
126 29. Cleghorn Ridge (**E**)*
128 30. Pilot Rock Road (**M**)*
130 31. Santiago Peak (**M**)

132 AREA 6
Big Bear, Lake Arrowhead

134 32. Grapevine Canyon (**M**)*
136 33. Willow Creek Road (**E**)*
138 34. Dishpan Springs (**D**)*
140 35. Holcomb Creek (**D**)*

144 36. Butler Peak (**E**)
146 37. John Bull Trail (**D**)*
148 38. Jacoby Canyon (**M**)
150 39. Gold Mountain (**D**)
152 40. Clarks Summit (**M**)
156 41. Skyline Drive (**E**)
158 42. Heartbreak Ridge (**D**)*
162 43. Rattlesnake Canyon (**M**)

164 AREA 7
Anza-Borrego Desert,
Ocotillo Wells, Truckhaven

166 44. Lower Coyote Canyon (**M**)
168 45. Calcite Mine (**D**)
170 46. Truckhaven (**D**)
174 47. Fonts Point (**E**)
176 48. The Slot (**D**)
178 49. Ocotillo Wells SVRA (**E**)*
182 50. Pumpkin Patch (**M**)*
184 51. Cross Over Trail (**M**)*

186 AREA 8
Anza-Borrego Desert,
Corral Canyon, Ocotillo

188 52. Oriflamme Canyon (**M**)
190 53. Blair Valley (**E**)
194 54. Pinyon Mountain Road (**D**)
198 55. Sandstone Canyon (**E**)
200 56. Canyon Sin Nombre (**E**)
202 57. Mud Caves/Diablo Dropoff (**D**)
206 58. Mortero Wash (**M**)
210 59. Los Pinos Lookout (**M**)*
214 60. Bronco Peak (**D**)*
216 61. Sidewinder (**D**)*
218 62. McCain Valley (**E**)*
220 63. Table Mountain (**M**)
222 64. Smugglers Cave/Elliot Mine (**D**)*

224 AREA 9
Superstition Mountain,
Imperial Sand Dunes

226 65. Superstition Mtn. Loop (**E**)*
230 66. Sand Dam Canyon (**M**)*
232 67. Knock-on-Wood (**D**)*
234 68. Sand Highway (**E**)*
236 69. Glamis/Oldsmobile Hill (**D**)*

238 AREA 10 Other Trails
240 70. Last Chance Canyon (**M**)
244 71. Trona Pinnacles (**E**)
246 72. Dumont Dunes (**D**)*
248 73. Sperry Wash (**E**)*
252 74. Sledgehammer Canyon (**D**)*
256 75. Berdoo Canyon (**M**)

6

Trail Locator Map

Easy Trails
Moderate Trails
Difficult Trails

*See individual area maps
for more detail.*

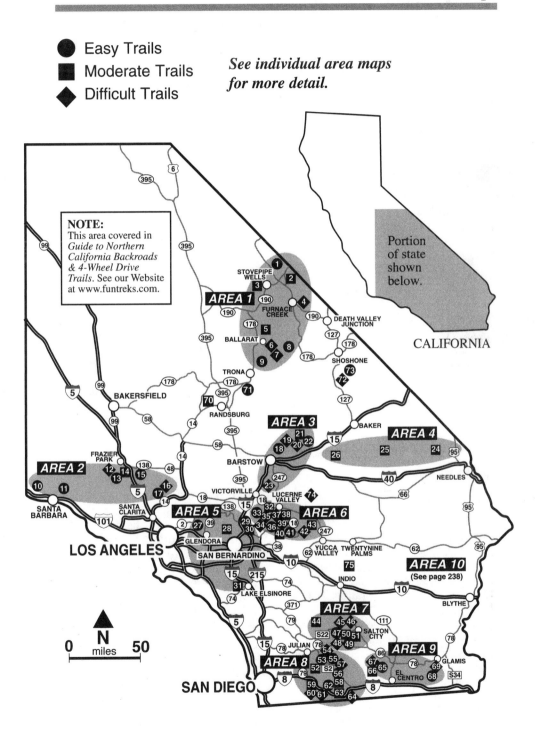

CALIFORNIA

Portion
of state
shown
below.

NOTE:
This area covered in
*Guide to Northern
California Backroads
& 4-Wheel Drive
Trails*. See our Website
at www.funtreks.com.

Trails Listed by Difficulty

● Easy

Trails are grouped into three major categories: easy, moderate and difficult. Within each group, trails at the top of the list are easier than at the bottom. If you drive a trail and find it too easy, try one lower on the list. Conversely, if you find a trail too difficult, try one higher on the list. You may have to skip several trails on the list to find a significant difference.

Easier

More Difficult

Pg.	No./Trail
218	62. McCain Valley
244	71. Trona Pinnacles
72	15. Liebre Mountain
174	47. Fonts Point
156	41. Skyline Drive
34	1. Titus Canyon
62	11. Agua Caliente Springs
190	53. Blair Valley
60	10. Santa Ynez Peak
198	55. Sandstone Canyon
54	8. Butte Valley
68	13. Alamo Mountain Loop
98	22. Mule Canyon Road
120	27. Rincon-Shortcut Road
144	36. Butler Peak
136	33. Willow Creek Road
248	73. Sperry Wash
78	17. Sierra Pelona Road
234	68. Sand Highway
200	56. Canyon Sin Nombre
178	49. Ocotillo Wells SVRA
126	29. Cleghorn Ridge
56	9. Fish Canyon Escape Trail
84	18. Wall Street Canyon Overlook
226	65. Superstition Mountain Loop

Trail Ratings Defined ➡

Trail ratings are very subjective. Conditions change for many reasons, including weather and time of year. An easy trail can quickly become difficult when washed out by a rainstorm or blocked by a fallen rock. You must be the final judge of a trail's condition on the day you drive it. If any part of a trail is difficult, the entire trail is rated difficult. You may be able to drive a significant portion of a trail before reaching the difficult spot. Read each trail description carefully for specific information.

Easy: Gravel, dirt, clay, sand, or mildly rocky road. Gentle grades. Water levels low except during periods of heavy runoff. Full-width single lane or wider with adequate room to pass most of the time. Where shelf conditions exist, road is wide and well-maintained with minor sideways tilt. Four-wheel drive recommended on most trails but some are suitable for two-wheel drive under dry conditions. Clay surface roads, when wet, can significantly increase difficulty.

■ Moderate ◆ Difficult

Pg.	No./Trail		Pg.	No./Trail
206	58. Mortero Wash		176	48. The Slot
162	43. Rattlesnake Canyon		202	57. Mud Caves/Diablo Dropoff
148	38. Jacoby Canyon		40	4. Echo Pass/Inyo Mine
256	75. Berdoo Canyon		50	7. Goler Wash/Mengel Pass
110	25. Mojave Road Central		150	39. Gold Mountain
128	30. Pilot Rock Road		236	69. Glamis/Oldsmobile Hill
106	24. Mojave Road East		168	45. Calcite Mine
130	31. Santiago Peak		246	72. Dumont Dunes
220	63. Table Mountain		46	6. Pleasant Canyon/South Park
188	52. Oriflamme Canyon		194	54. Pinyon Mountain Road
114	26. Mojave Road West		222	64. Smugglers Cave/Elliot Mine
36	2. Chloride City		158	42. Heartbreak Ridge
38	3. Cottonwood/Marble Canyon		74	16. Rowher Trail
152	40. Clarks Summit		140	35. Holcomb Creek
96	21. Phillips Loop		92	20. Odessa Canyon
134	32. Grapevine Canyon		138	34. Dishpan Springs
70	14. Pronghorn Trail		64	12. Lockwood/Miller Jeep Trail
184	51. Cross Over Trail		216	61. Sidewinder
44	5. Jail Canyon		170	46. Truckhaven
182	50. Pumpkin Patch		214	60. Bronco Peak
210	59. Los Pinos Lookout		146	37. John Bull Trail
122	28. Cucamonga Big Tree Trail		232	67. Knock-on-Wood
230	66. Sand Dam Canyon		100	23. Achy-Breaky
166	44. Lower Coyote Canyon		88	19. Doran Loop
240	70. Last Chance Canyon		252	74. Sledgehammer Canyon

Moderate: Rutted dirt or rocky road suitable for most sport utility vehicles. Careful tire placement often necessary. Four-wheel drive, low range, and high ground clearance required. Standard factory skid plates and tow hooks recommended on many trails. Undercarriage may scrape occasionally. Some grades fairly steep but manageable if dry. Soft sand possible. Sideways tilt will require caution. Narrow shelf roads possible. Backing may be necessary to pass. Water depths passable for stock high-clearance vehicles except during periods of heavy runoff. Mud holes may be present especially in the spring. Rock-stacking may be necessary in some cases. Brush may touch vehicle.

Difficult: Some trails suitable for more aggressive stock vehicles but most trails require vehicle modification. Lifts, differential lockers, aggressive articulation, and/or winches recommended in many cases. Skid plates and tow hooks required. Body damage possible. Grades can be steep with severe ground undulation. Sideways tilt can be extreme. Sand hills very steep with soft downslopes. Deep water crossings possible. Shelf roads extremely narrow; use caution in full-size vehicle. Read trail description carefully. Passing may be difficult with backing required for long distances. Brush may scratch sides of vehicle.

Trails Listed Alphabetically

Pg. No./Trail, Rating (Easy, Mod., Diff.)

100 23. Achy-Breaky (**D**)
62 11. Agua Caliente Springs (**E**)
68 13. Alamo Mountain Loop (**E**)
256 75. Berdoo Canyon (**M**)
190 53. Blair Valley (**E**)
214 60. Bronco Peak (**D**)
144 **36. Butler Peak (E)**
54 **8. Butte Valley (E)**
168 45. Calcite Mine (**D**)
200 56. Canyon Sin Nombre (**E**)
36 **2. Chloride City (M)**
152 **40. Clarks Summit (M)**
126 **29. Cleghorn Ridge (E)**
38 3. Cottonwood/Marble Cyn. (**M**)
184 51. Cross Over Trail (**M**)
122 **28. Cucamonga Big Tree Trail (M)**
138 **34. Dishpan Springs (D)**
88 19. Doran Loop (**D**)
246 72. Dumont Dunes (**D**)
40 **4. Echo Pass/Inyo Mine (D)**
56 9. Fish Canyon Escape Trail (**E**)
174 **47. Fonts Point (E)**
236 69. Glamis/Oldsmobile Hill (**D**)
150 39. Gold Mountain (**D**)
50 **7. Goler Wash/Mengel Pass (D)**
134 **32. Grapevine Canyon (M)**
158 42. Heartbreak Ridge (**D**)
140 35. Holcomb Creek (**D**)
148 38. Jacoby Canyon (**M**)
44 5. Jail Canyon (**M**)
146 **37. John Bull Trail (D)**
232 67. Knock-on-Wood (**D**)
240 70. Last Chance Canyon (**M**)
72 15. Liebre Mountain (**E**)
64 **12. Lockwood/Miller Jeep Tr. (D)**
210 59. Los Pinos Lookout (**M**)
166 **44. Lower Coyote Canyon (M)**
218 62. McCain Valley (**E**)
110 **25. Mojave Road Central (M)**

Pg. No./Trail, Rating (Easy, Mod., Diff.)

106 24. Mojave Road East (**M**)
114 **26. Mojave Road West (M)**
206 58. Mortero Wash (**M**)
202 57. Mud Caves/Diablo Dropoff (**D**)
98 22. Mule Canyon Road (**E**)
178 **49. Ocotillo Wells SVRA (E)**
92 **20. Odessa Canyon (D)**
188 52. Oriflamme Canyon (**M**)
96 21. Phillips Loop (**M**)
128 30. Pilot Rock Road (**M**)
194 **54. Pinyon Mountain Road (D)**
46 **6. Pleasant Cyn./South Park (D)**
70 14. Pronghorn Trail (**M**)
182 **50. Pumpkin Patch (M)**
162 43. Rattlesnake Canyon (**M**)
120 27. Rincon-Shortcut Road (**E**)
74 16. Rowher Trail (**D**)
230 66. Sand Dam Canyon (**M**)
234 **68. Sand Highway (E)**
198 **55. Sandstone Canyon (E)**
60 10. Santa Ynez Peak (**E**)
130 31. Santiago Peak (**M**)
216 61. Sidewinder (**D**)
78 17. Sierra Pelona Road (**E**)
156 **41. Skyline Drive (E)**
252 **74. Sledgehammer Canyon (D)**
222 **64. Smugglers Cave/Elliot Mine (D)**
248 73. Sperry Wash (**E**)
226 **65. Superstition Mtn. Loop (E)**
220 63. Table Mountain (**M**)
176 48. The Slot (**D**)
34 **1. Titus Canyon (E)**
244 71. Trona Pinnacles (**E**)
170 46. Truckhaven (**D**)
84 18. Wall Street Cyn. Overlook (**E**)
136 33. Willow Creek Road (**E**)

Author's favorite trails are shown in boldface type.

10

INTRODUCTION

First part of Odessa Canyon, Trail #20.

Introduction

Like so many people, I bought my first four-wheel-drive SUV for practical reasons—more cargo room and good traction in bad weather. At first, I stayed on pavement, never giving a second thought to what lies beyond. Then one day, my curiosity took me down a rough dirt road. I started tentatively, not knowing what to expect. Would I cut my tires? ...scratch my paint? ...damage my undercarriage? Gradually, as each new exciting mile passed without a problem, I became more confident. My vehicle was doing just fine and I was having a ball. Each new trail I drove brought more enjoyment. Today, I continue to drive my stock SUV on easy and moderate roads and the feeling hasn't changed. I love it. I look back and wonder why I wasted all those years clinging to the pavement.

In recent years, I've learned the hard-core side of four-wheeling. I joined a four-wheel-drive club and modified a second vehicle. I've tackled some of the toughest trails in Colorado, Utah, Arizona and California. I've learned the right way to do things and the wrong way, the best places to go and places to avoid. I've also learned how important it is to minimize impact on the environment by driving responsibly and staying on authorized routes at all times.

I wasn't happy with any guidebooks on the market, so I decided to write my own. To my surprise, the first one on Colorado sold well enough for me to quit my regular job and publish books full-time. This book is my fifth since 1998. To maintain accuracy, I continue to drive all the trails myself, write the directions, draw the maps and shoot the photographs. I get letters and e-mail from all over the world from happy customers telling how much fun they've had using my books. I know you'll feel the same way.

KEEPING IT SIMPLE

Everything about this book is designed to be simple and easy to use. As you flip through the book, notice how trail headings always appear at top of right-hand pages. Type is large and easy to read in a moving vehicle. Directions are written in plain narrative—no tables or abbreviations. Numerous photos show actual trail conditions, not just beautiful scenery. Maps are easy to read, starting with a statewide locator on page 7. Area maps zoom in closer on ten specific areas. Finally, an individual map is provided for each of 75 trails. Although GPS is not required to find your way, waypoints are provided for those who use them. Coordinates are listed in the appendix. Mileages are accurate and rounded to the nearest tenth of a mile. Your mileage will likely vary because of different driving habits and road conditions. When space allows, historical information may be included.

SELECTING THE RIGHT TRAIL FOR YOUR VEHICLE

It is important to select trails that are appropriate for your vehicle. Trails are divided into three general categories. A circle identifies easy trails, a square, moderate trails and a diamond, difficult trails. In addition, on pages 8 and 9, the trails are ranked from easiest to hardest within each of the three general categories explained below.

Easy: Suitable for all stock four-wheel-drive sport utility vehicles with high ground clearance and low range. Some trails can be driven in two-wheel drive without low range in dry weather. A few trails, under ideal conditions, are suitable for passenger cars.

Moderate: Suitable for most stock 4WD sport utility vehicles with high ground clearance and low range. For the toughest moderate trails, factory skid plates, tow points, and all-terrain tires are recommended. These options are available from your dealer or local four-wheel-drive shop.

Difficult: Suitable for some aggressive stock 4WD sport utility vehicles with very high ground clearance, excellent articulation, tow hooks, and a full skid plate package. All-terrain tires are a minimum, mud terrains preferred. A winch or differential lockers are recommended for the most difficult trails. Drivers who spend a great deal of time on the most difficult trails may find it necessary to modify their vehicles with higher ground clearance, oversized tires, and heavy duty accessories. A trail is rated difficult if any spot on the trail is difficult. You may be able to enjoy much of a trail before running into the difficult portion. Read the trail description carefully.

CALIFORNIA LAWS, LICENSING AND FEES

California has the greatest number of off-highway vehicle (OHV) enthusiasts in the nation and the number is growing rapidly. In the last twenty years OHV registrations have increased 83%. Unfortunately, since 1985, land available for OHV recreation has decreased 47%. Much of this land was lost in 1994 when Congress passed the California Desert Protection Act. Over 7 million acres of land were designated wilderness and closed to OHV recreation. To deal with this problem, California has enacted special licensing classifications, strict OHV laws and additional fees which are explained as follows:

Street-Legal Vehicles. This classification includes licensed SUVs, Jeeps and dual-purpose motorcycles. They are allowed on major highways, forest roads, state park roads and in most OHV areas. Fees are paid when license plates are purchased and vary with vehicle type. Normal highway laws apply.

Green-Sticker Vehicles. This category includes ATVs, dune buggies, sand rails and unlicensed dirt bikes. These vehicles are allowed in OHV areas and on certain BLM and forest lands. Green stickers cost $21 and are good for two years. (See OHV laws on next page.)

Red-Sticker Vehicles. ATVs and motorcycles made after January 1, 1997, must meet stricter emission standards. Those that don't get a red sticker, which is exactly the same as a green sticker except the riding period is limited. Cost is same as green sticker.

Recreation Fee Demonstration Program. This money is used for maintenance and to provide additional facilities at recreation sites. The most notable of these is Imperial Sand Dunes Recreation Area. Here an additional fee of $10/week or $30/year is collected at automated vending machines. The fee is for primary vehicle only. For example, if you tow several vehicles on a trailer, you pay just one fee. If you and a friend drive separate SUVs, you each pay the fee.

National Forest Adventure Pass. There are four national forests in southern California: Los Padres, Angeles, San Bernardino and Cleveland. You can drive through these forests without paying an additional fee; however, if you stop along the way to recreate, you are required to purchase an Adventure Pass which is good in all four forests. Cost is $5/day or $30/year. Fee does not apply to green-sticker vehicles. You can get passes at Forest Service offices and at many local vendors (see www.fsadventurepass.org).

ATVs & DIRT BIKES

This book is primarily a guide for street-legal, off-highway vehicles. It is not intended to be a comprehensive guide for green-sticker vehicles (specifically ATVs and dirt bikes). However, with so many OHV areas in southern California, it makes sense to identify trails that are common to both vehicle types. **The complete trail listing on page 6 identifies ATV and dirt-bike trails with an asterisk.** It means ATVs and dirt bikes are allowed either directly on the trail or an OHV area nearby. Usually, there's a centralized network of trails with parking for loading and unloading. Dual-purpose motorcycles (i.e. street-legal dirt bikes) can run on both primary roads and legal open land. The following is a simplified list of state OHV laws.

State OHV Laws:
- Riders must wear approved safety helmets.
- A safety course is required for riders under age 18.
- A safety certification is required along with parental supervision for riders under age 14.
- ATVs cannot carry passengers.
- No riding while under the influence of alcohol or drugs.
- Speed is limited to 15 mph near campsites and groups of people. You are the final judge of unsafe situations. Be extra careful.
- Vehicles must have muffler, spark arrester and brakes plus lights if used at night.

14

In addition to state laws, most OHV areas have additional rules. Some common ones include:

- Safety flags must be used.
- No glass containers are allowed.
- No open alcoholic beverage containers are allowed.
- Campers cannot dump sewage or gray water.
- In most areas, you must pack out your trash.

Irresponsible use of ATVs and dirt bikes is one of the biggest concerns of the Forest Service, BLM and other land management agencies and a major reason for trail closures. It is your responsibility to understand and obey laws wherever you ride. You must stay on designated routes when required.

OHV AREAS AND SVRAs

Despite many land closures, California still has nearly 100 off-highway vehicle (OHV) areas. These areas include upwards of 100,000 miles of unpaved roads and countless acres of open land. The seven State Vehicular Recreation Areas (SVRAs) alone comprise about 92,000 acres. The two largest state areas, Hungry Valley SVRA and Ocotillo Wells SVRA, are covered in this book. In addition, eight OHV areas are covered. They include Superstition Mountain, Corral Canyon, Johnson Valley, Imperial Sand Dunes, Dumont Dunes, Rowher Flat, Stoddard Valley and Lark Canyon. With the exception of Lark Canyon, all of these areas offer trails for street-legal vehicles. The largest and best areas for SUVs and Jeeps are Johnson Valley (140,000 acres), Superstition Mountain (13,000 acres), Ocotillo Wells (70,000 acres), Hungry Valley (19,000 acres) and Imperial Sand Dunes (33,000 acres counting Buttercup Valley). Non-state areas are administered by the National Forest Service or Bureau of Land Management. If you would like a detailed listing and a map of all OHV areas across the state, contact the Off-Highway Motor Vehicle Recreation (OHMVR) Division of the California State Parks (see appendix).

NATIONAL PARKS AND FORESTS

Death Valley National Park. Don't be frightened away from this park because of its ominous name. It's a great place to visit during the late fall, winter and early spring. Although it's open all year, not many people go four-wheeling during the summer. May through September, average high temperatures are near or above 100°, topping out at 116° in July. Highs above 120° are not unusual. Conversely, February averages a wonderful 72°. The park has an extensive network of primitive roads although many are graded and washboardy. **Only street-legal vehicles are allowed in the park.** This book concentrates on those roads that offer a bit more challenge; two have sections that are borderline difficult. Most of the best roads are centered around Furnace Creek which also has the most services and campgrounds. Park campgrounds are dry camping only. Just a few private full-hookup spaces are nearby. More full-hookup spaces are available in Stovepipe Wells. At the time of this writing, a park pass cost $10 and was good for seven days. (See appendix for contact information.)

Some trails on the west side of Death Valley National Park connect to trails in the Panamint Mountains. Even with the closure of renowned Surprise Canyon, the Panamint Mountains are a popular four-wheeling destination.

Joshua Tree National Park. There are just a handful of unpaved roads in this park. Berdoo Canyon (Trail #75), offers the most challenge. Fees are the same as Death Valley National Park. **Street-legal vehicles only.**

National Forests. With the exception of Lockwood/ Miller Jeep Trail, Hungry Valley and Rowher Flats, Los Padres and Angeles National Forests are devoid of any serious four-wheeling. Giant gates are everywhere. Cleveland National Forest has a bit more to offer, including challenging Corral Canyon. The best forest, by far, in southern California is San Bernardino National Forest. The most challenging trails are near Big Bear and Lake Arrowhead. The trails are well marked and most are adopted by four-wheel-drive clubs. You can still enjoy many scenic roads in all four forests. Remember, an Adventure Pass is required if you stop to recreate.

ANZA-BORREGO DESERT STATE PARK

This book documents eleven trails inside massive Anza-Borrego Desert State Park. Although some of the park is wilderness, many great high-clearance roads remain open. Four trails (#45, #48, #54,and #57) include some difficult terrain. It is very important to stay on designated roads inside the park; otherwise these, too, could someday be closed. **Only street-legal vehicles are allowed in the park.** Those with an urge to cross open land should head directly to nearby Ocotillo Wells State Vehicular Recreation Area. While visiting Anza-Borrego Desert State Park, make sure to stop at the unique and interesting visitor center located on the west end of Borrego Springs. When you arrive at the parking lot, the visitor center is completely invisible. Follow signs downhill east of the parking lot. The park charges no entry fees.

MOJAVE NATIONAL PRESERVE

The preserve has hundreds of miles of dirt roads for the well-prepared traveler. **Only street-legal vehicles are allowed,** and you must stay on existing roads at all times. Do not drive in washes. If you are seeking cross-country travel, do so in Rasor OHV area. Camping is permitted but don't create new campsites. Don't camp along paved roads or within a quarter mile of water sources. Bring your own firewood and use fire rings when provided. Pack out all trash, including fire ashes.

SAFETY TIPS

File a Flight Plan. Determine where you are going and when you plan to return. Be as specific as possible. Inform a friend or relative and call them when you return. If something goes wrong, you'll have the comfort of knowing that at least someone knows where you are.

Travel with another vehicle. Your chances of getting stuck in the back-country are immensely reduced with two vehicles. If one vehicle breaks down, you have a back-up.

Know location of closest hospital. Before you leave on any trip, check the location of the closest hospital or emergency facility in the area.

Carry extra maps. The maps in this book will clearly direct you along the trail. However, if you get lost or decide to venture down a spur road, you'll need additional maps with topographic information. Carry a compass or a GPS unit to orient yourself. At the end of each trail description, I have listed several maps that I found useful. Make sure you have at least one.

I wouldn't go anywhere without my *DeLorme Atlas & Gazetteer (Southern and Central California edition)*. Although it's a large-scale map, it has a surprising amount of backroad detail. It covers all of southern California and its booklet format is easy to use. Latitude and longitude are printed along the edge of each map. With the simplest GPS unit, you can quickly determine your location. The *California Road & Recreation Atlas* by Benchmark Maps is very similar to the Gazetteer. It has better graphics but doesn't show quite as much backroad detail. Either atlas will work just fine.

The Automobile Club of Southern California has great maps with good backroad detail. I used their maps for the Mojave Road inside the Mojave National Preserve and for the Imperial Sand Dunes Recreation Area.

The greatest amount of detail is shown on 7.5 minute U.S. Geological Survey Maps; however, each map covers a small area and many maps are required. Since I carry a laptop computer, I buy 7.5 minute maps on CDs. They are extremely economical and easy to use in this format, but they would be useless if something happened to my computer. I use them because they provide maximum detail for GPS tracking. I always carry paper maps.

Changing conditions. California's backcountry is fragile and under constant assault by forces of nature and man. Rock slides can occur or an entire road can be washed away from a single heavy rainstorm. A road may be closed without notice. Directional signs may be removed or vandalized. Route numbers are sometimes changed. Maps seldom keep up with changes and sometimes have mistakes. Take these factors into consideration when faced with a confusing situation. Rely on your own common sense.

High water, flash floods. Many of California's backroads cross or follow dry washes, small streams, and narrow canyons. Heavy rains can turn these places into raging torrents of water in minutes. Check weather forecasts and keep an eye on the sky. Be conservative and don't take chances. Cut your trip short if necessary. Don't attempt to cross a fast-flowing stream unless you've done it before and know what your vehicle can do. Wait if necessary; water levels usually go down quickly after a single rain shower. If you're in a narrow canyon and water begins to rise, drive perpendicularly out of the canyon if possible. If this is not possible, get out of your vehicle and climb to higher ground. Most people who die in flash floods attempt to outrun the rising water in their vehicles.

Inspect your vehicle carefully. Before you start into the backcountry, make sure your vehicle is in top operating condition. If you have a mechanic do the work, make sure he is reliable and understands four-wheeling. Tell him where you plan to take your vehicle. Pay particular attention to fluids, hoses, belts, battery, brakes, steering linkage, suspension system, driveline, and anything exposed under the vehicle. Tighten anything that may be loose. Inspect your tires carefully for potential weak spots and tread wear.

Wear your seat belt. You might think that because you're driving slowly, it's not necessary to wear your seat belt or use child restraints. I've learned through experience that you are much safer with a seat belt than without. Buckle up at all times.

Keep heads, arms, and legs inside a moving vehicle. Many trails are narrow. Brush, tree limbs, and rock overhangs may come very close to your vehicle. The driver must make it clear to every passenger to stay inside the vehicle at all times. Children, in particular, must not be allowed to stick their heads, arms, or legs out the windows.

Cliff edges. Watch children and be extremely careful around cliff edges. Hand rails are rarely provided. Watch for loose rock and stay away from these areas when it's wet, icy, or getting dark. If you climb up a rock wall, remember it's harder to get down than to climb up.

Lightning. During a storm, stay away from lone trees, cliff edges, and high points. Stay low to the ground or in your vehicle. Lightning can strike from a distant storm even when it's clear overhead.

Mines, tunnels, and old structures. Be careful around old mine buildings. Stay out of mines and tunnels. Don't let children play in these areas.

DESERT SURVIVAL

Self-reliance. Most of us live in populated areas and are accustomed to having other people around when things go wrong. In California's remote backcountry, you must be self-reliant. Don't count on anyone else's help. Try to anticipate what can go wrong and prepare accordingly.

Water, water, and more water. I can't stress enough the importance of carrying and drinking plenty of water—at least one gallon per person per day plus extra water for your vehicle. I leave an extra five-gallon container in my vehicle at all times. A canteen is handy if you have to walk out. Running out of water under certain circumstances can be a fatal mistake.

First Aid. Always carry a good first-aid kit. Take a first-aid course and learn the basics. Make sure the kit contains a good first-aid book.

What to do if you have mechanical problems or you get lost. Stay with your vehicle. There's always a chance that someone will come along if you stay near the road. Your vehicle is easier to see than you are. Your car can provide shelter from wind, rain, and cold. The desert can get very cold at night, especially if you get wet. During the day, desert heat will drive you out of your car. Seek shade. You're more likely to find a rock overhang than a shady tree. Don't sit on the hot ground. Dig down to cooler sand below or sit on something at least 18 inches above ground. Create your own shade with blankets or tarp attached to your car or build a lean-to. If necessary, dig a depression under your car and crawl underneath after exhaust pipes and engine have cooled. If you don't have a shovel, dig with a hub cap. Work slowly; don't overexert yourself. Rest as much as possible. Drink plenty of water; don't wait until you're thirsty. Wear light-colored, loose-fitting clothing that covers as much of your skin as possible. Wear a hat and use sunscreen. Collect firewood before dark. Build a fire before you need it. If you get lost or separated from your group, stay in one place.

If you're familiar with the area and know exactly how far it is to hike out and are absolutely sure you can make it, consider walking out as a last resort. Cover up with loose clothing, take plenty of water, food, and rain protection to stay dry. Travel at night when it's cooler if the terrain is not too treacherous. Make sure you can see where you're walking.

Try to draw attention to yourself. Make noise anyway you can—whistles, horns, whatever you have. Don't run down your car battery. Build a smoky fire. Three fires in a triangle 150 feet apart are an international distress signal. Use flares if you have them. Some are designed for day use, others for night. Use a reflective mirror if you see an airplane or anyone in the distance.

Take your cellphone but remember you're often out of a service area. Sometimes cellphones work if you can get to higher ground. If you have a CB radio, broadcast on channel 19 or emergency channel 9. Continue intermittently to call out even if no one responds. Make sure you give your location. HAM radios work well in the backcountry. Consider getting a license.

Hyperthermia. When your body overheats it's called hyperthermia. Symptoms include dry, flushed skin, inability to sweat, rapid heartbeat, and a rising body temperature. Hyperthermia is often preceded by cramps. They may not go away by drinking water alone. You may need food or salt. If hyperthermia is allowed to progress you could collapse from heatstroke, which is extremely serious and can be fatal if not treated quickly.

To prevent hyperthermia, stay in the shade, don't overexert yourself, wear loose-fitting clothing, and drink plenty of water. If work is required to find or make shade, conserve your energy as best as possible.

Dehydration. As your body sweats to cool itself, it dehydrates. You may be drinking water but not enough. Eating may make you nauseous. You won't want to eat or drink. As symptoms get worse, your mouth will become dry, you may become dizzy, develop a headache, and become short of breath. At some point, you may not be able to walk or care for yourself. You must prevent dehydration before it happens. Drink more than just to quench your thirst. If you must conserve water, rest as much as possible, try not to sweat, and don't eat a lot. Digestion requires body fluids. If you have plenty of water, drink it.

Hypothermia. It gets cold in the desert after the sun goes down. If it rains and gets windy, you could find yourself shivering in no time, especially if you've worked up a sweat during the day. Your hands and feet will become stiff. You may not be able to hold a match and start a fire. Again, prevention is the key. Put on a jacket before you begin to get cold. Stay dry. Change clothes if necessary. If you get too cold, blankets may not be enough to warm you. Build a fire, drink hot liquids, or cuddle up with someone else. Your car is a great shelter—use it.

CHECKLIST. No single list can be all inclusive. You must be the final judge of what you need. Here's a list of basic items:
- WATER, WATER, WATER. At least one gallon per person per day. It's also wise to carry extra water for your vehicle.
- Food for normal eating and high-energy foods for emergencies. Energy bars, dried fruit, and hard candy store well.
- Loose-fitting, light-colored clothing, sun hats, shoes, socks, coats, and boots. Wool clothing keeps you warm when you're wet.
- Sleeping bags in case you get stuck overnight even if you're not planning to camp.
- A good first-aid kit including a first-aid book. Other important items include: sunscreen, insect repellent, water purification tablets, safety pins, needles and thread, tweezers, pocket knife or all-purpose tool.
- Candles, matches, fire starter, and a lighter.
- An extra set of keys and glasses.
- Toilet paper, paper towels, wet wipes, and trash bags.
- A large plastic sheet or tarp.
- Rain gear, small tent or tarp, nylon cords.
- Detailed maps, compass, watch, and a knife.
- If you plan to make a fire, carry your own firewood. Make sure fires are allowed.

- A heavy-duty tow strap. (The kind without metal hooks on the ends.)
- A fire extinguisher. Make sure you can reach it quickly.
- Jumper cables, extra fan belts, stop-leak for radiator.
- Replacement fuses and electrical tape.
- Flashlight and extra batteries.
- Flares, signal mirror, police whistle.
- Extra oil and other engine fluids.
- A full tank of gas. If you carry extra gas, make sure it's in an approved container and properly stored.
- A good set of tools, work gloves, and a complete service manual for your vehicle.
- Baling wire and duct tape.
- An assortment of hoses, clamps, nuts, bolts, and washers.
- A full-size spare tire.
- A tire pressure gauge, electric tire pump that will plug into your cigarette lighter, and a can of nonflammable tire sealant.
- A jack that will lift your vehicle fairly high off the ground. Take a small board to place under the jack. Carry a high-lift jack if you can, especially on more difficult trails. Test your jack before you leave home.
- Shovel and axe. Folding shovels work great.
- Tire chains for winter mountain travel. They can also help if you get stuck in the mud.
- CB radio and/or cellular phone.
- Portable toilet.
- If you have a winch, carry a tree strap, clevis, and snatch block.

Maintenance. Backroad travel puts your vehicle under greater stress than normal highway driving. Follow maintenance directions in your owner's manual for severe driving conditions. This usually calls for changing oil, oil filter, and air filter more frequently as well as more frequent fluid checks and lubrications. Inspect your tires carefully; they take a lot of extra abuse. After your trip, make sure you wash your vehicle. Use a high pressure spray to thoroughly clean the underside and wheel wells. Automatic car washes usually are not adequate. Do it yourself, if you want your vehicle in good shape for the next trip.

YOUR RESPONSIBILITIES AS A BACKCOUNTRY DRIVER

Make sure you know and follow backcountry, *Tread Lightly* guidelines. Consider joining the national *Tread Lightly* organization (see appendix for contact information). Although much damage is done by deliberate violators, some is done by well-intentioned, ignorant drivers.

Stay on the trail. This is the single most important rule of back-country driving. Leaving the trail causes unnecessary erosion, kills vegetation, and spoils the beauty of the land. Scars remain for years. Don't widen the trail by driving around rocks and muddy spots and don't short cut switchbacks. When you have to pass another vehicle, do so at designated pull-overs. Sometimes the edge of the trail is defined by a line of rocks. Don't move the rocks or cross over them. Drivers who leave existing trails risk fines and cause trails to be closed. Practice diligently to leave no trace of your passage.

The Desert Tortoise. The Desert Tortoise is a *threatened species* and their population is being monitored as part of the Desert Tortoise Recovery plan. If you see a Desert Tortoise anytime during your travels, stay clear. Do not pick up or harass. They store water in their bladders which they may empty if frightened which could be fatal. They like shade, so check under your vehicle before driving away.

Wilderness Areas. It is a serious offense to drive in a designated wilderness. These areas are usually well marked and clearly shown on maps.

Private Property. Pass through private land quietly and stay on the road at all times. Don't disturb livestock. Leave gates the way you find them unless posted otherwise.

Ruins and archaeological sites. It is a federal crime to disturb archaeological sites. Don't touch them or climb inside. Do not remove or touch historical artifacts. Don't camp or picnic near an archaeological site.

Trash disposal and litter. Carry plastic trash bags and pack out your own trash, including cigarette butts. Where waste receptacles are provided, use them. When possible, clean up after others. Keep a litter bag handy and pick up trash along the trail.

When nature calls. The disposal of solid human waste and toilet paper is becoming a big problem as more visitors head into the backcountry. Arid climates do not decompose these materials as fast as they are being left behind. It is generally advisable to carry a portable toilet. Otherwise, keep a small shovel handy and bury feces 4 to 6 inches deep, away from trails, campsites and at least 300 feet from any water source, which includes dry washes. Seal toilet paper and feminine hygiene products in a small plastic bag and discard with your trash.

Campfires. Fire prevention is extremely important in southern California. Regulations vary across the state and restrictions may apply when fire danger is high. Always use fire rings when they are provided. Try to build fires in spots where others have had a fire. Bring your own firewood whenever possible and know local regulations for firewood gathering. Thoroughly douse all campfires. Carry out fire debris with your trash. Consider using a propane camping stove instead of building a fire. Stoves are very convenient for cooking and are environmentally preferred.

Washing, cleaning, and bathing. If you must use soap, use biodegradable soap but never around lakes or streams. Heat water without using soap to clean utensils whenever possible.

BACKCOUNTRY DRIVING LESSONS

Trail Etiquette. A little common courtesy goes a long way in making everyone's travel in the backcountry more enjoyable. After all, we're all out to have fun. Take your time and be considerate of others. If you see someone approaching from behind, look for a wide spot on the trail, pull over and let him pass. Conversely, if you get behind a slowpoke, back off or look for a scenic spot to pull over for a while. Stretch your legs and take a few pictures. When you're out of your vehicle, pick a wide spot where you can pull over so others can get by. A horn is rarely needed in the backcountry. Don't play your radio loudly. When you see bikers, pull over and let them pass. Ask if they have enough water. Don't let your pet bark or chase wildlife.

The basics. If you have never shifted into low range, grab your owner's manual now and start practicing. Read the rest of this book, then try some of the easy trails. Gradually you'll become more proficient and eventually you'll be ready to move up in difficulty.

Low and slow. Your vehicle was designed to go over rocky and bumpy terrain but only at slow speed. Get used to driving slowly in first gear low range. This will allow you to idle over obstacles without stalling. You don't need to shift back and forth constantly. Get into a low gear and stay there as much as possible so your engine can operate at high RPM and at maximum power. If you have a standard transmission, your goal should be to use your clutch as little as possible. As you encounter resistance on an obstacle or an uphill grade, just give it a little gas. As you start downhill, allow the engine's resistance to act as a brake. If the engine alone will not stop you from accelerating, then help a little with the brake. When you need more power but not more speed, press on the gas and feather the brake a little at the same time. This takes a little practice, but you will be amazed at the control you have. This technique works equally well with automatic transmissions.

Rocks and other high points. Never attempt to straddle a rock that is large enough to strike your differentials, transfer case or other low-hanging parts of your undercarriage. Instead, drive over the highest point with your tire, which is designed to take the abuse. This will lift your undercarriage over the obstacle. As you enter a rocky area, look ahead to determine where the high points are, then make every effort to cross them with your tires. Learn the low points of your undercarriage.

Using a spotter. Sometimes there are so many rocks you get confused. In this case, have someone get out and guide you. They should stand at a safe distance in front, watching your tires and undercarriage. With hand signals, they can direct you left or right. If you are alone, don't be embarrassed to spot for yourself by getting in and out of your vehicle several times.

Those clunking sounds. Having made every attempt to avoid dragging bottom, you'll find it's not always possible. It is inevitable that a rock will contact your undercarriage eventually. The sound can be quite unnerving the first time it happens. If you are driving slowly and have proper skid plates, damage is unlikely. Look for a different line, back up and try again. If unsuccessful, read on.

Crossing large rocks. Sometimes a rock is too large to drive over or at such a steep angle your bumper hits the rock before your tire. Stack rocks on each side to form a ramp. Once over the obstacle, make sure you put the rocks back where you found them. The next driver to come along may prefer the challenge of crossing the rock in its more difficult state.

Getting high centered. You may drive over a large rock or into a rut, causing you to get lodged on the object. If this happens, don't panic. First ask your passengers to get out to see if less weight helps. Try rocking the vehicle. If this doesn't work, jack up your vehicle and place a few rocks under the tires so that when you let the jack down, you take the weight off the high point. Determine whether driving forward or reverse is best and try again. You may have to repeat this procedure several times if you are seriously high centered. Eventually you will learn what you can and cannot drive over.

Look in all directions. Unlike highway driving in which your primary need for attention is straight ahead, backcountry driving requires you to look in all directions. Objects can block your path from above, below, and from the sides. Trees fall, branches droop, and rocks slide, making the trail an ever-changing obstacle course.

Scout ahead. If you are on an unfamiliar trail and are concerned that the trail is becoming too difficult, get out of your vehicle and walk the trail ahead of you. This gives you an opportunity to pick an easy place to turn around before you get into trouble. If you have to turn around, back up or pull ahead until you find a wide flat spot. Don't try to turn in a narrow confined area. This can damage the trail and perhaps tip over your vehicle.

Anticipate. Shift into four-wheel drive or low range before it is needed. If you wait until it is needed, conditions might be too difficult, e.g., halfway up a hillside.

Blind curves. When approaching blind curves, always assume that there is a speeding vehicle coming from the opposite direction. This will prepare you for the worst. Be aware that many people drive on the wrong side of the road to stay away from the outer edge of a trail. Whenever possible, keep your windows open and your radio off so that you can hear an approaching vehicle. You can usually hear motorcycles and ATVs. Quiet SUVs are the biggest problem. Collisions do occur, so be careful.

Driving uphill. The difficulty of hill climbing is often misjudged by

24

the novice four-wheeler. You should have good tires, adequate power, and be shifted into four-wheel drive low. There are four factors that determine difficulty:

Length of the hill. If the hill is very long, it is less likely that momentum will carry you to the top. Short hills are easier.

Traction. Smooth rock is easier to climb than dirt.

Bumpiness. If the road surface undulates to the point where all four tires do not stay on the ground at the same time, you will have great difficulty climbing even a moderately steep hill.

Steepness. This can be difficult to judge, so examine a hill carefully before you attempt it. Walk up the hill if necessary to make sure it is not steeper at the top. If you are not absolutely sure you can climb a hill, don't attempt it. Practice on smaller hills first.

If you attempt a hill, approach it straight on and stay that way all the way to the top. Do not turn sideways or try to drive across the hill. Do not use excessive speed but keep moving at a steady pace. Make sure no one is coming up from the other side. Position a spotter at the top of the hill if necessary. Do not spin your tires because this can turn you sideways to the hill. If you feel you are coming to a stop due to lack of traction, turn your steering wheel back and forth quickly. This will give you additional grip. If you stall, use your brake and restart your engine. You may also have to use your emergency brake. If you start to slide backwards even with your brake on, you may have to ease up on the brake enough to regain steering control. Don't allow your wheels to lock up. If you don't make it to the top of the hill, shift into reverse and back down slowly in a straight line. Try the hill again but only if you think you learned enough to make a difference. As you approach the top of the hill, ease off the gas so you are in control before starting down the other side.

Driving downhill. Make sure you are in four-wheel drive. Examine the hill carefully and determine the best route that will allow you to go straight down the hill. Do not turn sideways. Use the lowest gears possible, allowing the engine's compression to hold you back. Do not ride the clutch. Feather the brakes slightly if additional slowing is needed. Do not allow the wheels to lock up. This will cause loss of steering and possibly cause you to slide sideways. The natural reaction when you begin to slide is to press harder on the brakes. Try to stay off the brakes. If you continue to slide despite these efforts, turn in the direction of the slide as you would on ice or snow and accelerate slightly. This will help maintain steering control.

Parking on a steep hill. Put your vehicle in reverse gear if pointing downhill and in forward gear if pointing uphill. For automatic transmissions, shift to park. Set your emergency brake hard and block your tires.

Tippy situations. No one can tell you how far your vehicle can safely lean. You must learn the limitations through practice. Remember that sport utility vehicles have a higher center of gravity and are less stable than a passenger car. However, don't get paranoid. Your vehicle will likely lean a lot more than you think. Drive slowly to avoid bouncing over. A good way to learn is to watch an experienced driver with a vehicle similar to yours. This is an advantage to traveling with a group. Once you see how far other vehicles can lean, you will become more comfortable in these situations. Remember, too, that you're likely to slide sideways before you tip over. This can be just as dangerous in certain situations. Use extreme caution if the road surface is slippery from loose gravel, mud, or wet clay. Turn around if necessary.

Crossing streams and water holes. You must know the high water point of your vehicle before entering any body of water. Several factors can determine this point, including the height of the air intake and the location of the computer module (newer vehicles). Water sucked into the air intake is a very serious matter. If you don't know where these items are located, check with your dealer or a good four-wheel drive shop. A low fan can throw water on the engine and cause it to stall. You may have to disconnect your fan belt. Water can be sucked into your differentials so check them regularly after crossing deep streams.

After you understand your vehicle's capabilities, you must assess the stream conditions. First determine the depth of the water. If you are with a group, let the most experienced driver cross first. Follow his line if he is successful. If you are alone, you might wait for someone else to come along. Sometimes you can use a long stick to check the depth of small streams or water holes. Check for deep holes, large obstacles, and muddy sections. If you can't determine the water depth, don't cross. A winch line or long tow strap can be used as a safety line to pull someone back if he gets into trouble, but attach it before entering the water. It must also be long enough for him to reach shallow water on the other side. Once in the water, drive slowly but steadily. This creates a small wake which helps form an air pocket around the engine. I've seen people put a piece of cardboard or canvas over the front of their vehicle to enhance the wake affect. This only works if you keep moving. After exiting a stream, test your brakes. You may have to ride them lightly for a short distance until they dry out. Always cross streams at designated water crossings. Don't drive in the direction of the stream. Try to minimize disruption of the water habitat.

Mud. Don't make new mud holes or enlarge existing ones. Stay home if you have reason to believe the trail will be too wet. Some trails, however, have permanent mud holes that you must cross. Mud can build up suction around your tires and be very difficult to get through. Always check a mud hole carefully to see how deep it is. Take a stick and poke around. Check the other side. If there are no tracks coming out, don't go in. If you decide to cross, keep moving at a steady pace and, if necessary, turn the steering wheel back and forth quickly for additional traction. If you get stuck, dig around the tires to break the suction and place anything hard under the tires for traction. It may be necessary to back out. If you are with a friend, and you are doubtful if you can get through without help, attach a tow strap before you enter so that you can be pulled back. But beware, sometimes the mud can be so bad, even a friend can't pull you out. Your only protection against this happening is to use your head and not go in the mud in the first place. When I've seen people stuck this badly, it is usually due to a total disregard for the obvious. If you can't get through the mud, search for an alternate route but don't widen the trail.

Ruts. If you get stuck in a rut and have no one to pull you out, dig a small trench from the rut to the right or left at a 45-degree angle. The dirt you remove from this trench should be used to fill the rut ahead of the turning point. If both tires are in parallel ruts, make sure the trenches are parallel. Drive out following the new rut. Repair any damage after you get out.

Gullies or washouts. If you are running parallel to a washed-out section of the trail, straddle it. If it becomes too large to straddle, drive down the middle. The goal is to center your vehicle so you remain as level as possible. This may require that you drive on the outer edges of your tires, so drive slowly and watch for any sharp objects. If you begin to tilt too far in one direction, turn in the direction of the tilt until you level out again. Sometimes it helps to have a spotter. To cross a gully from one side to the other, approach at a 45-degree angle and let each tire walk over independently.

Ravines. Crossing a ravine is similar to crossing a gully. Approach on an angle and let each tire go through independently. If the ravine is large with steep sides, you may not be able to cross at an angle because it could cause a rollover. If you don't cross at an angle, two things can happen. You will drag the front or rear of your vehicle, or you will high center on the edge of the ravine. If this is the case, ask yourself if you really need to cross the ravine. If you must cross, your only solution is to stack rocks to lift the vehicle at critical points.

Sand. Dry sand is more difficult than wet sand (unless it's quicksand). In either case, keep moving so that your momentum helps carry you through. Stay in a higher gear and use a little extra power but don't use excessive power and spin your tires. If necessary, turn your steering wheel back and forth quickly to give your tires a fresh grip. Airing down your tires is often necessary. Experiment with different tire pressures. Make sure you have a way to air up after you get through the sand. If you do get stuck, wet the sand in front of your tires. Try rocking the vehicle. If necessary, use your floor mats under the tires.

Sand Dunes. Limit yourself to smaller dunes. Stay off the soft side of the dune where the wind is depositing the sand. Soft sand will not support your vehicle. Worse than getting stuck, you could roll over. To avoid digging in, don't accelerate quickly or slam on your brakes. When helping someone else get unstuck, be careful not to spin your wheels or you'll get stuck. Use a winch if you have one.

Washboard roads. Washboard roads are a natural part of backcountry travel. Vibration from these roads can be annoying. It is a problem for everybody so don't think there is something wrong with your vehicle. Experiment with different speeds to find the smoothest ride. Slowing down is usually best, but some conditions may be improved by speeding up a little. Be careful around curves where you could lose traction and slide. Check your tires to make sure they are not overinflated.

Airing down. There may be times when you need to let air out of your tires to get more traction or improve your ride, e.g., when driving through sand, going up a steep hill, or driving on washboard roads. It is usually safe to let air out of your tires until they bulge slightly, provided you are not traveling at high speed. If you let out too much air, your tires may come off the rims, or the sidewalls may become vulnerable to damage by sharp objects. Consider how or where you will reinflate. A small air pump that plugs into your cigarette lighter is handy for this purpose. Airing down on hard-core trails is essential. I've seen some wheelers with larger tires air down to as little as 3-5 lbs. A typical SUV can usually be aired down to 18 to 20 lbs. without noticeable handling difficulties at low speeds.

Winching. Next to tow points and skid plates, a winch is one of the best investments you can make. If you drive more difficult trails and you don't have a winch, travel with someone who does. I've known some hard-core wheelers who have gone for years without owning a winch but they always travel with a group. If you never intend to buy a winch, carry a high-lift jack or come-along. Although these tools are slow and inconvenient when used in place of a winch, they can get you out of difficulty when there is no other way.

If you own a winch, make sure you also have these five basic winch accessories:

1. Heavy-duty work gloves.

2. A tree strap—looks like a tow strap but is shorter. It has a loop on each end.

3. A snatch block—a pulley that opens on the side so you can slip it over your winch cable.

4. A clevis—a heavy U-shaped device with a pin that screws across one end. This enables you to connect straps together and to your vehicle. It has many other uses.

5. A heavy-duty chain with grab hooks to wrap around rocks. It's also handy when trying to pull another vehicle that does not have tow points.

Winching tips:

• Your winch cable should be lined up straight with the pulling vehicle. If you can't pull straight, attach a snatch block to a large tree or rock to form an angle. This technique also works for pulling a fallen tree off the trail.

28

• If your winch cable bunches up at one end of the spool but there's still room for the cable, let it go and rewind the cable later.

• When winching from trees, attach to the largest tree possible using your tree strap and clevis. If no tree is large enough, wrap several smaller trees. The strap should be put as low as possible on the tree. Finding a decent size tree in the desert may be impossible.

• Keep your engine running while winching to provide maximum electrical power to the battery.

• Help the winch by driving the stuck vehicle slowly. Be in the lowest gear possible and go as slowly as possible without spinning your tires. Don't allow slack in the winch cable. This can start a jerking motion that could break the cable.

• If there is not enough power to pull the stuck vehicle, attach a snatch block to the stuck vehicle and double the winch cable back to the starting point. This block-and-tackle technique will double your pulling power.

• Set the emergency brake on the anchor vehicle and block the wheels if necessary. In some cases, you may have to connect the anchor vehicle to another vehicle or tree.

• Throw a blanket or heavy coat over the winch cable while pulling. This will slow the end of the winch cable if it breaks and snaps back.

• Make sure there are at least 5 wraps of the winch cable left on the spool.

• Never hook the winch cable to itself. Use a tree strap and clevis. Never allow the winch cable to kink. This creates a weak spot in the cable.

• If tow points are not available on the stuck vehicle, attach to the vehicle's frame, not the bumper. Use your large chain to wrap around the frame. If you are helping a stranger, make sure he understands that you are not responsible for damage to his vehicle.

• Never straddle or stand close to the winch cable while it is under stress.

• When finished winching, don't let the end of the cable wind into the spool. It can become jammed and damage your winch. Attach the hook to some other part of your vehicle like a tow point.

FINAL COMMENTS

I've made every effort to make this book as accurate and as easy to use as possible. If you have ideas for improvements or find any significant errors, please write to me at FunTreks, Inc., P.O. Box 3127, Monument, CO 80132-3127. Or, send e-mail to: *books@funtreks.com*. Whether you're a novice or expert, I hope this book makes your backcountry experience safer, easier, and more fun.

Map Legend

～～	Interstate
～	Paved Road*
～	Easy Trail*
～	Moderate Trail*
～	Difficult Trail*
....	Other Road*
～	Described in text
....	Hiking Trail
— ·· — · — ·	Boundaries & Divides
⊔⊔⊔⊔⊔⊔	Cliff, Canyon
+++++++	Railroad
 MT. PEALE	Mountain Peak
	Lake, Sand Dune
Ⓝ	Map Orientation
(25)	Interstate
(50)	U.S. Highway
(35)	State & County Road
586	Forest Service Road
EP26	BLM Road
Start here	Starting point of trail

👫	Toilet
⛽	Gas
Ⓟ	Parking
⛱	Picnic Area
⛺	Camping
⛏	Mine
🚶	Hiking
🏠	Cabin
〰	Water Crossing
🎣	Fishing
🏍	ATVs, Dirt bikes
📷	Scenic Point
🌾	Windmill
🐕	Ghost town
◣	Major Obstacle
⚑05	GPS Waypoint

Scale indicated by grid

Scale is different for each map; check grid size at bottom of map.

* These items repeated on each map for your convenience. See Mini Key.

THE TRAILS

The Squeeze on Pinyon Mountain Road (Trail #54).

AREA 1

Death Valley
National Park,
Panamint
Mountains

1. Titus Canyon
2. Chloride City
3. Cottonwood/
   Marble Canyon
4. Echo Pass/
   Inyo Mine
5. Jail Canyon

6. Pleasant Canyon/
   South Park
7. Goler Wash/
   Mengel Pass
8. Butte Valley
9. Fish Canyon
   Escape Trail

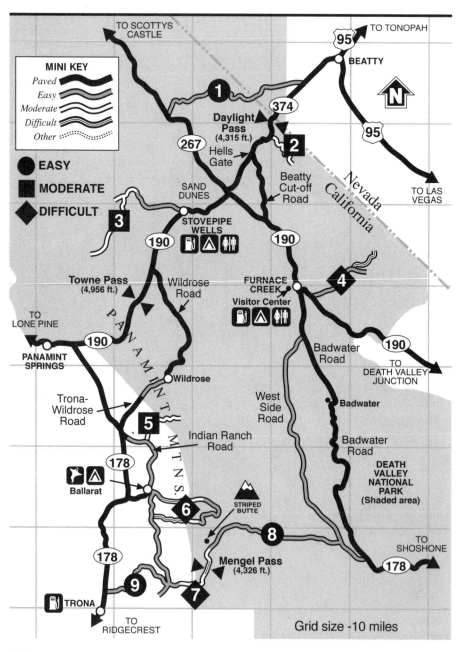

MINI KEY

Paved
Easy
Moderate
Difficult
Other

● EASY
■ MODERATE
◆ DIFFICULT

TO SCOTTYS CASTLE

TO TONOPAH

95

BEATTY

N

1

374

Daylight
Pass
(4,315 ft.)

267

Hells
Gate

2

95

TO LAS VEGAS

Beatty
Cut-off
Road

Nevada
California

SAND
DUNES

3

STOVEPIPE
WELLS

190

190

Towne Pass
(4,956 ft.)

Wildrose
Road

FURNACE
CREEK

Visitor Center

4

TO
LONE PINE

190

PANAMINT
SPRINGS

Wildrose

Badwater
Road

190

TO
DEATH VALLEY
JUNCTION

Trona-
Wildrose
Road

West
Side
Road

Badwater

5

Indian Ranch
Road

178

Ballarat

PANAMINT MTNS.

6

STRIPED
BUTTE

Badwater
Road

DEATH
VALLEY
NATIONAL
PARK
(Shaded area)

8

TO
SHOSHONE

9

Mengel Pass
(4,326 ft.)

7

178

178

TRONA

TO
RIDGECREST

Grid size -10 miles

32

Death Valley National Park, Panamint Mountains

There are scores of backroads in Death Valley and Death Valley National Park. The routes selected here are some of the best, offering more challenging terrain and interesting destinations while minimizing long, washboard drives. All routes are day trips from Furnace Creek and Stovepipe Wells. Although a long drive from coastal cities, the park offers a truly memorable backcountry experience that no one should miss. Allow at least three or four days to see the park—longer, if possible. Obviously, winter, early spring and late fall are the best times to visit. While at the visitor center, ask about the park's *Adopt-a-Cabin* program—a little-publicized, unique opportunity to enhance your trip. On the way to Death Valley, be sure to stop at the ghost town of Ballarat off Highway 178. Although few structures remain, the town offers dry camping and access to some of the most interesting mountain terrain in California. Serious four-wheelers flock to the area every November to attend *Panamint Valley Days*. Information about this event is available on the Internet.

Russel Camp accessed from trails 7 or 8. Part of Death Valley N.P. *Adopt-a-Cabin* program.

The road climbs out of Titanothere Canyon towards Red Pass on the way to Titus Canyon.

Park near this sign and walk across road to the mine.

The Narrows of Titus Canyon.

Leadfield Mine has a few remaining structures.

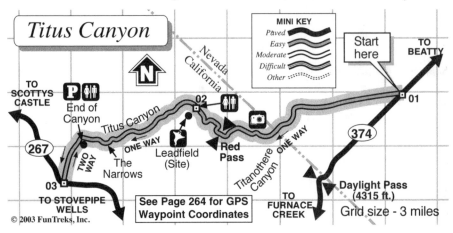

Titus Canyon

MINI KEY
Paved
Easy
Moderate
Difficult
Other

Start here

TO BEATTY

Nevada
California

TO SCOTTYS CASTLE

P

End of Canyon

Titus Canyon

ONE WAY

02

01

374

TWO WAY

The Narrows

Leadfield (Site)

Red Pass

Titanothere Canyon ONE WAY

267

03

TO STOVEPIPE WELLS

See Page 264 for GPS Waypoint Coordinates

TO FURNACE CREEK

Daylight Pass (4315 ft.)

Grid size - 3 miles

© 2003 FunTreks, Inc.

34

Titus Canyon ①

Location: Southwest of Beatty, Nevada, northeast of Stovepipe Wells and north of Furnace Creek.

Difficulty: Easy. A well-maintained gravel road but steep and narrow in a few places. Four-wheel drive seldom necessary under dry conditions. Road is closed when rain is expected due to extreme flash-flood danger through narrowest part of Titus Canyon. May also close with winter snows.

Features: Perhaps the most popular backroad in Death Valley National Park. Very scenic after the first 10 miles. A few buildings remain at the Leadfield Mine. Interesting geologic rock formations and a few petroglyphs. The road is one-way east to west. Street-legal vehicles only.

Time & Distance: Total 26.8 miles. Allow about 2 hours plus travel time.

To Get There: Head northeast on Hwy. 374 towards Beatty, NV. Turn left about 7 miles east of Daylight Pass on a well-marked road.

Trail Description: Reset your odometer at the start [01]. Head west on a wide gravel road. After about 10 miles, drop into Titanothere Canyon and begin a long climb to Red Pass. In places, the road is narrow with significant drop-offs. Cross Red Pass at 12.5 before reaching Leadfield at 15.7 (02). Watch for interesting folded rock layers at 16.1 after you've entered Titus Canyon. The canyon narrows at 22.7 miles before ending dramatically at 24.1. A parking area begins two-way traffic down a wide gravel road which reaches paved Hwy. 267 at 26.8 miles (03).

Return Trip: Turn left on Hwy. 267 to return to Hwy. 190. Right goes north to Scottys Castle. Picnic area just north of Hwy. 190 on Hwy. 267.

Services: I found a porta-potty at Leadfield and a vault toilet at canyon end.

Historical Highlights: The town of Leadfield never delivered on its promise of rich lead claims and lasted less than a year despite getting a post office in 1926. The canyon is named after mining engineer Morris Titus, who died prospecting the canyon in 1906.

Maps: Death Valley N.P. map, USGS 250,000-scale map of Death Valley, California/ Nevada, DeLorme Atlas & Gazetteer.

Back door of cabin near Chloride City leads to mine.

Grave marker.

Road ends at Chloride Cliff with view of Death Valley and Panamint Mountains.

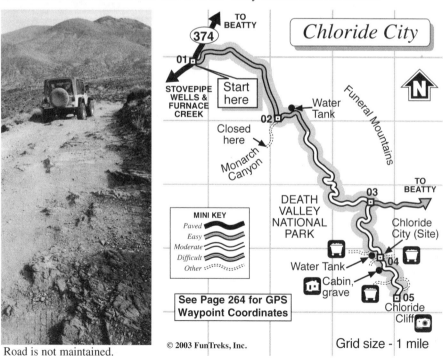

Chloride City

TO BEATTY

374

01

STOVEPIPE WELLS & FURNACE CREEK

Start here

02

Closed here

Monarch Canyon

Water Tank

Funeral Mountains

N

03

TO BEATTY

DEATH VALLEY NATIONAL PARK

Chloride City (Site)

Water Tank

Cabin, grave

04

05

Chloride Cliff

MINI KEY

Paved
Easy
Moderate
Difficult
Other

See Page 264 for GPS Waypoint Coordinates

© 2003 FunTreks, Inc.

Grid size - 1 mile

Road is not maintained.

Chloride City **2**

Location: Southwest of Beatty, Nevada, northeast of Stovepipe Wells.

Difficulty: Moderate. Starts easy then climbs mild, rocky switchbacks. Suitable for stock SUVs with high ground clearance and 4WD.

Features: A fun trail in a remote area. Many mines and a few small cabins. Scenic view of Death Valley from Chloride Cliff. Street-legal vehicles only.

Time & Distance: Takes about an hour to cover 6.6 miles one-way to Chloride City. Add another 0.8 miles to Chloride Cliff.

To Get There: Head northeast on Hwy. 374 towards Beatty, NV. Turn right 3.4 miles after Hells Gate. Watch for a small road marked with Jeep sign.

Trail Description: Reset your odometer at the start (01). Follow two-track road as it weaves through low brush. Bear right at 1.4 miles. At 2.2 miles (02) bear left at T. Road to right is blocked after short distance but you can hike into Monarch Canyon. Continue straight uphill past a water tank on the left at 2.5 miles. You'll pass several nice camping spots as the road climbs and deteriorates. Shift into low range. Bear left at 4.7. Bear right at a triangular intersection at 5.3 miles (03). Road to left is an easy, long trip to Beatty. Bear left at a T when you reach a ridge above water tank at 6.3. A five-way intersection at 6.6 miles (04) marks the center of Chloride City site. Pick your way uphill through maze of roads past grave marker and a cabin on the right. From grave, return to main road and continue uphill. Pass a second cabin hidden by a ridge to reach Chloride Cliff at 7.4 miles (05).

Return Trip: Return the way you came or take alternate road to Beatty.

Services: Rest area at Hells Gate on Hwy. 374. No services on trail.

Historical Highlights: Chloride City was first established in the early 1870s when silver was discovered at Chloride Cliff. Poor profits led to the town's abandonment by 1880. New investors reopened the mine in 1908. Enough ore was discovered to warrant construction of a cyanide mill in 1916, but by 1918 the town, once again, shut down.

Maps: Death Valley N.P. map, USGS 100,000-scale map, Death Valley Junction 36116-A1-TM-100, DeLorme Atlas & Gazetteer.

Drop into rocky wash after parking area.

Relax in the shade of this large cave.

Cottonwood Canyon narrows at end.

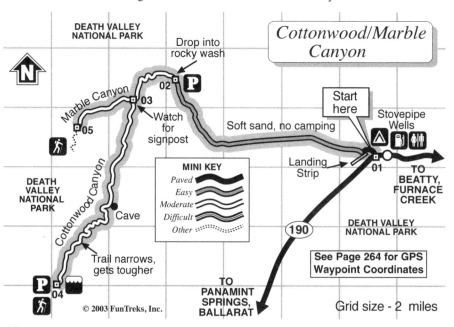

DEATH VALLEY
NATIONAL PARK

Drop into
rocky wash

Cottonwood/Marble
Canyon

Marble Canyon

02 P

03

05

Watch
for
signpost

Start
here

Stovepipe
Wells

Soft sand, no camping

01

TO
BEATTY,
FURNACE
CREEK

DEATH
VALLEY
NATIONAL
PARK

Cottonwood Canyon

Cave

Landing
Strip

MINI KEY
Paved
Easy
Moderate
Difficult
Other

Trail narrows,
gets tougher

P
04

190

DEATH VALLEY
NATIONAL PARK

See Page 264 for GPS
Waypoint Coordinates

TO
PANAMINT
SPRINGS,
BALLARAT

© 2003 FunTreks, Inc.

Grid size - 2 miles

Cottonwood/Marble Canyon 3

Location: Directly west of Stovepipe Wells in Death Valley National Park.

Difficulty: Moderate. Starts easy then drops into rocky wash. If you are the first vehicle in after a heavy rain, you may have to blaze your own trail and conditions could be difficult. The most challenging section is at the end of Cottonwood Canyon. Do not drive this trail if rain is forecast.

Features: Surface water at end of Cottonwood Canyon. Gigantic cave along Cottonwood Canyon. Great hike at end of Marble Canyon features many different marbleized rock formations. Street-legal vehicles only.

Time & Distance: Allow 5 to 6 hours to explore both canyons and return to start. Cottonwood Canyon is 19.5 miles from Hwy. 190 and takes about 2 hours one-way. Marble Canyon is 2.7 miles and takes about 1/2 hour one-way from Cottonwood Canyon.

To Get There: Take Hwy. 190 to Stovepipe Wells in Death Valley National Park. Head north on paved road that enters large campground west of gas station and general store.

Trail Description: Reset your odometer as you pull off Hwy. 190 [01]. Stay left of campground entrance. Bear right of air strip at 0.4 miles onto sandy road. Road is deeply graded through soft sand. Gradually the road narrows and gets rockier as it turns north and drops into wide wash after parking area at 8.5 miles [02]. Stay left at 10.8 miles [03] where Marble Canyon goes right. Faded signpost is hard to see. Stay right at 12.5 to avoid wilderness. Cave on left at 14.9 miles. Bear left in main wash at 16.2 and 18.1 miles. At 17.5 miles, the canyon narrows and gradually gets tougher. Trail ends at 19.5 miles [04] but you can hike farther following small stream. Return to **Marble Canyon** entrance and turn left. *Reset odometer.* Bear left at 0.2 miles. The park no longer allows vehicles past the 2.7-mile point [05]. Hike another 1.1 miles to see outstanding marbleized rock formations.

Return Trip: Return the way you came.

Services: Gas, food, restrooms, lodging and camping in Stovepipe Wells.

Maps: Death Valley N.P. map, USGS 100,000-scale map, Saline Valley, CA-NV 36117-E1-TM-100, DeLorme Atlas & Gazetteer.

First part of the trail to the Inyo Mine is easy enough for any SUV.

Eye of the Needle

The mill at Inyo Mine shut down in 1938.

Difficult rocky ledges going up to Echo Pass.

Approaching Echo Pass.

40

Echo Pass/ Inyo Mine 4

Location: East of Furnace Creek in Death Valley National Park.

Difficulty: Difficult. Although a little rocky in places, the first part of the trip to Inyo Mine is easy and suitable for just about any SUV. The last portion of the trip to Echo Pass is mostly moderate but has one difficult spot. Stock SUVs should have very high ground clearance and good articulation. Even then, a winch or tow strap may be needed for this one section. Vehicles with big tires and differential lockers should have no problem.

Features: A popular route because much of the trip is easy and the start is close to Furnace Creek and the visitor center. Pass through Echo Canyon featuring *Eye of the Needle*. Visit Inyo Mine where several cabins and significant mining structures remain. Climb high into the Funeral Mountains with great views along the route to Echo Pass. Street-legal vehicles only.

Time & Distance: The 9.6-mile drive to Inyo Mine takes about an hour one-way. Echo Pass is another 5.2 miles. This part of the trip could take another hour or two one-way, depending upon the capability of your vehicle. With stops along the way, you can easily spend 5 to 6 hours for the whole trip. (The route continues on past Echo Pass to Amargosa Valley in Nevada, a significant distance and a long drive back to the start. I did not drive this part of the trip.)

To Get There: Head south on Hwy. 190 from Furnace Creek. Stay on Hwy. 190 about 2 miles past the Furnace Creek Inn. Turn left on a well-defined road displaying a Jeep symbol.

Trail Description: Reset your odometer as you pull off Hwy. 190 [01]. Head northeast on a mildly rocky road. Climb gradually across an open area before reaching Echo Canyon after 3.4 miles. Watch for *Eye of the Needle* on the left at 4.7 miles. Gradually, the canyon widens again. Stay right at 7.8 miles. At 9.1 miles (02) stay right to reach the Inyo Mine. A sign here indicates Amargosa is left. You'll come back to this point later for Echo Pass. Stop at a small parking area on the left at 9.6 miles (03) to visit the Inyo Mine. The road is closed past this point. When visiting the mine area, remember to leave everything as you find it. It is a federal crime to remove anything from an historical site.

　　To reach Echo Pass, return 0.6 miles and turn right at the Amargosa sign (02). *Reset your odometer.* Follow a single, two-track road north. At

0.2 miles, bear left. A right here would drop down a steep, rocky bank and shortcut the trail. At 0.3 miles, a barricade indicates the road is closed straight ahead but the trail continues around to the right. You can stop here and hike to the Schwaub Townsite in less than a mile. Not much is left at the site but a few scattered rusty cans. At 0.4 miles the earlier mentioned shortcut joins on the right. You continue straight. The trail varies from easy to moderate as it winds back and forth through a narrow canyon. There are mines along the way but most are hidden. Watch for clues of their existence in the form of scattered metal pipes and cables lying on the ground.

Somewhere around 3.0 miles you'll encounter several difficult rocky ledges (see photo). Stock vehicles will have a tough time here. Hardcore enthusiasts will be disappointed that this stretch isn't longer. At 3.5 miles make a hard left uphill. Then at 3.7 miles, bear left downhill on a better traveled road. Go over the top of a rounded hill at about 4.2 miles and continue down the other side. Bear right at 4.4 and left at 4.8 as you wind up and down rolling hills. Echo Pass is at the top of a hill at 5.2 miles (04). The pass is not obvious or very dramatic. I elected to turn around at this point.

Return Trip: Return the way you came.

Services: Complete services, including gas, are available at Furnace Creek, largest of the burgs serving Death Valley National Park. Furnace Creek Visitor Center is also located here. Many of the services are located inside Furnace Creek Ranch. Open to the public, the ranch has a general store, a gift shop, restaurants and a post office. Furnace Creek Campground, closest to the Visitor Center, fills up first with overflow going to Sunset and Texas Spring Campgrounds. The campgrounds take large RVs and motor homes. Campgrounds have flush toilets but hookups and showers are not available. The park is open all year.

Historical Highlights: Inyo Mine had two periods of activity: the first from 1905 to 1912, the second from about 1932 to 1938. The town included a boarding house, a blacksmith shop and company store in 1907. A 25-ton ball mill was built in the later period but shut down in 1938. Schwaub was a short-lived tent town named after Charles Schwaub, a well-known industrialist known for his support of mining in the boom town of Rhyolite near Beatty.

Maps: Death Valley N.P. visitor map, USGS 250,000-scale map, Death Valley, CA-NV, DeLorme Atlas & Gazetteer. Schwaub can be found on USGS 7.5 minute map Lees Camp, CA/NV. 36116-E6-TF-024.

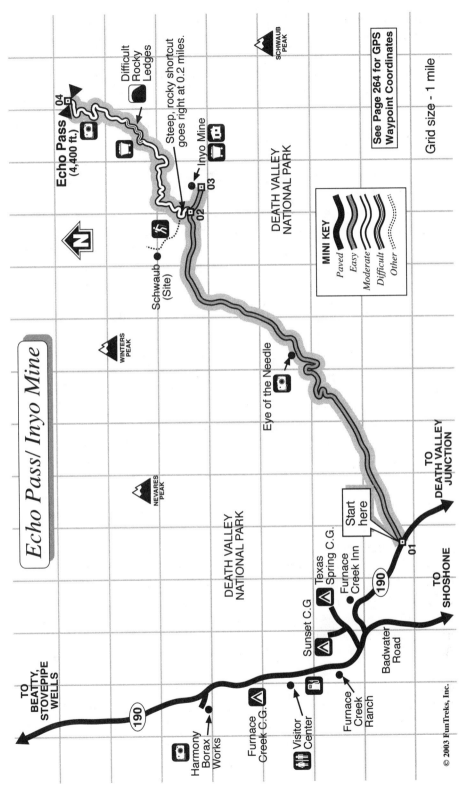

Echo Pass / Inyo Mine

Echo Pass (4,400 ft.)

Difficult Rocky Ledges

Steep, rocky shortcut goes right at 0.2 miles.

Inyo Mine

04

03

02

SCHWAUB PEAK

DEATH VALLEY NATIONAL PARK

Schwaub (Site)

WINTERS PEAK

Eye of the Needle

NEVARES PEAK

DEATH VALLEY NATIONAL PARK

Start here

TO DEATH VALLEY JUNCTION

01

190

TO SHOSHONE

Badwater Road

Texas Spring C.G.

Furnace Creek Inn

Sunset C.G

Furnace Creek Ranch

190

TO BEATTY, STOVEPIPE WELLS

Harmony Borax Works

Furnace Creek C.G.

Visitor Center

MINI KEY

Paved
Easy
Moderate
Difficult
Other

See Page 264 for GPS Waypoint Coordinates

Grid size - 1 mile

© 2003 FunTreks, Inc.

43

First part of trip crosses heavily eroded alluvial fan. Rains can quickly increase difficulty.

Small *Adopt-a-Cabin* at end of trail is short hike to mine at right.

Mill at Corona Mine.

Jail Canyon changes with each rain.

Jail Canyon

Panamint

Jail Canyon

04

Corona Mine

DEATH VALLEY
NATIONAL PARK

Mountains

03

Enter
National
Park

02

MINI KEY

Paved
Easy
Moderate
Difficult
Other

Indian
Ranch
Road

Start
here

See Page 264 for GPS
Waypoint Coordinates

TO
HWY.
178

01

SURPRISE
CANYON
WILDERNESS

TO
BALLARAT

Grid size - 1 mile

© 2003 FunTreks, Inc.

Jail Canyon 5

Location: East of Hwy. 178 and north of Ballarat.

Difficulty: Moderate. This trail crosses an alluvial fan and then winds its way up a major canyon which is highly susceptible to erosion. Conditions drastically worsen after each new flash flood. Stay out if rain is predicted.

Features: The end of this trail features an *Adopt-a-Cabin* and an amazingly intact 3-stamp mill at the Corona Mine. Street-legal vehicles only in park.

Time & Distance: Once on the trail, allow 3 to 4 hours to get in and back out. The drive is 5.6 miles one way.

To Get There: Drive north from Trona on Hwy. 178. Past the turn for Ballarat, continue north on Hwy. 178 another 9.2 miles to Indian Ranch Road on the right. If you are coming south from Panamint Springs on Hwy. 178, turn left about 0.4 miles south of where the road forks to Wildrose. Head east on Indian Ranch Road 4.1 miles to the trail on the left. From Ballarat, go north on Indian Ranch Road 7.8 miles and turn right.

Trail Description: Reset your odometer at the start [01]. Head north on a poorly defined road. A sign indicates you are entering Surprise Canyon Wilderness. Enter Death Valley National Park after 2.0 miles (02). Note huge pieces of mining debris on the right at 2.8. The road drops down into a large wash at 3.1 miles (03) then climbs out on the other side. At 3.7 miles the canyon narrows. Stay left at 5.2 miles—the road on the right is closed. At 5.4 miles continue straight where another canyon goes right. Pick your way through various mining debris until you reach the end of the trail at 5.6 miles (04). Park by the cabin and hike a short distance to the Corona Mine.

Return Trip: Return the way you came.

Services: Gas available at Trona. No services in Ballarat or along the trail.

Historical Highlights: Originally called the Gem Mine, the Corona Mine saw its heyday in 1899. A flood destroyed most of the mill in 1901. The mill was powered by a water wheel, a first for Death Valley.

Maps: USGS 100,000-scale map, Darwin Hills, CA 36117-A1-TM-100, DeLorme Atlas & Gazetteer.

Looking up to Pleasant Canyon from Ballarat.

Rocky section on Pleasant Canyon.

Part of Clair Camp below Radcliff Mine.

3-ton weight limit on bridge above Briggs Camp.

Narrow ledge just before bridge.

Briggs Cabin must be seen inside to appreciate.

Snow above 6,000 ft. in February.

46

Pleasant Canyon/ South Park

SPECIAL NOTE: *Just before press time, a section of road just west of the bridge was blocked by a rock slide. You will have to turn around at this point until this section is repaired. Contact the BLM in Barstow for status.*

Location: East of the ghost town of Ballarat, northeast of Trona.

Difficulty: Difficult. Most of this trail is easy to moderate; however, the steepest, narrowest sections of both Pleasant Canyon and South Park Canyon are susceptible to water damage and rock movement, sometimes creating difficult conditions. When I drove the trail, stock SUVs would have had difficulty negotiating these stretches. South Park Canyon is quite steep and is always difficult going up from west to east. A narrow wooden bridge above Briggs Cabin has a weight limit of 3 tons. Large vehicles loaded with gear can easily exceed this weight limit. **DO NOT ATTEMPT TO CROSS THIS BRIDGE IF YOU HAVE ANY DOUBT YOUR LOADED VEHICLE WEIGHS MORE THAN 6,000 LBS.** Dangerous ice and snow may be present at higher elevations in the winter. Some tight brush in places.

Features: A scenic, high elevation trail. Many mines and structures along the way, especially at Clair Camp. Briggs Cabin is, by far, the most elaborate and best stocked of all the *Adopt-a-Cabins*. Briggs and Stone cabin are maintained by volunteers (Friends of Briggs). The cabins are on private land owned by C.R. Briggs Corporation which graciously allows you to use the cabins for free. Street-legal vehicles only inside Death Valley N. P.

Time & Distance: Allow 6 to 8 hours driving time for this 23.3-mile adventure. Plan to camp overnight if you explore side roads and hiking trails.

To Get There: Take Hwy. 178 north from Trona. Turn right on Ballarat Road and head east to the ghost town of Ballarat. Leave from the intersection of Ballarat Road and Wingate Road just south of the general store.

Trail Description: Reset your odometer at the start [01]. Bear right at 0.5 miles where Jackpot Canyon goes left. The trail becomes steep and brushy within the first mile and gets rockier as you climb, with the toughest spots coming between miles 3 and 4. Pass through an open gate at 6.0 miles (02) as you enter Clair Camp. There's much to see here so take a few minutes and look around, but watch out for snakes and rusty nails. Continue straight at 7.0 where a side road goes right to World Beater Mine. Water piped from a nearby spring fills a makeshift bathtub on the left at 8.3. At 8.4 you enter Death Valley National Park. Bear right at 8.6 where a side road goes left to

Cooper Mine. Bear right at 9.2 then continue straight at 10.0 miles where a lesser road goes left. Go right at 10.1. Go right of a cabin at 10.2 on a steep rocky road which climbs to a saddle above 6,800 feet at 10.7 miles (03). (Note: this route bypasses the higher and longer route over Rogers Pass. Our group took this shortcut because of deepening snow.)

As you descend from the saddle to Middle Park, several difficult side roads go left. Continue straight downhill on the main trail. Once on the valley floor, bear right at 12.8 then continue straight at 12.9 (04). A right turn here would take you part way down Middle Park Canyon. Bear right uphill at 13.0. Continue straight and drop downhill into South Park at 13.2. Stay right downhill at 13.7. Several sheds mark a mine location at 13.8. Bear right here, followed by another right immediately. Another right soon follows at 13.9 miles (05). Head west across South Park. Continue straight at 15.6 and start your descent into South Park Canyon. You leave Death Valley National Park at Colter Spring, an overgrown tunnel of brush at 16.7 miles. A side trip to Thorndike Mine goes left at 17.6. You continue straight. Cross a dramatic narrow ledge and wooden bridge at 17.8 miles (06). (Maximum load limit of bridge is 6,000 lbs. Don't risk your life if you have the slightest doubt your vehicle weighs more than this.)

Below the bridge, take a short side trip to Briggs Cabin on the right. If a flag is flying, the cabin is occupied. Ask if you can take a tour inside—you'll be amazed. Return to the main road and continue down the mountain. Make a left at 19.3 before the canyon finally narrows and ends. From here, a shelf road twists dramatically up then down the mountainside. Bear right at 20.9 where a difficult shortcut goes left straight down the mountainside. Wingate Road is finally reached at 23.3 miles (07).

Return Trip: Turn right and head back to Ballarat in 3.9 miles.

Services: Gas, food and water are available at Trona, about 25 miles south of Ballarat. To avoid driving back and forth, carry extra gas. No services are available in Ballarat or along the trail. Until recently, a general store operated in Ballarat; however, when I was there in February, 2002, the store was closed. A caretaker was living there to collect for camping. A very small fee was charged for a bare spot on the desert floor.

Historical Highlights: Between 1897 and 1917, Ballarat's population grew to about 400. It once had 3 hotels, 7 saloons, a post office and a school. Although the town served as a supply center for all the mines in the area, it was primarily supported by the nearby Radcliffe and World Beater Mines, which you'll pass as you go up Pleasant Canyon. The cemetery in Ballarat contains the grave of *Seldom Seen Sam*, Ballarat's most colorful inhabitant.

Maps: USGS 100,000-scale map, Darwin Hills, CA 36117-A1-TM-100, Sidekick Map Panamint Mountains, DeLorme Atlas & Gazetteer.

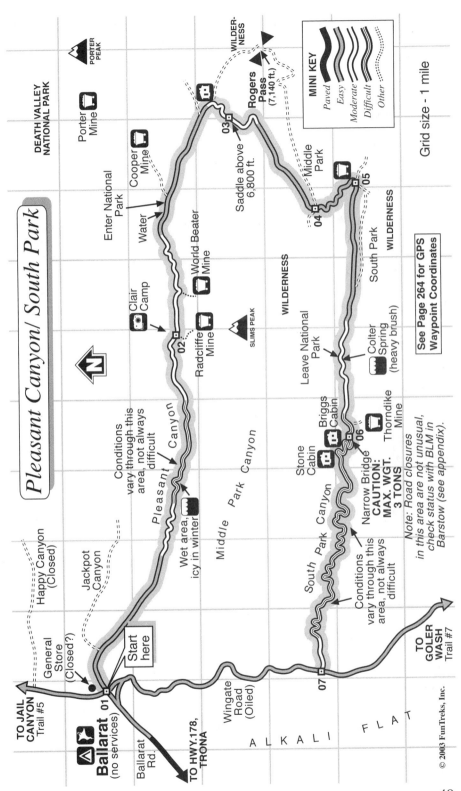

Pleasant Canyon/ South Park

DEATH VALLEY NATIONAL PARK

PORTER PEAK

Porter Mine

Cooper Mine

Enter National Park

Water

World Beater Mine

Clair Camp

Radcliffe Mine

SLIMS PEAK

02

WILDERNESS

Pleasant Canyon

Middle Park Canyon

Conditions vary through this area, not always difficult

Wet area, icy in winter

Happy Canyon (Closed)

Jackpot Canyon

General Store (Closed?)

Start here

Ballarat 01 (no services)

Ballarat Rd.

TO HWY.178, TRONA

TO JAIL CANYON Trail #5

Wingate Road (Oiled)

A L K A L I   F L A T

© 2003 FunTreks, Inc.

Rogers Pass (7,140 ft.)

WILDER-NESS

03

Saddle above 6,800 ft.

Middle Park

04

05

South Park WILDERNESS

Leave National Park

Colter Spring (heavy brush)

Stone Cabin

Briggs Cabin

06

Thorndike Mine

Narrow Bridge CAUTION: MAX. WGT. 3 TONS

South Park Canyon

Conditions vary through this area, not always difficult

07

TO GOLER WASH Trail #7

Note: Road closures in this area are not unusual, check status with BLM in Barstow (see appendix).

See Page 264 for GPS Waypoint Coordinates

MINI KEY

Paved
Easy
Moderate
Difficult
Other

Grid size - 1 mile

49

Goler Wash is narrow and steep at the start.

Optional side road above Lotus Camp.

Barker Cabin (Charles Manson's hideout)

Rocky and steep climbing to Mengel Pass.

All vehicles must be street legal inside park.

Goler Wash/ Mengel Pass ◆7

Location: South of Ballarat, northeast of Trona.

Difficulty: Difficult. Most of this trail is easy to moderate. Only one short stretch over Mengel Pass is difficult. Under normal circumstances, high-clearance 4x4 SUVs can reach this point without a problem. Those with skid plates should also be able to get over Mengel Pass but some caution must be taken to avoid undercarriage damage. Some rock stacking may be necessary. In addition, there is always the possibility that a flash flood through the canyon could make it more difficult. This trail is extremely remote. Make sure your gas tank is full and carry plenty of water. Street-legal vehicles only inside Death Valley National Park.

Features: Camp nearby in the ghost town of Ballarat. Along the trail, see mines and outstanding *Adopt-a-Cabins* including Barker Ranch, once the hideout of serial killer Charles Manson and his gang. Other cabins include Russel Camp (my favorite) and the Geologist's Cabin, popular because it is very tight and clean. The other cabins are mice infested and are posted with danger signs explaining the deadly Hantavirus which is spread by inhaling dust from mice droppings. People stay in the cabins despite the warnings.

Time & Distance: Allow about 2 hours to reach Mengel Pass, a distance of 10.6 miles. Plan at least 5 to 6 hours for the whole trip.

To Get There: From Ballarat, head south on Wingate Road 15.1 miles and turn left uphill. The first half of Wingate Road services the active Briggs Mine so you may see cars going in and out. You can also reach the start of Goler Wash by driving Fish Canyon (Trail #9). If you are heading to Furnace Creek in Death Valley National Park, you can continue across Butte Valley (Trail #8) to Badwater Road. Make sure you have plenty of gas.

Trail Description: Reset your odometer as you turn left off Wingate Road [01]. Proceed uphill on a rocky road marked P52. Enter Goler Wash at 1.4 miles where a single lane road winds through a narrow canyon. The road has been improved here but is susceptible to damage from erosion. You may see burro droppings along the route but you'll seldom see a burro. A very short side trip on the right at 3.8 miles (02) leads to tiny Newman Cabin. Burros will tear up the cabin if the door is left open so close it when you leave. Lotus Mine Camp is reached at 4.7 miles. A nasty side road on the right climbs high up the mountainside to Lotus Mine.

Stay left at 5.2 where a dead-end road goes right. Bear left at 5.8 miles just before you enter Death Valley National Park. At 6.0 miles (03), turn right for a side trip to the Barker Ranch and the Manson hideout. Bear right at 6.4 then make a hard left at 6.6 miles (04) where the road splits 3 ways. Pass through a gate and close it. The cabin contains supplies and interesting memorabilia. The road continues a short distance but ends at a Wilderness boundary just short of Myers Ranch, now burned down.

Return to the main trail (03) and *reset your odometer*. Turn right and continue up Goler Wash. Bear left at 0.2. Make an important right turn uphill at 0.7. Stay right after climbing some steep ridges. It flattens out for a short distance on a sandy road. The road splits at 2.4 miles as it gets rockier. You can go either way. A large grave marker identifies Mengel Pass at 3.3 miles (05). Continue straight down the other side on the steepest, rockiest part of the trail. The road gradually flattens out as you drop into Butte Valley.

A fork at 4.7 miles (06) goes left to Russel Camp. Straight continues to a convergence of roads at Anvil Spring at 5.4 miles (07) just below the Geologist Cabin. To get to Russel Camp, make two left turns and go about 0.4 miles back into a smaller valley. Come back out and turn left uphill to reach Mengel's Cabin. The long road heading northeast across the valley goes past Striped Butte and eventually reaches Highway 178 (See Trail #8).

Return Trip: Return the way you came for Ballarat and Trona. To reach Furnace Creek, continue across Butte Valley. (See directions for Trail #8).

Services: Return to Trona which is about 50 miles from the start of Goler Wash. Ballarat has no services. From Butte Valley, full services can be found in Shoshone.

Historical Highlights: The Lotus Mine is located some 2,800 feet above the base camp along Goler Wash. At one time, two aerial tramlines serviced the mine. Carl Mengel owned the mine until 1935. He lived in the cabin shown on the map (opposite page) from 1912 to 1944. His ashes are entombed in the stone monument at the pass.

Serial killer Charles Manson and his gang moved into the cabin at Barker Ranch in 1968. He was apprehended there October 12, 1969, for his involvement in the Tate-LaBianca murders which occurred two months earlier. He was found huddled inside a cabinet after multiple searches of the cabin.

Maps: Death Valley N.P. map, USGS 100,000-scale map, Ridgecrest, CA, 35117-E1-TM-100, Sidekick Map Panamint Mountains, DeLorme Atlas & Gazetteer.

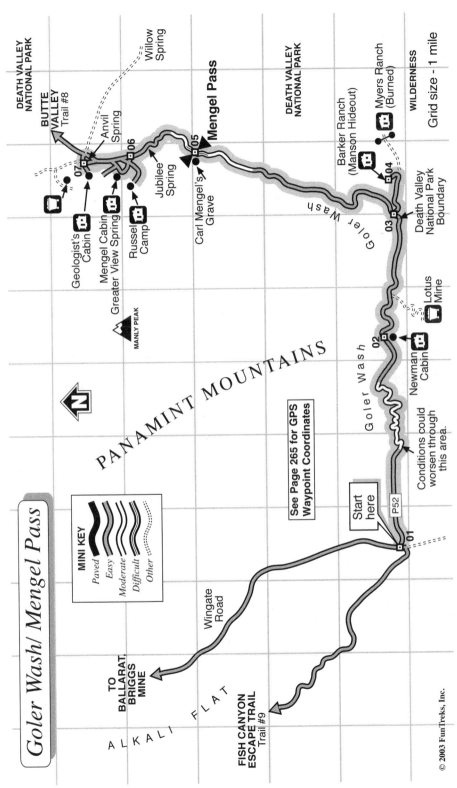

Goler Wash / Mengel Pass

MINI KEY
- Paved
- Easy
- Moderate
- Difficult
- Other

See Page 265 for GPS Waypoint Coordinates

DEATH VALLEY NATIONAL PARK

BUTTE VALLEY Trail #8

Willow Spring

Anvil Spring

Mengel Pass

07
06
05

Geologist's Cabin

Mengel Cabin
Greater View Spring

Russel Camp

Jubilee Spring

Carl Mengel's Grave

MANLY PEAK

N

PANAMINT MOUNTAINS

DEATH VALLEY NATIONAL PARK

Barker Ranch (Manson Hideout)

Myers Ranch (Burned)

04

WILDERNESS

Grid size - 1 mile

Death Valley National Park Boundary

03

Goler Wash

Lotus Mine

02

Newman Cabin

Conditions could worsen through this area.

Goler Wash

Start here

P52

01

Wingate Road

TO BALLARAT, BRIGGS MINE

ALKALI FLAT

FISH CANYON ESCAPE TRAIL Trail #9

© 2003 FunTreks, Inc.

53

Looking across Butte Valley at Striped Butte from Geologist's Cabin.

Well-preserved mill for Gold Hill Mine.

Entire route is suitable for stock SUVs.

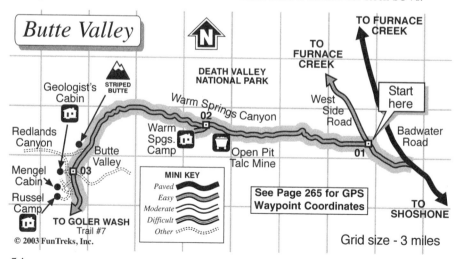

Butte Valley

N

TO FURNACE CREEK

TO FURNACE CREEK

Start here

Badwater Road

West Side Road

DEATH VALLEY NATIONAL PARK

Geologist's Cabin

STRIPED BUTTE

Warm Springs Canyon

02

Redlands Canyon

Butte Valley

Warm Spgs. Camp

Open Pit Talc Mine

Mengel Cabin

03

Russel Camp

TO GOLER WASH
Trail #7

© 2003 FunTreks, Inc.

01

TO SHOSHONE

MINI KEY
Paved
Easy
Moderate
Difficult
Other

See Page 265 for GPS Waypoint Coordinates

Grid size - 3 miles

54

Location: South of Furnace Creek, west of Shoshone.

Difficulty: Easy. Mildly rocky road suitable for stock SUVs. Explore side roads in Butte Valley if seeking more challenge.

Features: See unusual talc mines. Visit desert oasis fed by natural warm springs. Explore beautiful Butte Valley on numerous side roads. Tour historic *Adopt-a-Cabins*. Connects to Trail #7. Street-legal vehicles only.

Time & Distance: Allow 2 hours to reach Geologist's Cabin at 22.8 miles.

To Get There: From Highway 190 south of Furnace Creek, drive 42 miles south on Badwater Road. Turn right on well-marked West Side Road. Head west then north a total of 3.0 miles to Butte Valley Road on left.

Trail Description: Reset your odometer at the start [01]. Head west on wide, uneventful Butte Valley Road. First talc mine on left at 9.1 miles followed by several others, including a large open pit mine. Entrance to Warm Springs Camp on left at 10.9 miles (02). Kiosk explains camp. Note posted warnings. Follow steep hiking trail behind cabins to warm springs that created this oasis. Examine Gold Hill mill. Return to main road (02) and *reset odometer*. Continue west on rockier road as it winds through narrower Warm Springs Canyon. Continue straight at 7.3 miles as Striped Butte begins to come into view. Road surface changes to smoother sandy soil. Major crossroads reached at 11.9 miles (03). Slight right goes to Anvil Spring and Geologist's Cabin. Hard left for Willow Spring. Straight to Mengel Cabin, Russel Camp and Goler Wash (Trail #7). Road that heads north from Geologist's Cabin leads to Redlands Canyon where you'll find interesting and challenging side roads. Many mines and a few mine structures dot the area.

Return Trip: Return the way you came or exit via Goler Wash (Trail #7). This route has a short section of difficult terrain over Mengel Pass.

Services: None along trail. Make sure you have plenty of water and gas before heading into this remote area. Full services in Furnace Creek and Shoshone, which is about 31 miles southeast of start on Highway 178.

Maps: Death Valley N.P. visitor map, USGS 250,000-scale map, Trona, CA, Sidekick Map Panamint Mountains, DeLorme Atlas & Gazetteer.

Road P170 along dry lake bed.

Looking across Panamint Valley at C.R. Briggs Mine.

Route joins Escape Trail at this sign.

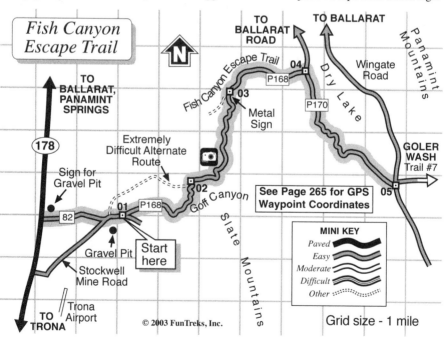

Fish Canyon Escape Trail

See Page 265 for GPS Waypoint Coordinates

MINI KEY
Paved
Easy
Moderate
Difficult
Other

Grid size - 1 mile

© 2003 FunTreks, Inc.

56

Fish Canyon Escape Trail ⑨

Location: Northeast of Ridgecrest and Trona.

Difficulty: Easy. Mildly rocky road, steep in places. OK for stock SUVs.

Features: Follows historic Death Valley escape route of early emigrants. Fun shortcut to start of Goler Wash (Trail #7).

Time & Distance: Allow 2 hours one way for this 12.4-mile trip.

To Get There: Head north about 6 miles from Trona on Hwy. 178. Turn right on Road 82 at sign for *Valley Sand & Gravel*. Bear left at 1.6 miles on large gravel road. At 1.9 miles bear left on Road P168. (Sign reads P 68)

Trail Description: Reset your odometer at the start [01]. Follow road towards foothills. Bear left at 1.4 and 1.7 miles. At 2.4 miles bear left uphill. Ignore lesser roads and continue straight at 2.7 (02) where road joins on left. Great views of Panamint Valley unfold as you meander along high ridges. Drop steeply to sign which explains *Escape Trail* (ET) at 5.9 miles (03). Bear right to continue. (Trail to historic points on left was badly washed out.) Follow rocky wash downhill. Bear right at 6.5 at sign for P168. Continue heading east on rocky, faint road following ET arrow signs and cairns. At 8.3 miles (04) turn right at T on P170. Road follows edge of dry lake. Bear left at 9.6 as road joins on right. Wingate Road reached at 12.4 miles (05). Entrance to Goler Wash (P52) is across road to left.

Return Trip: Left on Wingate Road goes to Ballarat in 15.1 miles.

Services: Return to Trona. None in Ballarat or along trail.

Historical Highlights: In 1849, William Manly led a party of emigrants across America in search of riches in California. His party got lost in the Death Valley area and wandered hopelessly for months. He scouted ahead and finally found a way out. When he returned for his party, only two families, the Bennetts and Arcanes, were still alive. The route described here is part of his escape route. In 1894, Manly wrote a book, *Death Valley in '49* chronicling his harrowing adventure. It's fascinating reading.

Maps: Not aware of any map that shows complete route. Portions of route can be found on USGS 100,000-scale map, Ridgecrest, CA.

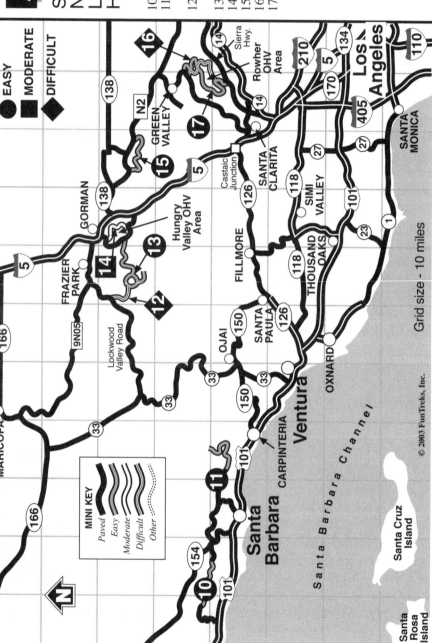

AREA 2

Santa Barbara, North of Los Angeles, Hungry Valley

10. Santa Ynez Peak
11. Agua Caliente Springs
12. Lockwood/ Miller Jeep Trail
13. Alamo Mtn. Loop
14. Pronghorn Trail
15. Leibre Mountain
16. Rowher Trail
17. Sierra Pelona Road

● EASY
■ MODERATE
◆ DIFFICULT

MINI KEY
Paved
Easy
Moderate
Difficult
Other

Grid size - 10 miles

© 2003 FunTreks, Inc.

N

Santa Barbara, North of Los Angeles, Hungry Valley

Many 4-wheel-drive roads close to Los Angeles have been gated closed over the years. There are, however, a few good trails still open. I've selected some of the best based on information from local users. At the top of the list is *Lockwood/Miller Jeep Trail*, known statewide as one of the better hardcore trails in Southern California. It's near my favorite OHV area, Hungry Valley. In addition to great ATV and dirt-bike trails, this area has interesting SUV and Jeep roads. Moderate *Pronghorn Trail* is just one example. West of the park is adjoining *Alamo Mountain Loop*, an easy, scenic drive that climbs high into the Los Padres National Forest. Northeast of Santa Clarita, you'll find exciting Rowher OHV Area, again offering a wide array of trails for all motorized recreationalists, including super-steep *Rowher Trail*. No Southern California backroad book would be complete without ocean views. For these, I ventured west to Santa Barbara where I enjoyed *Santa Ynez Peak* and *Agua Caliente Springs*. These little-used backroads look down from high above the city to spectacular beach and coastal views, weather permitting.

Vast Hungry Valley OHV Area covers 19,000 acres and has 130 miles of designated trails.

59

Looking north to Lake Cachuma, a county recreation area.

Just a few rough spots.

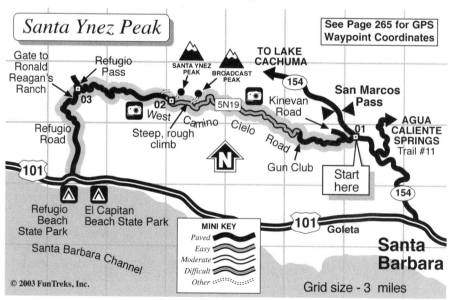

Gate to Ronald Reagan's Ranch is marked *Rancho Dos Vista*.

Santa Ynez Peak

See Page 265 for GPS
Waypoint Coordinates

Gate to
Ronald
Reagan's
Ranch

Refugio
Pass

SANTA YNEZ
PEAK

BROADCAST
PEAK

TO LAKE
CACHUMA

154

San Marcos
Pass

03

02
West

5N19

Kinevan
Road

01

AGUA
CALIENTE
SPRINGS
Trail #11

Refugio
Road

Camino

Cielo

Road

Steep, rough
climb

N

Gun Club

Start
here

154

101

Refugio
Beach
State Park

El Capitan
Beach State Park

MINI KEY

Paved
Easy
Moderate
Difficult
Other

101

Goleta

Santa Barbara Channel

Santa
Barbara

© 2003 FunTreks, Inc.

Grid size - 3 miles

60

Santa Ynez Peak ⑩

Location: Northwest of Santa Barbara.

Difficulty: Easy. Part of the road is paved, but it's a very enjoyable drive. The dirt portion is steep and rough in a few places. Suitable for all high-clearance stock SUVs. Climbs over 4,000 feet.

Features: Follows a ridge across the Santa Ynez Mountains which parallel the coastline. Great views both north and south most of the way. Mornings are often foggy, obscuring southern views of the ocean—afternoons are best. Pass the gate to Ronald Reagan's Ranch just below Refugio Pass. Maps show his ranch as *Rancho del Cielo* but the gate says *Rancho Dos Vista.*

Time & Distance: From the start of the trail to Highway 101 is 26.3 miles. Allow about 3 hours.

To Get There: From Hwy. 101 west of Santa Barbara, head north on Hwy. 154. Turn left at a sign for Kinevan Road after about 7.2 miles.

Trail Description: Reset your odometer at the start [01]. Head west on a narrow paved road as it weaves through a residential area. Bear left after 0.2 miles on West Camino Cielo Road. The pavement ends at 4.0 miles after going by the Westchester Gun Club. The road is rough in places as it winds up and down along a ridge. Under no circumstances are you to leave the main road, which is clearly fenced on both sides. Lake Cachuma can be seen to the north and, if you're lucky, the coastline can be seen to the south. I drove this trail in the morning and the fog never cleared along the ocean. At 12.0 miles, a gated service road to the right goes uphill to Broadcast Peak. You can't miss it—it's covered with radio towers. Continue straight as the main road climbs steeply up a rocky section. At 13.2 miles (02) another service road goes right to Santa Ynez Peak. Continue west on a paved road at 13.7 miles. At Refugio Pass, bear left downhill on Refugio Road at 19.3 miles (03). Pass the gate to Reagan's Ranch at 19.8. Continue downhill on a long but beautiful drive to Hwy. 101 at 26.3 miles.

Return Trip: Head east on 101 to return to Santa Barbara.

Services: None on trail. RV camp at Refugio and El Capitan State Beaches.

Maps: Los Padres National Forest, USGS 250,000-scale map, Los Angeles, CA, DeLorme Atlas & Gazetteer.

Santa Barbara coastline barely visible through clearing fog.

Descent into Blue Canyon.

Unrestricted hot spring at end of trail.

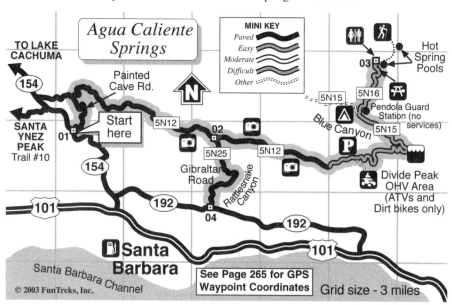

Agua Caliente Springs

TO LAKE CACHUMA

154

Painted Cave Rd.

N

SANTA YNEZ PEAK
Trail #10

154

01

Start here

5N12

02

5N25

5N12

Gibraltar Road

Rattlesnake Canyon

04

192

101

192

MINI KEY
Paved
Easy
Moderate
Difficult
Other

5N15

5N16

Hot Spring Pools

03

Blue Canyon

Pendola Guard Station (no services)

5N15

P

Divide Peak OHV Area
(ATVs and Dirt bikes only)

🅿 Santa Barbara

Santa Barbara Channel

© 2003 FunTreks, Inc.

See Page 265 for GPS Waypoint Coordinates

Grid size - 3 miles

Agua Caliente Springs 🕚

Location: North of Santa Barbara.

Difficulty: Easy. First part of route is a narrow, winding, poorly maintained paved road. After that, a bumpy dirt road descends steeply into canyon. Suitable for any SUV. Very hot in summer. Day use only at hot springs.

Features: See Painted Cave, an historical landmark featuring Chumash Indian rock art. Dirt road ends at picnic spot with unique hot spring pool, vault toilet and dressing area. A hiking trail leads to another hot spring. Trip concludes with a spectacular drive down Rattlesnake Canyon. Route passes Divide Peak OHV Area. (For ATVs and dirt bikes only.)

Time & Distance: About 30 miles from Hwy. 154 to the hot springs. Then 18 miles back to the turn for Gibraltar Road. The drive down Rattlesnake Canyon is another 7 miles. Allow 4 to 5 hours driving time altogether.

To Get There: From Hwy. 101 west of Santa Barbara, head north on Hwy. 154. Turn right on Painted Cave Road after about 5.6 miles.

Trail Description: *Reset odometer at start of Painted Cave Road* [01]. After steep, winding climb, pass Painted Cave on left at 2.4 miles. At 3.2 miles, turn right uphill on rutted paved road. Road winds along ridge and enters forest. Driver needs to pay attention and not be distracted by views. Bear left at 12.3 miles (02) where F.S. 5N25 goes downhill. You will come back to this spot later. Bear left at 19.1 miles when pavement ends. You'll soon pass parking area for Divide Peak OHV area. Concrete water crossing at 24.4. Bear right at 27.5 on F.S. 5N16. More water crossings before reaching end of trail at 30.1 miles (03). Hiking trail leads to another hot spring in about 1/8 mile. Return to F.S. 5N25 (Gibraltar Road) and turn left downhill. *Reset odometer.* Turn left when Gibraltar meets El Cielito at 6.2 miles. Cross over Mountain Road before reaching Hwy. 192 at 6.7 miles (04).

Return Trip: Left on Hwy. 192 to Hwy. 101, right goes back to Hwy. 154. Make sure you have a street map for Santa Barbara—streets are confusing.

Services: Vault toilet at hot spring. Full services in Santa Barbara.

Maps: Santa Barbara Street Map, Los Padres Nat. Forest, USGS 250,000-scale map, Los Angeles, CA, DeLorme Atlas & Gazetteer.

Steep and rocky after crossing Lockwood Creek at start.

Official trail marker.

Stock SUVs not recommended.

Last two miles of Miller Jeep Trail are tough.

Lockwood Creek Trail includes several long, continuous climbs.

Lockwood/ Miller Jeep Trail ◆12◆

Location: Southwest of Frazier Park, west of Hungry Valley OHV Area.

Difficulty: Difficult. Very hilly, steep and rocky. Not recommended for stock SUVs. Tough section at beginning of trail is fairly typical of conditions all along the route. Last few miles of Miller Jeep Trail are toughest part of trip. Lockers and oversized tires recommended. Don't drive alone.

Features: Very convenient to Los Angeles. One of few remaining hardcore trails in this part of California. Campgrounds along trail offer no amenities; however, those in Hungry Valley OHV Area include ramadas and picnic tables. Descent from Alamo Mountain is very scenic. Route is open to ATVs and dirt bikes. Stay on designated route at all times.

Time & Distance: Difficult portion of route is 12 miles and takes 4 to 5 hours assuming no problems along the way. Add another 15 miles of easy road to descend Alamo Mountain. Allow a full day for the entire trip.

To Get There: Exit Interstate 5 at Frazier Park. Head west on Frazier Mountain Road approximately 7 miles to Lake-of-the-Woods. Turn left on Lockwood Valley Road and go about 5 miles. Bear left when the road forks at a sign for Lockwood Creek Campground (Road 8N12). *Reset odometer.* Follow a well-defined graded road, ignoring smaller side roads. Bear right at 1.3 miles. At 2.2 miles, bear right into a cabled-off, open area. (I wasn't sure if this was the camping area or just parking.) Head southwest to an opening on the other side. A sign identifies the start of Lockwood Trail as route #127. A larger sign points out that this is adopted by the Point Magu 4WD Club.

Trail Description: Reset odometer at the start [01]. The trail drops down to Lockwood Creek then climbs steeply up the other side. You'll need low range immediately. (The trail has been rerouted in recent years to avoid following the creek. Under no circumstances are you to drive in the creek except to cross it.) Go either way at 0.5 miles. The trail is a mixture of soft powdery soil and rock. It would likely be very muddy if wet. You'll climb a ridge and drop down into a valley on the other side. At 2.1 miles (02), Yellowjacket Trail 7N15 goes left. This spot is a popular camping area. As you come around a corner, you'll see a fire ring followed by a steep hill to the left. Go up this hill.

At 4.7 miles a poorly marked road goes left to Cottonwood Campground (as shown on my forest map). You continue straight. A rock challenge on the left at 4.9 miles (03) is called *Kabob Hill*. It can be bypassed on the right. Continue straight at 5.3 miles where a sign identifies *Elk Ridge*. You'll descend very tight switchbacks before reaching the next valley floor. You'll cross Lockwood Creek again before reaching a T at 8.2 miles. Turn right at the T. You'll soon enter a sandy clearing at 9.1 miles (04). My forest map identified this spot as Sunset Campground, a nice shady spot to take a break. A side trip here goes right up Piru Creek.

Reset your odometer at this clearing (04) and bear left. Bear left at the next two closely spaced forks. The second fork begins the *Miller Jeep Trail*. A sign here identifies it as adopted by the Bakersfield Trail Blazers. After 2.8 miles of steep, rocky terrain, you reach the top of Alamo Mountain and a shady clearing which is the Dutchman Campground (05). Turn left to reach the Alamo Mountain Loop Road which is close enough to see. The shortest way down the mountain is to turn left on this well-defined road.

Return Trip: Follow Alamo Mountain Loop Road 2.6 miles and turn sharp left downhill (06). The road becomes paved about halfway down. It switchbacks and crosses over a concrete water crossing. This is a popular spot to park and cool your feet in the creek. From this point, the road becomes Gold Hill Road. Approximately 15 miles from the end of *Miller Jeep Trail*, you'll reach the intersection of Gold Hill Road and Hungry Valley Road (07). Right is the shortest way back to I-5. Left takes you past many campsites and the main entrance to Hungry Valley OHV Area.

Services: Plenty of eating places and gas stations in Gorman and at the I-5 interchange at Frazier Park. If you have an RV, there's a dump station and water hose at the Flying J Truck Stop at the Frazier Park interchange. Campgrounds in the Hungry Valley OHV Area have ramadas and vault toilets.

Maps: Los Padres National Forest, USGS 250,000-scale map, Los Angeles, CA, DeLorme Atlas & Gazetteer. If you camp in Hungry Valley OHV Area, you'll get a color map when you pay your entry fee. It does not show the Lockwood/ Miller Jeep Trail, but it has all the routes inside the park.

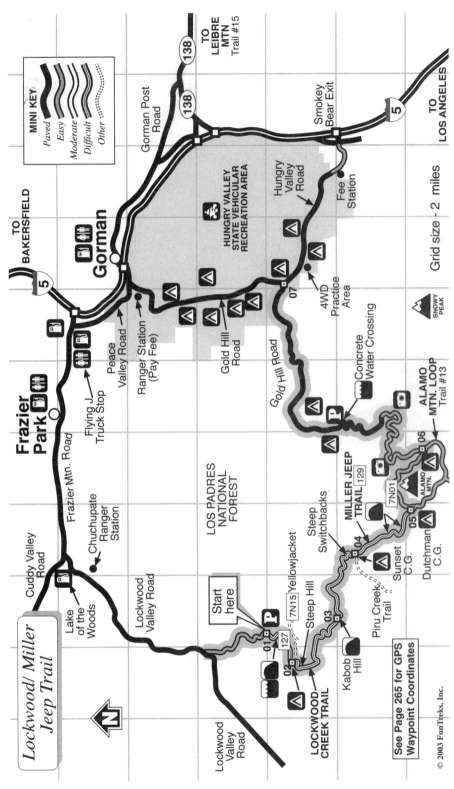

Lockwood/ Miller Jeep Trail

MINI KEY
Paved
Easy
Moderate
Difficult
Other

N

TO BAKERSFIELD

Frazier Park

Gorman

TO LEIBRE MTN Trail #15

138
138

Gorman Post Road

5

5
TO LOS ANGELES

Smokey Bear Exit

HUNGRY VALLEY STATE VEHICULAR RECREATION AREA

Hungry Valley Road

Fee Station

Flying J Truck Stop

Peace Valley Road

Ranger Station (Pay Fee)

Gold Hill Road

07

4WD Practice Area

SNOWY PEAK

Concrete Water Crossing

ALAMO MTN. LOOP Trail #13

06

ALAMO MTN.

05

Dutchman C.G.

7N01

MILLER JEEP TRAIL 129

04

Sunset C.G.

Piru Creek Trail

Steep Switchbacks

LOS PADRES NATIONAL FOREST

Cuddy Valley Road

Frazier Mtn. Road

Chuchupate Ranger Station

Lockwood Valley Road

Lake of the Woods

Lockwood Valley Road

Start here

03

Steep Hill

7N15 Yellowjacket

P

01

127

02

Kabob Hill

LOCKWOOD CREEK TRAIL

Grid size - 2 miles

See Page 265 for GPS Waypoint Coordinates

© 2003 FunTreks, Inc.

Great views heading down the mountain.

Keep your camera handy.

Many blind curves; drive cautiously.

Dry camp only at Dutchman Campground.

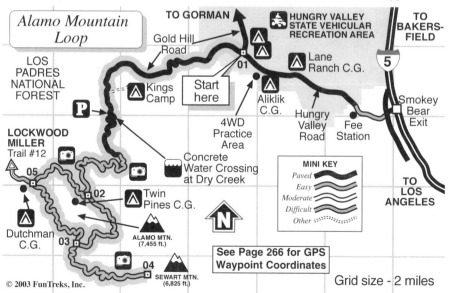

Alamo Mountain Loop

TO GORMAN

HUNGRY VALLEY STATE VEHICULAR RECREATION AREA

TO BAKERS-FIELD

Gold Hill Road

LOS PADRES NATIONAL FOREST

Lane Ranch C.G.

5

Kings Camp

Start here

Aliklik C.G.

Smokey Bear Exit

P

4WD Practice Area

Hungry Valley Road

Fee Station

LOCKWOOD MILLER
Trail #12

Concrete Water Crossing at Dry Creek

01

MINI KEY

Paved
Easy
Moderate
Difficult
Other

TO LOS ANGELES

05

02

Twin Pines C.G.

N

Dutchman C.G.

03

ALAMO MTN.
(7,455 ft.)

See Page 266 for GPS Waypoint Coordinates

© 2003 FunTreks, Inc.

04

SEWART MTN.
(6,825 ft.)

Grid size - 2 miles

Alamo Mountain Loop ⑬

Location: Southwest of Frazier Park and Hungry Valley OHV Area.

Difficulty: Easy. Well-maintained gravel road suitable for any stock SUV. Single lane with many blind turns on loop portion. Side trip to Sewart Mountain is even narrower.

Features: A scenic, relaxing mountain drive that climbs to cooler temperatures above 6,000 feet. Dry camp in shady forest. Watch for wildlife.

Time & Distance: The entire trip as described here returning to starting point is about 42 miles. Allow 3 to 4 leisurely hours.

To Get There: From points south, exit I-5 at Smokey Bear Exit and head northwest on Hungry Valley Road about 5 miles to Gold Hill Road. From points north, exit I-5 at Gorman. Go west on Peace Valley Road to entrance of Hungry Valley OHV Area and turn left. Follow Gold Hill Road about 5 miles south until it intersects with Hungry Valley Road. No fee is required if you are just passing through the OHV area but you must tell the ranger.

Trail Description: Reset odometer at the start where Hungry Valley Road intersects with Gold Hill Road (01). Follow paved Gold Hill Road west. Cross Dry Creek after 6 miles and begin to climb. Pavement ends in another two miles. Intersect with loop at 12.5 miles (02). You can go either way; I went left. At 15.8 miles (03) bear left at a T to take a side trip to Sewart Mountain. You must turn around at the end of this narrow but enjoyable road in another 3.9 miles (04). *Reset your odometer at Waypoint 03* before continuing on around the loop. At 3.3 miles (05) a road goes left to Dutchman Campground and the end of difficult Miller Jeep Trail (Trail #12). Go straight to continue around the loop back to where you started at 6.0 miles (02).

Return Trip: Turn left and head back down the mountain on the same road you came up.

Services: Many campgrounds with toilets and ramadas in Hungry Valley OHV Area (fee area). Food and gas in Gorman and Frazier Park. A Flying J Truck Stop at the Frazier Park interchange has an RV dump station.

Maps: Los Padres Nat. Forest, USGS 100,000-scale map, Lancaster, CA N3430-W11800, Hungry Valley OHV map, DeLorme Atlas & Gazetteer.

Pronghorn is very narrow, tippy and steep.   Manmade 4WD Practice Area, difficult part.

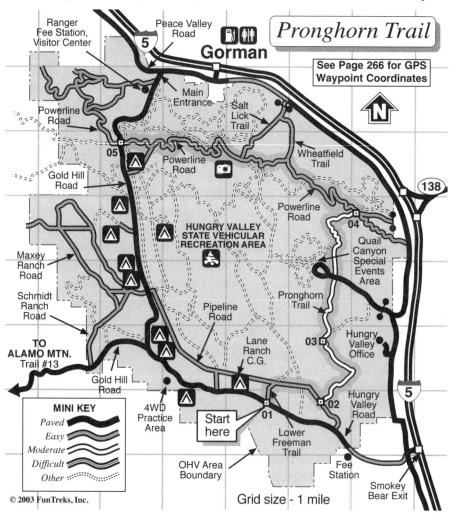

Ranger Fee Station, Visitor Center

Peace Valley Road

Gorman

5

Pronghorn Trail

See Page 266 for GPS
Waypoint Coordinates

N

Main Entrance

Salt Lick Trail

Powerline Road

05

Powerline Road

Gold Hill Road

Wheatfield Trail

138

Powerline Road

04

HUNGRY VALLEY
STATE VEHICULAR
RECREATION AREA

Quail Canyon Special Events Area

Maxey Ranch Road

Pronghorn Trail

Schmidt Ranch Road

Pipeline Road

03

Hungry Valley Office

TO
ALAMO MTN.
Trail #13

Lane Ranch C.G.

02

Hungry Valley Road

Gold Hill Road

01

4WD Practice Area

Start here

Lower Freeman Trail

Hungry Valley Road

5

MINI KEY

Paved
Easy
Moderate
Difficult
Other

OHV Area Boundary

Fee Station

Smokey Bear Exit

© 2003 FunTreks, Inc.

Grid size - 1 mile

Pronghorn Trail 14

Location: South of Gorman in the Hungry Valley OHV Area.

Difficulty: Moderate. Narrow, tippy and steep in places. No long vehicles.

Features: Get an inside look at Hungry Valley OHV Area. Offers trails for ATVs, dirt bikes and 4WD vehicles. Manmade 4WD Practice Area on south side of park has easy, moderate and difficult practice hills. Great camping.

Time & Distance: As described here, 12.7 miles including Powerline Road. Allow 1 to 2 hours plus additional time for side trips.

To Get There: From south side, exit I-5 at Smokey Bear Exit and head west on Hungry Valley Road. I entered at Lower Freeman Trail about 3 miles from I-5. You would likely drive trail in opposite direction if entering from the north. Exit I-5 at Gorman. Take Peace Valley Rd. west to park entrance.

Trail Description: Reset odometer at the start [01]. Head north on Lower Freeman Trail. Turn right on Pipeline Road at 0.3 miles. At 1.3 miles (02) turn left (north) on Pronghorn Trail. Trail is not bad until 2.9 miles (03) when you climb a steep rock and the trail seems to disappear. Be careful here—if you go the wrong way you could tip over. Get out and look around. The trail goes sharply west as you climb over the rock. Cross paved Quail Canyon Road at 4.3. Go straight at 4.7 where difficult Quail Pass Trail goes left. Trail becomes extremely narrow with very tight turns. Watch for speeding ATVs and dirt bikes. *Reset odometer* when you reach Powerline Road at 6.0 miles (04). Turn left and follow an easy road along a scenic ridge. Bear left at 0.3 and 1.0 miles following power lines. Many side roads to explore along the way. Go straight at 1.6 and left at 2.7. Bear right at 6.0 before returning to paved Gold Hill Road at 6.7 miles (05).

Return Trip: Turn left to get back to start or right for Gorman.

Services: Many campgrounds with vault toilets and ramadas in OHV Area (fee area). Food and gas in Gorman and Frazier Park. A Flying J Truck Stop at the Frazier Park interchange has an RV dump station.

Maps: Be sure to get a map of Hungry Valley when you check in at park entrance. It's a great color map with excellent detail. It also includes park regulations and safety tips. See appendix for address and phone number.

Enjoy great views as you climb constant switchbacks along first two miles of trail.

Southern view from Liebre Mountain.

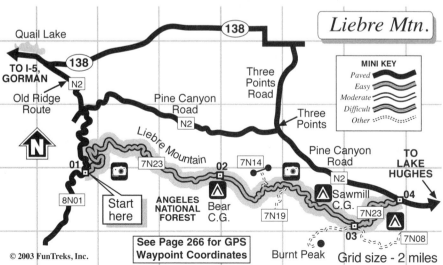

Campgrounds have no water.

Quail Lake

138

Liebre Mtn.

TO I-5, GORMAN

138

N2

Old Ridge Route

Pine Canyon Road

N2

Three Points Road

MINI KEY

Paved
Easy
Moderate
Difficult
Other

Three Points

Liebre Mountain

Pine Canyon Road

N2

TO LAKE HUGHES

01

7N23

02

7N14

04

8N01

Start here

ANGELES NATIONAL FOREST

Bear C.G.

7N19

Sawmill C.G.

7N23

03

7N08

© 2003 FunTreks, Inc.

See Page 266 for GPS Waypoint Coordinates

Burnt Peak

Grid size - 2 miles

Liebre Mountain ⑮

Location: North of Los Angeles between Gorman and Lake Hughes.

Difficulty: Easy. Well-maintained gravel road suitable for any stock SUV.

Features: Stressless drive with great views along both sides of a high ridge. Several side roads to explore. Enjoy secluded camping at two little-used primitive campgrounds. Hike the Pacific Crest National Scenic Trail which crosses the road several times along the same ridge.

Time & Distance: Takes a little more than an hour to drive the 12.6 miles described here. Trip can be extended another 10 miles by continuing on Sawmill Mountain Road, F.S. 7N08 to Lake Hughes.

To Get There: Exit Interstate 5 east on Hwy. 138 south of Gorman. Bear right on The Old Ridge Route (N2) at the eastern end of Quail Lake. Head uphill, continuing straight through a 4-way intersection at 2.2 miles. After another 3 miles on a deteriorating paved road, turn left on F.S. 7N23.

Trail Description: Reset odometer at the start [01]. Climb scenic switchbacks before leveling off along the ridgeline of Liebre Mountain. Continue straight past Bear Campground on right at 3.2 miles [02]. Bear right at 4.3, passing a scenic overlook to left. Bear right at 5.3 where 7N14 goes left. This side road is closed just down the hill. Continue straight where a side road goes right to Atmore Meadows at 6.2. At 8.2 miles, Sawmill Campground is hidden in the trees on the left. You bear right. Turn left downhill on 7N23 at a large circular area at 9.5 miles [03]. (You can continue east another 10 miles to Lake Hughes on F.S. 7N08 or head southwest to Burnt Peak.) As you continue downhill on a wide washboard road, bear left at 10.6 miles before reaching paved N2 at 12.6 miles [04].

Return Trip: Left takes you back to Interstate 5 and Gorman. Right goes to Lake Hughes, Elizabeth Lake, and eventually to the Rowher OHV Area. The I-5 interchange at Frazier Park has an RV dump station at Flying J.

Services: Gas and food in Frazier Park, Gorman and Lake Hughes. Sawmill and Bear Campgrounds have substandard pit toilets.

Maps: Angeles National Forest, USGS 100,000-scale map, Lancaster, CA N3430-W11800, DeLorme Atlas & Gazetteer.

Bouquet Reservoir and start of trail.   Lower section of trail on south side.

One of several points where trails cross.   Dirt bike rider comes up south side.

Staging Area 2 is near lower end of Rowher Trail. Vault toilets but no water.

Location: North of Los Angeles, northeast of Santa Clarita, southeast of Green Valley and west of Palmdale.

Difficulty: Difficult. Extremely steep and rutted. A long and relentless climb up one side of a mountain and down the other. Vehicles must have low-range gears and plenty of power. Lockers or excellent articulation are a must. The trail is mostly dirt and would be impassable if wet. Avoid getting sideways on the steepest hills or risk a rollover. Very challenging for ATV riders and dirt bikers. Route-finding can be confusing through a network of crisscrossing trails.

Features: The state of California has set aside about 20 square miles of tough mountainside for vehicular recreation. Eighteen trails plus forest roads cover the area. Most of the trails are for ATVs and dirt bikes. Rowher Trail, Lookout Trail and the forest roads are suitable for Jeeps and SUVs. A fun ATV and dirt-bike course, next to Staging Area 1, has been set up for kids. The gentle, twisting course is lined with bales of hay for safety. Engine size is limited to 90cc.

Time & Distance: Rowher Trail, starting from Bouquet Canyon Road, is 5.2 miles long. Add another 4.7 miles to reach the park entrance on Sierra Highway. Allow about 3 hours for the entire trip.

To Get There: Most Jeepers run this trail from the back side of Rowher OHV Area to the front as described here. The trail starts from Bouquet Canyon Road south of the reservoir near mile marker 6.8. From the south side, take Bouquet Canyon Road north from Santa Clarita. From the north side at Green Valley, take Spunky Canyon Road south to Bouquet Canyon Road then go southwest.

　　To reach the start of Rowher Trail from Staging Area 1, follow directions for Sierra Pelona Road (Trail #17). When you reach Bouquet Canyon Road, turn left and go 0.4 miles. Rowher trail leaves from a wide parking area on the left. You can also drive Rowher Trail in the opposite direction described here.

Trail Description: *Reset odometer at the start* [01]. The trail winds through a tight ravine and quickly tests you with a steep, short climb. Don't go any farther if you have trouble with this section because it gets worse. The trail then swings right and heads straight uphill. You will cross the easier 6N08 at 0.6 and 0.9 miles. It's easy to accidentally get off Rowher onto 6N08. To stay on Rowher Trail, just keep going up the hardest way. Continue straight uphill as you cross 6N07 at 1.6 miles (02). Bear left at 1.7 as the trail temporarily gets easier at the top of the mountain. You'll pass a wide parking area at 2.0 miles as you head east. Trails head in many directions from this point so pay attention to trail markers. Continue heading east a little farther to avoid going down the Lookout Trail. You'll run into 6N07 again at 2.2 miles. It's hard to tell the difference between Rowher Trail and easier 6N07 but it doesn't make much difference which trail you're on until 2.6 miles (03). Here Rowher Trail (also marked A1) turns right and heads steeply downhill.

Rowher Trail splits many times but eventually comes back together. Select the the best route for you. I tended to take right forks. A nasty spot at 3.0 miles (04) is very steep and rutted. Make sure you stay pointed downhill. If you find yourself getting sideways, you may have to accelerate slightly to maintain steering control; otherwise a rollover is possible. Do not press on the brake so hard that your wheels lock up. This makes it difficult to steer. Bear right at 3.8 miles (05). By now you can see your destination at the bottom of the hill. Finally, after more steep descents, you reach a rocky ravine below a dirt road. Climb up a steep bank to the road at 5.2 miles (06).

Reset your odometer at the dirt road and turn right. Turn left when you reach Staging Area 2 at 0.3 miles. A rough road winds back and forth before reaching Staging Area 1 at 1.9 miles (07). (Trail #17 goes right here.) Bear left and follow a wide gravel road southwest. It becomes paved before reaching the Sierra Highway at 4.7 miles (08) near mile 40.

Return Trip: Turn right to head back to Los Angeles. You'll eventually run into divided Highway 14. Left goes to Highway 14 in the direction of Palmdale.

Services: Vault toilets at each of the three staging areas inside the park. No water is available. A few picnic tables are scattered about.

Regulations: All state regulations for ATVs and dirt bikes apply. Riders under 14 years old must be supervised by a parent. Riders 14 to 17 must possess a state ATV certificate or be supervised by an adult with a certificate. Riders 18 or older must have a state ATV certificate.

Maps: Detailed map of the Rowher Flat OHV Area (available at the Saugus Ranger District, Angeles National Forest), USGS 7.5-minute map Sleepy Valley and Green Valley, CA. Detail trail maps of the area are posted on information boards at each staging area.

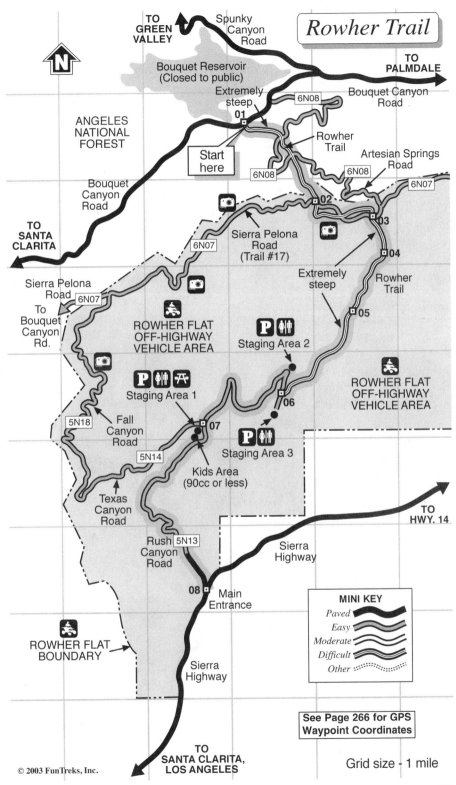

TO GREEN VALLEY

Spunky Canyon Road

Rowher Trail

Bouquet Reservoir
(Closed to public)

TO PALMDALE

Extremely steep

6N08

Bouquet Canyon Road

01

Rowher Trail

Start here

6N08

Artesian Springs Road

6N08

6N07

ANGELES NATIONAL FOREST

Bouquet Canyon Road

02

03

04

TO SANTA CLARITA

6N07

Sierra Pelona Road
(Trail #17)

Extremely steep

Rowher Trail

Sierra Pelona Road

6N07

05

To Bouquet Canyon Rd.

ROWHER FLAT OFF-HIGHWAY VEHICLE AREA

P Staging Area 2

ROWHER FLAT OFF-HIGHWAY VEHICLE AREA

5N18

P Staging Area 1

06

Fall Canyon Road

07

5N14

P Staging Area 3

Kids Area
(90cc or less)

Texas Canyon Road

TO HWY. 14

Rush Canyon Road

5N13

Sierra Highway

08 Main Entrance

MINI KEY

Paved
Easy
Moderate
Difficult
Other

ROWHER FLAT BOUNDARY

Sierra Highway

See Page 266 for GPS Waypoint Coordinates

© 2003 FunTreks, Inc.

TO SANTA CLARITA, LOS ANGELES

Grid size - 1 mile

Heading up Fall Canyon Road towards Sierra Pelona Road.

View of Bouquet Reservoir from Sierra Pelona Road.

Entrance to Kids Area.

Many trails for ATVs and dirt bikes.

Sierra Pelona Road 🟤17

Location: North of Los Angeles, northeast of Santa Clarita, southeast of Green Valley and west of Palmdale.

Difficulty: Easy. Single-lane shelf road much of the way with adequate room to pass most of the time. Mildly steep in places with vertical dropoffs at the top. Since the road is seldom graded, enough rough spots remain to make the drive fun. Suitable for all stock SUVs with decent ground clearance. Skid plates helpful.

Features: A rugged backcountry drive that climbs high to the ridgeline of the Sierra Pelona. After traversing the ridge for several scenic miles, it switchbacks down the northern side of the mountain, which has outstanding views of Bouquet Reservoir. Most of the route is inside Rowher Flat OHV Area with trails for ATVs, dirt bikes and serious 4x4s. You'll pass by Staging Area 1, which accesses a special ATV and dirt bike track for kids. This unique course is lined with hay bales for safety. Maximum engine size is 90cc. Bouquet Reservoir is a water storage lake and is not open for public recreation.

Time & Distance: The entire trip from pavement to pavement is 17.6 miles. Allow at least 2 hours. Explore several side roads at the top of the mountain to extend the trip.

To Get There: From Los Angeles, take Interstate 5 to Antelope Valley Freeway 14. Cut over east to the Sierra Highway at Rt. 126 or wait until you are farther north. Last chance to cut over would be at Sand Canyon Road. Head north on the Sierra Highway to about mile 40. Turn left into well-marked Rowher Flat OHV Area.

Trail Description: Reset odometer as you turn west off Sierra Highway [01]. Follow a paved road west. The pavement soon changes to wide gravel. You'll reach Staging Area 1 on the left at 2.8 miles. You can see the kids track below the road before reaching the staging area. Just past the staging area on the left is Texas Canyon Road 5N14. It's simply marked as Route #1. *Reset your odometer here* (02). Head west downhill. Watch for speeding dirt bikes dropping down from the staging area. At 1.9 miles (03) you must turn sharply right uphill on Fall Canyon Road 5N18. The road now begins an earnest climb. Stay on the main road as dirt bike trails branch off. You reach Sierra Pelona Road 6N07 at 5.5 miles (04). Turn right and continue to climb as the road switchbacks across the face of the mountain. Enjoy great views of the vast valley below. More difficult side roads branch off, but the main road is easy to follow. Bear right at 5.5 miles. Bear right again at 7.4 as views of Bouquet Reservoir can be seen to the left. Go right again at 8.1. At 8.9 continue straight as you cross over Rowher Trail. (This was WAYPOINT 03 in the Rowher Trail description.) Bear left at 9.4 and go straight at 9.8. This area is confusing. Just continue to head east staying on the easier road.

At 10.0 miles (05) turn left on Artesian Springs Road 6N08. It winds down the mountainside as it crosses steeper Rowher Trail at 11.8 and 12.7 miles. The road heads into shaded forest fed by water from numerous artesian springs. Paved Bouquet Canyon Road is reached at 14.8 miles (06). (The start of difficult Rowher Trail #16 is 0.4 miles to the left.)

Return Trip: Left takes you to Santa Clarita where you can go west to Interstate 5 or east to Highway 14. Right takes you to Green Valley or Palmdale.

Services: Vault toilets and picnic tables at Staging Area 1. No water anywhere. Make sure you are self sufficient.

Maps: Angeles National Forest, USGS 7.5-minute map Sleepy Valley and Green Valley, CA, DeLorme Atlas & Gazetteer. Detail trail maps of Rowher Flats OHV Area are posted on information boards at each staging area.

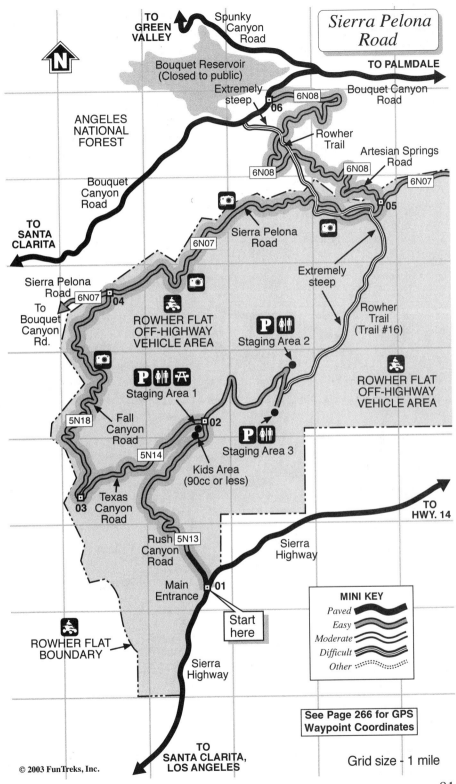

TO GREEN VALLEY

Spunky Canyon Road

Sierra Pelona Road

TO PALMDALE

Bouquet Reservoir (Closed to public)

Extremely steep

6N08

06

Bouquet Canyon Road

Rowher Trail

ANGELES NATIONAL FOREST

6N08

6N08

Artesian Springs Road

6N07

05

Bouquet Canyon Road

Sierra Pelona Road

6N07

Extremely steep

Rowher Trail (Trail #16)

TO SANTA CLARITA

Sierra Pelona Road

6N07

To Bouquet Canyon Rd.

04

ROWHER FLAT OFF-HIGHWAY VEHICLE AREA

P

Staging Area 2

ROWHER FLAT OFF-HIGHWAY VEHICLE AREA

P

Staging Area 1

5N18

Fall Canyon Road

02

5N14

Kids Area (90cc or less)

P

Staging Area 3

03

Texas Canyon Road

Rush Canyon Road

5N13

Sierra Highway

TO HWY. 14

Main Entrance

01

Start here

Sierra Highway

ROWHER FLAT BOUNDARY

MINI KEY

Paved
Easy
Moderate
Difficult
Other

See Page 266 for GPS Waypoint Coordinates

© 2003 FunTreks, Inc.

TO SANTA CLARITA, LOS ANGELES

Grid size - 1 mile

81

AREA 3

Barstow, Calico Mountains

18. Wall St. Canyon Overlook
19. Doran Loop
20. Odessa Canyon
21. Phillips Loop
22. Mule Canyon Road
23. Achy-Breaky

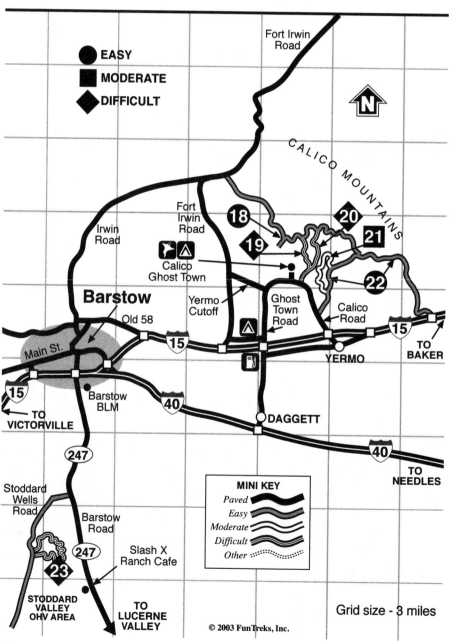

Grid size - 3 miles

© 2003 FunTreks, Inc.

82

Barstow, Calico Mountains

The Calico Mountains provide a unique 4-wheeling opportunity for all skill levels. The slightest driver error at the entrance to *Doran Loop* will likely result in serious body damage even for vehicles with 35-inch tires. *Odessa Canyon* is difficult but manageable. With the exception of moderate *Phillips Loop*, most of the remaining roads are easy. But be careful, some roads have sections of clay that become extremely slippery when wet. Many unsuspecting drivers have slid off *Mule Canyon Road* after a heavy rain. Evidence of extensive mining is apparent throughout the area. Although many people explore the mines, they should be considered extremely dangerous. When the sun is at the right angle, the mountains become a mix of beautiful colors, thus the name *Calico* Mountains. Make sure to visit restored *Calico Ghost Town*, a major tourist attraction that you pass on the way to the trails. South of Barstow, I've included one difficult trail, *Achy-Breaky*, that is representative of many trails inside Stoddard Valley OHV Area. (In both the Calico Mountains and Stoddard Valley OHV Area, watch out for the Desert Tortoise. See page 22 for complete explanation.)

Calico Ghost Town located just west of Doran and Odessa Canyons, Trails #19 and #20.

High ridge above Hidden Valley.

Exposed catacombs of Bismarck Mine.

Horseback riders may also be using the trail.

Take a short side trip to see this stone cabin.

Looking down into Wall Street Canyon.

Wall St. Canyon Overlook (18)

Location: Northeast of Barstow, north of Yermo.

Difficulty: Easy. Much of the route is single lane but there is adequate room to pass. A few steep places along Mule Canyon Road are a clay surface which is very slippery after a good rain. This trail is suitable for stock SUVs with 4-wheel drive and good ground clearance. The roughest part of the trail is just before you get to the overlook.

Features: A fun drive through the heart of the Calico Mountains. Provides a unique look into Wall Street Canyon. See many mines and a stone cabin. (If you see a Desert Tortoise, do not pick up or harass. See page 22.)

Time & Distance: Allow 2 to 3 hours for this 14-mile trip. Add time for side trips.

To Get There: Exit Interstate 15 at well-marked Ghost Town Road. Head north and follow the loop around to the east. Continue past the entrance to Calico Ghost Town at 3.4 miles. The road now becomes Calico Road. Continue past the entrance to Doran and Odessa Canyons marked with a post that says Doran Scenic Drive at 3.9 miles. Turn left at 5.4 miles onto Mule Canyon Road. You can also exit I-15 at Calico Road near Yermo and head north about a mile to Mule Canyon Road on the right.

Trail Description: Reset odometer at the start of Mule Canyon Road [01]. Head uphill on a rocky road. Continue straight at 0.6 miles. Continue straight at 1.6 miles (02) where Phillips Loop (Trail #21) goes left. This spot is identified by a large rock formation called Camp Rock. Many people camp here and use this area to unload ATVs and dirt bikes. Bear right at 2.0 miles where Phillips Loop returns to Mule Canyon Road. A steep, winding section at 2.7 miles is very slippery if wet. Bear left at 3.1 and 3.4 miles as the road winds through undulating terrain. Continue straight at 3.6 and 3.8 miles.

    At 4.3 miles (03), an arrow on a large rock in the middle of the road points left. *Reset your odometer* here and head north along Tin Can Alley. Watch for rusty tin cans from bygone mining days scattered along the road. Bear left at 0.4 miles. Continue straight at 1.4 as another road joins on the left. Bear left at 1.6 and the road soon gets steeper. Continue straight at 2.3 miles as you cross over a high ridge. Bear left at 2.4 and right at 2.6. At the bottom of the hill at 2.8 miles (04), bear left on another road. (If you continue straight uphill, the road is closed just ahead.)

Bear right at 3.0 miles (05). (This intersection is the end of Odessa Canyon Trail #20). Continue straight past a parking area for Sweetwater Spring Hiking Trail at 3.2. Continue straight at 3.5 where a lesser road goes right. After climbing over a saddle, bear right at 3.7 and start downhill on a rougher road. You can see Bismarck Mine below. When you reach the mine at 4.0 miles (06), bear sharp right downhill. Follow the lowest road downhill. Keep bearing to the left as several branches go right. At 4.4 miles (07) bear left downhill. Continue straight downhill at 4.7 as the road gets rougher. Bear left downhill at 4.9 miles (08). The trail ends at 5.1 miles (09) at a small turnaround area. Walk in a southwest direction to some jagged boulders. Be careful—there's a 100-ft. drop to Wall Street Canyon below. You can't see it until you are right on the edge.

Reset your odometer and start back up the hill. At 0.2 miles (08) bear left. Turn left out of a sandy wash at 0.7 miles (10). (Before turning here, you may want to see the stone cabin just around the corner to the right.) Bear left at 1.1 and 1.3 miles. Soon after that, bear right on a better road at a 4-way intersection. Continue heading north and west on the best traveled road until reaching paved Ft. Irwin Road at 4.5 miles (11).

Return Trip: Turn left on Ft. Irwin Road. It swings south and returns to Interstate 15. To get back to Ghost Town Road, turn left off Ft. Irwin Road on the Yermo Cutoff Road after about 5 miles.

Historical Highlights: The Calico Mining district was one of the richest in California. About $86 million in silver was extracted from over 500 mines during the 1880s. The Bismarck Mine was one of the largest. Its unusual exposed catacombs resulted from modern-day strip mining. An entire mountain was carved away, exposing the original network of underground shafts. Miners used to hike up Wall Street Canyon from the town of Calico and climb a 100-ft. ladder at the end of the canyon. The trail described here looks down into the canyon where the miners climbed out. The town of Calico began in 1881. By 1887 there were 22 saloons and many other busi-nesses serving a population of about 1,200. In 1966, Walter Knott, founder of Knott's Berry Farm, donated the town to San Bernardino County. The restored town is kept alive by private donations and a modest entry fee.

Services: Gas at I-15 and Ghost Town Road. Good food at Peggy Sue's Cafe (see map). Full hookups available at KOA Campgrounds and Calico Ghost Town Campgrounds (see map). Many people dry camp on the road into Odessa Canyon and along the first part of Mule Canyon Road.

Maps: USGS 100,000-scale map, Newberry Springs, CA, Sidekick Map of Calico Mountains, DeLorme Atlas & Gazetteer.

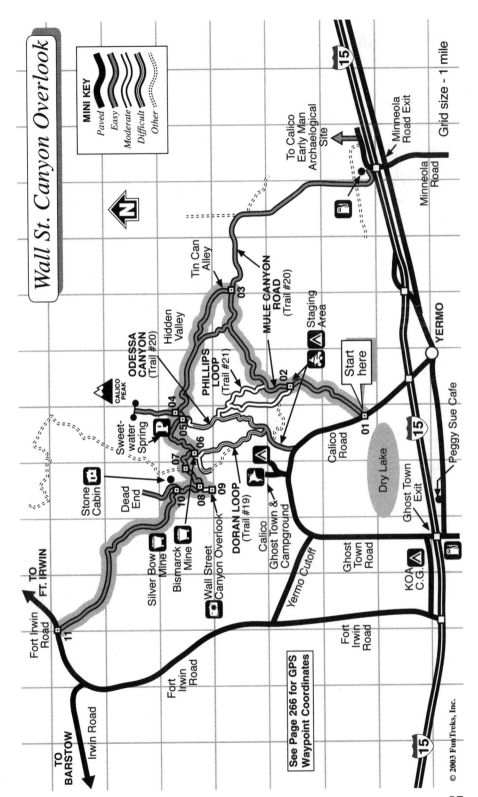

Wall St. Canyon Overlook

MINI KEY
Paved
Easy
Moderate
Difficult
Other

N

To Calico Early Man Archaeological Site

Minneola Road Exit

Minneola Road

15

Grid size - 1 mile

Tin Can Alley

03

MULE CANYON ROAD (Trail #20)

Hidden Valley

ODESSA CANYON (Trail #20)

PHILLIPS LOOP (Trail #21)

CALICO PEAK

Sweet-water Spring

P

04

05

06

02

Staging Area

Start here

01

Calico Road

Dry Lake

YERMO

15

Peggy Sue Cafe

Ghost Town Exit

Stone Cabin

Dead End

07

10   08   09

Silver Bow Mine

Bismarck Mine

Wall Street Canyon Overlook

DORAN LOOP (Trail #19)

Calico

Ghost Town & Campground

Yermo Cutoff

Ghost Town Road

KOA C.G.

Fort Irwin Road

TO FT. IRWIN

11   Fort Irwin Road

Fort Irwin Road

TO BARSTOW

Irwin Road

See Page 266 for GPS Waypoint Coordinates

© 2003 FunTreks, Inc.

87

Crowd gathers at first obstacle during High Desert Roundup.

Upper section easier compared to start.

Use side walls of tires to lift vehicle over boulders.   Strategic rock placement is important.

88

Doran Loop ◆19

Location: Northeast of Barstow, north of Yermo. Directly east of Calico Ghost Town.

Difficulty: Difficult. The first obstacle is extreme. Boulders are several feet high and widely spaced. Side walls of tires must be used to lift a vehicle over the boulders. This maneuver is very difficult and usually requires the help of an experienced spotter. A vehicle can easily slip off the side of a boulder, causing serious body damage. The remainder of the trail consists of several steep rock ledges, difficult but comparatively easier than the first obstacle.

You can avoid the first obstacle by taking a bypass located on the west side of the wash about 0.3 miles north of the paved road as you entered (see map). Doran Loop can also be driven in the opposite direction as described in Trail #20. The bypass is easier to find coming downhill.

Features: This trail includes scenic high points and passes the massive Bismarck Mine. However, these features can be accessed from other trails. The primary reason people drive this trail uphill is the challenge of the first obstacle. (If you see a Desert Tortoise, do not pick up or harass. See pg. 22.)

Time & Distance: The loop portion of the trail is about 5 miles around. After completing the first obstacle, allow about 3 hours to drive the remainder of the loop.

To Get There: Exit Interstate 15 at Ghost Town Road and head north following signs to Calico Ghost Town. Go east 0.5 miles past the entrance to the ghost town and turn left on a road marked *Doran Scenic Drive.*

Trail Description: Reset odometer at the start as you leave the paved road [01]. Head north on an easy gravel road. The road enters a wash and splits in various directions. Keep right following the best traveled route. As you continue northeast on the main road, look left for tunnels cut into the hillside. This is a popular play area for ATVs, dirt bikes, and small 4x4s. Continue straight at 0.4 miles. (The small road to the right cuts across to Phillips Loop and Mule Canyon. This is a fun drive for short 4x4s, ATVs and dirt bikes.) At 0.6 miles (02) bear left at a well-defined fork. (Right goes to Odessa Canyon, Trail #20.) After a narrow passage, the trail enters a wide, high-walled canyon. Park in this area and inspect the first obstacle on the north end of the canyon at 0.7 miles (03).

Reset your odometer above the first obstacle and continue uphill. At 0.1 miles, note the bypass on the left. Pass through a narrow spot at 0.4 then ignore a road that joins on the right. Ledges get rougher as you climb what is officially Bismarck Canyon. Note sections of eroded pavement along the way. The last ledge is completed at 1.3 miles. Continue right uphill at 1.5 miles (04). (The road to the left climbs to a scenic high point, then drops back to the main trail on a difficult route.) The main road swings to the right as you continue uphill to a wide spot above Bismarck Mine. From here, bear left downhill and pass through the mine area at 1.7 miles (05).

Reset your odometer at the mine. Bear right after the mine and climb a steep rocky hill to the left. Turn left at 0.3 miles at the top of the hill. Continue north along the side of a hill as the road swings right and drops into a drainage grade at 0.5 (06). Stay on the main road heading east, ignoring lesser roads. A road joins on the right at 0.7 before reaching a parking area for Sweetwater Spring Hiking Trail. Bear right past the parking area before an intersection at 1.0 miles (07).

Reset your odometer here (07) Turn right and head down Odessa Canyon. At 0.4 stay in the canyon as a road goes right uphill. At 0.6 miles (08) continue straight downhill, staying in the canyon as side roads exit. The trail gradually narrows with increasing rough sections. Eroded pavement only makes the trail more difficult. Be careful at one very narrow spot where a miscue can tip you against vertical canyon walls. Various ledges and sharp rock projections remain before reaching a final challenging boulder field at 1.9 miles. After maneuvering through this boulder field, follow an easy road out of a narrow canyon. At 2.1 miles (02) continue straight at the fork you encountered coming in. Continue down the wash to the main paved road at 2.7 miles (01).

Return Trip: Right returns the way you came in. Left takes you past Mule Canyon Road towards Yermo.

Historical Highlights: The eroded paved portions of this trail are remnants of Doran Scenic Drive, constructed in the 1930s and popular for about a decade.

Services: Gas, food and a KOA Campground at Ghost Town Road and Interstate 15. Calico Ghost Town also has a full-hookup campground. Many people camp in the dry wash along the start of the trail. This area also serves as a staging area for ATVs and dirt bikes.

Maps: USGS 7.5-minute map Yermo, CA, N3452.5-W11645/7.5., Sidekick Map of Calico Mountains, DeLorme Atlas & Gazetteer.

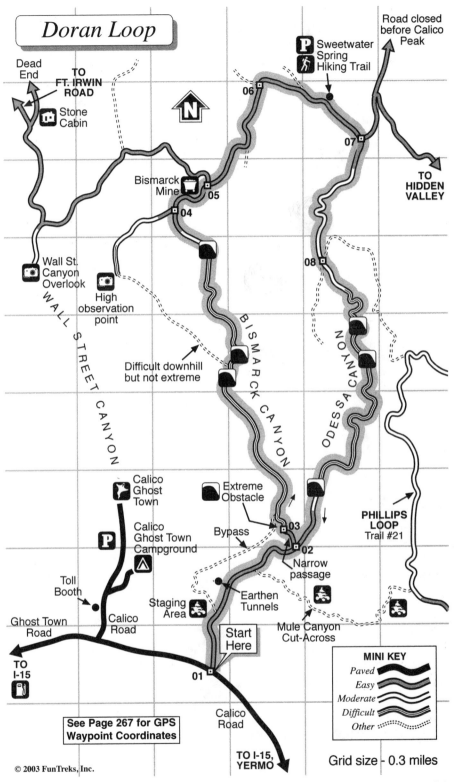

Doran Loop

Road closed before Calico Peak

Dead End

TO FT. IRWIN ROAD

Stone Cabin

N

P — Sweetwater Spring Hiking Trail

06

07

TO HIDDEN VALLEY

Bismarck Mine
05
04

08

Wall St. Canyon Overlook

High observation point

WALL STREET CANYON

BISMARCK CANYON

ODESSA CANYON

Difficult downhill but not extreme

Extreme Obstacle

PHILLIPS LOOP Trail #21

Calico Ghost Town

P

Calico Ghost Town Campground

Bypass

03

02

Narrow passage

Toll Booth

Staging Area

Earthen Tunnels

Mule Canyon Cut-Across

Ghost Town Road

Calico Road

TO I-15

Start Here

01

Calico Road

See Page 267 for GPS Waypoint Coordinates

TO I-15, YERMO

© 2003 FunTreks, Inc.

MINI KEY
Paved
Easy
Moderate
Difficult
Other

Grid size - 0.3 miles

The entrance to Odessa Canyon is a popular place to dry camp.

Optional play area.

Dirt bikers enjoy the trail.

Trail is not for long wheel-based vehicles.

This vehicle got jammed against the wall.

Odessa Canyon ◆20◆

Location: Northeast of Barstow, north of Yermo. Directly east of Calico Ghost Town.

Difficulty: Difficult. Very challenging but easier than Trail #19 if you take the bypass. Narrow and rocky in places. Not for large vehicles or stock SUVs. Differential lockers, skid plates and high ground clearance required.

Features: Perhaps the most popular route in the Calico Mountains. Visit Bismarck Mine, Wall Street Canyon Overlook and Hidden Valley. Many additional mines along the route. Great views at the top. (If you see a Desert Tortoise, do not pick up or harass. See page 22.)

Time & Distance: Approximately 6.2 miles as described here counting the easy section at the start. Allow 3 to 4 hours but add time for side trips.

To Get There: Exit Interstate 15 at Ghost Town Road and head north following signs to Calico Ghost Town. Go east 0.5 miles past the entrance to the ghost town and turn left on a road marked *Doran Scenic Drive.*

Trail Description: Reset odometer at the start as you leave the paved road [01]. Head north on an easy gravel road. The road enters a wash and splits in various directions. Keep right following the best traveled route. As you continue northeast on the main road, look left for tunnels cut into the hillside. This is a popular play area for ATVs, dirt bikes, and small 4x4s. Continue straight at 0.4 miles. (The small road to the right cuts across to Phillips Loop and Mule Canyon. This is a fun drive for short wheel-based vehicles. See complete description in Trail #21.)
    At 0.6 miles (02) bear right at a well defined fork. The canyon narrows and gets rougher. The first boulder field at 0.8 miles is the toughest part of the trip. Even short wheel-based vehicles will find it a tight squeeze. After that, it smooths out for a while with intermittent small obstacles. The canyon tightens again by 1.3 miles with several narrow ledges made more difficult by remnants of the old paved road. Continue straight at 1.8 where a road exits the canyon on the left. Continue straight in the canyon at 2.1 miles (03) where a road crosses. (A right turn here would take you to Phillips Loop Trail #21.) Stay right at 2.3 miles where a road exits the canyon on the left. Odessa Canyon ends at an intersection at 2.7 miles (04).
    Reset your odometer and turn left (04). (If you go straight at this intersection, you can reach Hidden Valley, Tin Can Alley and Mule Canyon

Road. This route is described in Wall Street Canyon Overlook Trail #18 going in the opposite direction.) At 0.2 miles pass the Sweetwater Spring Hiking Trail parking area on the right. Bear left at 0.3 on a larger road. Bear left uphill at 0.5 (05) and head south across the side of a hill. When you reach a high point at 0.7 miles, bear right. Drop down a steep rocky hill. You can see Bismarck Mine below. You reach the mine at 0.9 miles (06).

Reset your odometer and bear left uphill. (If you go right downhill at the mine, you would be on the Wall Street Canyon Overlook Trail #18.) When you reach a wide flat spot above the mine, turn right and head downhill. At 0.2 miles (07) make a right then an immediate left downhill. (The uphill road climbs to a high observation point then drops down the mountain on a difficult road before connecting back into Bismarck Canyon.) Drop down a ledge mixed with pavement at 0.4 miles. The canyon drops earnestly now with more rocky ledges. You'll pass a large sign painted on the rocks marked "Danger Keep Out." Bear right at 1.3 miles where a road climbs out of the canyon on the left. Immediately, pass through a very narrow spot in the canyon.

At 1.6 miles (08), a side road climbs out of the canyon on the right. This is the bypass for the major obstacle pictured in Trail #19. Walk down and inspect the obstacle before proceeding. The obstacle is extreme and body damage is likely. If you go down the obstacle the trail takes you back to the fork you passed on the way in (02).

To take the bypass, turn right uphill out of the canyon (08). You get a great bird's eye view of the obstacle from the bypass. Follow a high scenic ridge southwest. It provides great views of Odessa Canyon below. The trail soon turns left off the ridge and drops into a narrow canyon twisting through boulders. When you reach the bottom of the canyon, turn right to reach the paved road at 2.6 miles (01).

Return Trip: Right returns the way you came in. Left takes you past Mule Canyon Road towards Yermo.

Historical Highlights: The eroded paved portions of this trail are remnants of the old Doran Scenic Drive, constructed in the 1930s and popular for about a decade.

Services: Gas, food and a KOA Campground at Ghost Town Road and Interstate 15. Calico Ghost Town also has a full-hookup campground. Many people camp in the dry wash along the start of the trail. This area also serves as a staging area for ATVs and dirt bikes.

Maps: USGS 7.5-minute map Yermo, CA, N3452.5-W11645/7.5., Sidekick Map of Calico Mountains, DeLorme Atlas & Gazetteer.

94

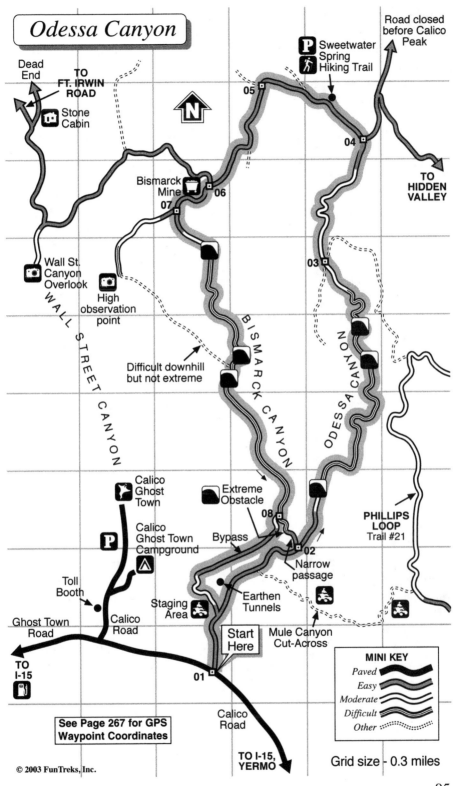

Odessa Canyon

Road closed before Calico Peak

TO FT. IRWIN ROAD

Dead End

Stone Cabin

N

P Sweetwater Spring Hiking Trail

05

04

TO HIDDEN VALLEY

Bismarck Mine

06

07

Wall St. Canyon Overlook

High observation point

03

BISMARCK CANYON

ODESSA CANYON

Difficult downhill but not extreme

Calico Ghost Town

P

Calico Ghost Town Campground

Extreme Obstacle

Bypass

08

02

PHILLIPS LOOP Trail #21

Narrow passage

Toll Booth

Staging Area

Earthen Tunnels

Mule Canyon Cut-Across

Ghost Town Road

Calico Road

Start Here

TO I-15

01

MINI KEY
Paved
Easy
Moderate
Difficult
Other

Calico Road

See Page 267 for GPS Waypoint Coordinates

TO I-15, YERMO

Grid size - 0.3 miles

© 2003 FunTreks, Inc.

95

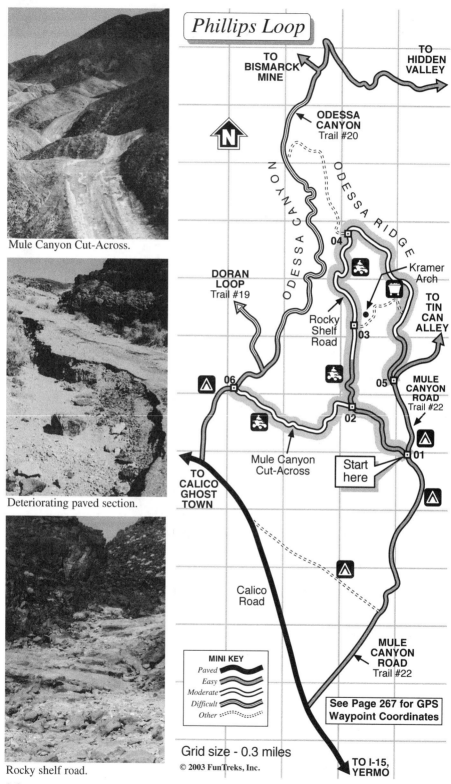

Mule Canyon Cut-Across.

Deteriorating paved section.

Rocky shelf road.

Phillips Loop

TO BISMARCK MINE

TO HIDDEN VALLEY

ODESSA CANYON
Trail #20

ODESSA CANYON

ODESSA RIDGE

Kramer Arch

TO TIN CAN ALLEY

04

DORAN LOOP
Trail #19

Rocky Shelf Road

03

05

MULE CANYON ROAD
Trail #22

06

02

Mule Canyon Cut-Across

Start here

01

TO CALICO GHOST TOWN

Calico Road

MULE CANYON ROAD
Trail #22

MINI KEY
Paved
Easy
Moderate
Difficult
Other

See Page 267 for GPS Waypoint Coordinates

Grid size - 0.3 miles

© 2003 FunTreks, Inc.

TO I-15, YERMO

96

Phillips Loop 21

Location: Northeast of Barstow, north of Yermo.

Difficulty: Moderate. Steep rocky climbs. Stretches of badly eroded pavement. Stock SUVs need skid plates and high ground clearance.

Features: Short but interesting trip. See Kramer Arch and various mines. Add some interest by entering via Mule Canyon Cut-Across. (If you see a Desert Tortoise, do not pick up or harass. See page 22.)

Time & Distance: Takes less than an hour for this 2.7-mile loop.

To Get There: Follow directions to Mule Canyon Road Trail #22. Phillips Loop goes left 1.6 miles north on Mule Canyon Road.

To reach Phillips Loop via Mule Canyon Cut-Across, follow directions for Odessa Canyon Trail #20. Turn right 0.4 miles (06) north of the paved road. This fun, roller-coaster ride is for short wheel-based vehicles only. Once on the cut-across road, make a right at 0.4, a left at 0.5, a right at 0.7 before reaching Phillips Loop at 0.8 miles (02).

Trail Description: *Reset odometer at the start as you turn left off Mule Canyon Road* (01). Bear right at 0.4 (02) where the cut-across road joins on the left. Bear right at 0.5 and 0.7 as the dirt road changes to a reddish color. Climb a badly eroded section of pavement to a flat area where the road forks at 0.9 miles (03). Right shortcuts Phillips Loop and goes past interesting Kramer Arch. Phillips Loop continues straight uphill on a tough, rocky shelf road then enters a sandy wash. Stay right in the wash at 1.5. After more bad pavement, turn right at 1.6 miles (04) and head downhill along Odessa Ridge. Bear right downhill at 1.9 miles. Continue straight at 2.3 miles where the previously mentioned shortcut joins on the right. Reconnect with Mule Canyon Road at 2.7 miles (05). Continue south down Mule Canyon Road to paved Calico Road.

Return Trip: Right on Calico Road takes you back to Calico Ghost Town. About a mile to the left is Interstate 15.

Services: Gas and food at Interstate 15 and Ghost Town Road. Dry camp along Mule Canyon Road near the start of trail.

Maps: USGS 7.5-minute map Yermo, CA, N3452.5-W11645/7.5., Sidekick Map of Calico Mountains, DeLorme Atlas & Gazetteer.

Camp with views of Calico Peak and Hidden Valley.

This stretch of clay surface road is slippery when wet.

Easy road for stock SUVs.

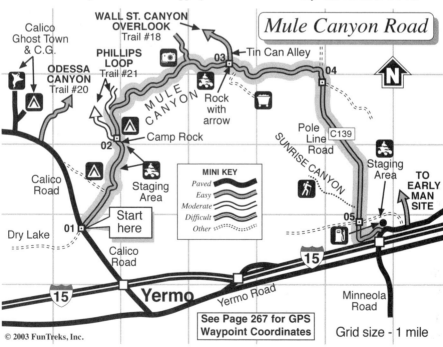

Mule Canyon Road

Calico Ghost Town & C.G.

WALL ST. CANYON OVERLOOK
Trail #18

Tin Can Alley

03

04

ODESSA CANYON
Trail #20

PHILLIPS LOOP
Trail #21

N

MULE CANYON

Rock with arrow

Pole Line Road   C139

02

Camp Rock

SUNRISE CANYON

Staging Area

TO EARLY MAN SITE

Calico Road

Staging Area

MINI KEY

Paved
Easy
Moderate
Difficult
Other

05

Start here

Dry Lake

01

Calico Road

15

15   Yermo   Yermo Road

Minneola Road

© 2003 FunTreks, Inc.

See Page 267 for GPS Waypoint Coordinates

Grid size - 1 mile

98

Mule Canyon Road

Location: Northeast of Barstow, north of Yermo.

Difficulty: Easy. The road gets little maintenance but is relatively smooth. Suitable for all stock SUVs. Stay off the western half of this road when wet. Several steep sections have a clay surface that is very slippery after a rain.

Features: This short drive gives you a glimpse of the area and some idea of what the other trails are like. See evidence of historic mining activity. Pick a spot you like and dry camp just about anywhere. Limited-use area for ATVs and dirt bikes. Retrace portion of historic Twenty-Mule Team Route (western half of route). Visit Early Man Archeological Site at end of trip. (If you see a Desert Tortoise, do not pick up or harass. See page 22.)

Time & Distance: Takes about an hour for this 8.7-mile drive.

To Get There: Exit Interstate 15 on Calico Road at Yermo. Go north about a mile and turn right at a small signpost for Mule Canyon Road.

Trail Description: Reset odometer at the start [01]. Head north on a bumpy road. Continue straight at 0.6 miles where a road goes left. Good camping along the road near Camp Rock at 1.6 miles (02) where Phillips Loop goes left. This is a popular area for ATVs and dirt bikes, but obey signs where marked for limited use. Stay right at 2.0 miles where Phillips Loop returns. Begin climbing through moonscape-like terrain before reaching a long hill at 2.7 miles. A clay road surface here becomes extremely slippery when wet. Vehicles have slid off the road and tumbled into the nearby ravine. Bear left at 3.1 to avoid following an old railroad bed. Continue straight at 3.4, 3.6 and 3.8. Evidence of heavy mining through this area. Go straight again at 4.3 miles (03) where a big rock with an arrow points left to Tin Can Alley. Bear right at 5.8 and 6.0 miles (04) and follow a power line downhill. At 8.2 miles (05) continue straight downhill to Interstate 15 then turn left to reach the Minneola Exit at 8.7 miles.

Return Trip: West on Interstate 15 takes you back to Yermo and Barstow.

Services: Best bet for food and gas is to return to Ghost Town Road 2 miles west on I-15. Visit Early Man Archaeological Site just to the east.

Maps: USGS 7.5-minute map Yermo, CA, N3452.5-W11645/7.5., Sidekick Map of Calico Mountains, DeLorme Atlas & Gazetteer.

This steep climb is just the first of many.   Over 100 vehicles participated in this run.

This vehicle got high-centered.   The trail is not always obvious.

Hundreds of motor homes camp during High Desert Roundup on Memorial Day weekend.

Achy-Breaky ◆23◆

Location: South of Barstow in the Stoddard Valley OHV Area. Northeast of Victorville.

Difficulty: Difficult. Menacing desert terrain with numerous steep, rocky climbs. Large, sharp rocks require tight maneuvering, increasing the likelihood of tire damage. High clearance, skid plates and differential lockers required. No stock vehicles. A complex network of poorly defined roads makes route-finding very difficult. Even with GPS, you will likely make some wrong turns. Very hot in summer. Carry plenty of water. Never drive this trail alone.

Features: This trail is similar to other rock-crawling trails inside Stoddard Valley OHV Area. The 54,679-acre park is open to cross-country travel for all off-road vehicles. Elevations range from 2,800 to 5,000 feet. The trail circles around the base of Watkins Peak, weaving in and out of numerous side canyons. Some good views from high points along the route but most of the trip is not scenic. I drove this trail on Memorial Day weekend as part of the annual High Desert Roundup sponsored by the California Association of 4-Wheel Drive Clubs. Hundreds of RVs show up for the event. Over a hundred 4x4s participated in the single-day, Achy-Breaky run. (Please watch out for Desert Tortoises. Do not pick up or harass. See page 22.)

Time & Distance: Allow 4 to 5 hours with a small group of well-equipped vehicles. With more vehicles, allow a full day. The loop is just 6.2 miles.

To Get There: From Barstow, head south on Barstow Road (Hwy. 247) approximately 4.7 miles. Turn right on Stoddard Wells Road into the Stoddard Valley OHV Area. You'll see a brown information kiosk after you turn. After a half mile, the road swings left and heads south/southwest. You'll reach the crest of a hill in another 3 miles. Turn left at the top of the hill onto an unmarked dirt road. (Base camp for the High Desert Roundup was another mile down the road on the right.)

Trail Description: Reset odometer at the start [01]. Before the first 10th of a mile, turn left downhill following a rocky cut at a convergence of roads. Before 0.2 miles turn right out of the cut and climb a steep hill. Drop down the other side into another rocky cut. Bear left downhill at 0.5 miles. After a sharp ledge, bear left again at 0.6 miles (02) where a road joins on the right. Later, you'll return to this spot. At 0.7 continue straight or bear right uphill to climb *The Staircase*, a big ledge that's harder than it looks.

At 0.8 miles (03), turn right, following a sandy wash. Turn left uphill out of the wash at 1.0 miles (04). This is an optional challenge. Climb a steep, loose hill, then turn right across a ridge and immediately drop back down into the wash at 1.3 miles (05). **Don't turn when you get to the wash.** Go another 30 feet across the wash then turn left on a lesser road. At 1.6 miles (06) turn right on a faint road. (There may not be any tracks at all.) Ignore crossroads until 1.7 miles (07) where you bear right and climb a small ridge. Make a left at 1.8 (08) and drop downhill across the face of a slope.

At 1.9 miles (09) turn right uphill in a narrow, rocky ravine. Traverse a tough obstacle at 2.1 miles or go around it. Climb a short ridge and drop down. After reaching a dramatic high point at 2.3 miles (10), bear left downhill. Bear right down a steep grade at 2.4. When you reach the bottom, turn right steeply uphill. Continue over the crest of another hill at 2.5 miles (11). At the bottom, turn right at 2.6 and follow another rocky cut. By 2.8 miles you should be able to see a couple of lonely telephone poles at the top of the hill. Continue uphill through sharp rock, a grueling test of tires. I had to bypass one section and got very off-camber.

Bear left and follow a ridgeline at 3.0 miles (12). Bear right and drop down the ridge at 3.1 miles (13). Stay left in a cut then turn right uphill after 3.2 miles (14). At another ridge, turn left at a telephone pole following a two-track road. Bear left at 3.4 miles (15). Continue south as you go up and down hills. Turn right on a better road at the bottom of a big valley at 3.9 miles (16). Turn left downhill at 3.9+ then climb another hill. Head southwest until 4.2 miles (17) then bear right at a fork.

Make a right at 4.4 (18), following a sandy valley. Go straight at 4.6. Driver's choice at 4.8 miles (19) (right goes through the *Rock Garden*). I made a left downhill. Make a slight right at 5.0 miles (20). Turn left at the top of a knoll at 5.1. Stay on the main trail for about 30 feet, then make a hard right up a steep hill. Stay in a rocky cut for a while. Go the way water would flow. You can bypass a nasty spot at 5.6 miles (21) before running into a portion of the trail you were on at the beginning. Turn left at 5.8 miles (03) and follow the sandy wash back to Stoddard Wells Road at 6.2 miles (22).

Return Trip: Right takes you back to Highway 247. Left takes you on a long trip back to Interstate 15 near Victorville.

Services: In Barstow or Victorville. The Slash X Ranch Cafe, about 9 miles south of Barstow on Hwy. 247, is a popular gathering place with good food and drinks. For emergencies, use Channel 9 on a CB radio or try 911 on a cell phone. The Barstow BLM office is just south of I-15 on Hwy. 247.

Maps: USGS 7.5-minute map Barstow SE, CA, 34117-G1-TF-024, DeLorme Atlas & Gazetteer.

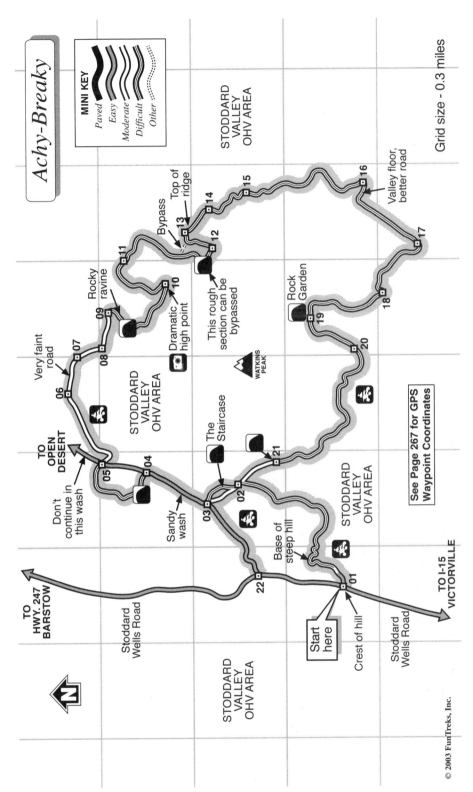

Achy-Breaky

MINI KEY
Paved
Easy
Moderate
Difficult
Other

Grid size - 0.3 miles

STODDARD VALLEY OHV AREA

Top of ridge

Bypass

Valley floor, better road

Rocky ravine

This rough section can be bypassed

Very faint road

Dramatic high point

Rock Garden

STODDARD VALLEY OHV AREA

WATKINS PEAK

TO OPEN DESERT

The Staircase

Don't continue in this wash

Sandy wash

Base of steep hill

STODDARD VALLEY OHV AREA

See Page 267 for GPS Waypoint Coordinates

TO HWY. 247 BARSTOW

Stoddard Wells Road

N

TO I-15 VICTORVILLE

Start here

Crest of hill

Stoddard Wells Road

STODDARD VALLEY OHV AREA

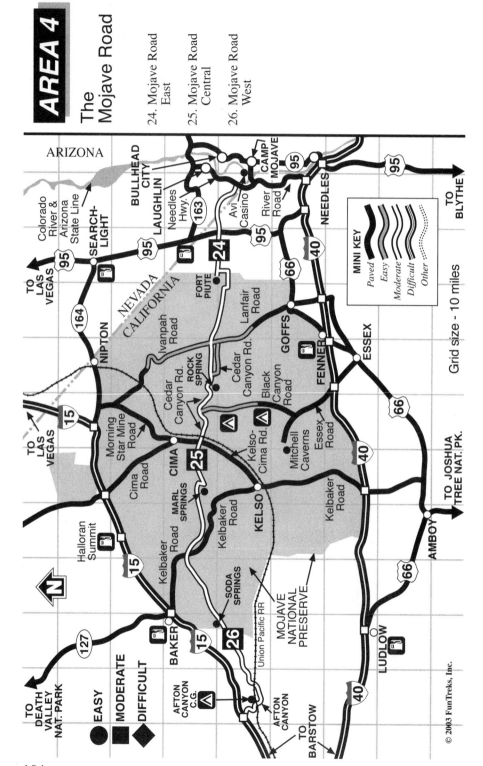

MINI KEY
Paved
Easy
Moderate
Difficult
Other

Grid size - 10 miles

ARIZONA

Colorado River & Arizona State Line

BULLHEAD CITY
LAUGHLIN
SEARCH-LIGHT
NEVADA
CALIFORNIA
NIPTON
FORT PIUTE
Lanfair Road
Ivanpah Road
Cedar Canyon Rd.
ROCK SPRING
Cedar Canyon Rd.
Black Canyon Road
GOFFS
Morning Star Mine Road
CIMA
MARL SPRINGS
Cima Road
Kelso-Cima Rd.
Mitchell Caverns
Essex Road
KELSO
Kelbaker Road
Kelbaker Road
Halloran Summit
SODA SPRINGS
Union Pacific RR
MOJAVE NATIONAL PRESERVE
BAKER
AFTON CANYON C.G.
AFTON CANYON
LUDLOW
AMBOY
FENNER
ESSEX
NEEDLES
CAMP MOJAVE
Avi Casino
River Road
Needles Hwy.

TO LAS VEGAS
TO LAS VEGAS
TO DEATH VALLEY NAT. PARK
TO JOSHUA TREE NAT. PK.
TO BLYTHE
TO BARSTOW

Needles Hwy.

95
164
95
95
95
95
163
24
25
26
15
15
15
15
127
164
40
40
40
66
66
66
66

EASY
MODERATE
DIFFICULT

N

© 2003 FunTreks, Inc.

104

The Mojave Road

If you're prioritizing trips, put the Mojave Road high on your list. Set aside a long weekend and mark it on your calendar. Although the trail offers no hardcore challenges, it's a trail everyone should experience at least once. Rich in history and stark beauty, this remote adventure provides memories for a lifetime. Make sure to pack a tent, plenty of water, food and above all, enough gas to go 150 miles. Although the trail itself is only 120 miles (as described here), you'll have to drive farther for gas. The trail can be driven in either direction, but most people go east to west. Don't go alone, but keep your travel group small. The trip offers subtle pleasures that are often missed when traveling with a large group. Be aware that Soda Dry Lake, on the western part of the trip, can become impassable after heavy rains. The trail is well-marked with rock cairns and is easy to follow most of the way. However, one long section of open desert has blowing sand that can obliterate any trace of the trail. Fortunately, natural landmarks make it nearly impossible to get lost for long. To fully appreciate this trip, I highly recommend you read Dennis G. Casebier's book, the *Mojave Road Guide, An Adventure Through Time*. This 160-page book is the most complete, authoritative guidebook on the Mojave Road and is a pleasure to read.

Cairn marks lonely stretch of sand-blown road on western part of trip.

ATVs allowed at start only.

Dropping into Lanfair Valley.

A few spots along the trail test articulation.

The Penny Can Tree.

Ruins of Fort Piute.

Cool temps in February make for a pleasant lunch break.

Location: The Mojave road crosses the Mojave National Preserve between Bullhead City, AZ and Barstow, CA. The eastern part runs between the Needles Highway and Ivanpah Road.

Difficulty: Moderate. Most of this trail is easy with a mix of desert sand and mild rocks. The climb to Fort Piute is a bit rockier and is borderline moderate. Larger washes have steep, sandy banks which can be challenging. You are a long way from services so carry plenty of water and gas. Dangerously hot in summer. Suitable for stock 4x4 SUVs with high ground clearance. Although many roads cross the trail, route-finding is easy because the main trail is marked with cairns (always on the right). They may be knocked over or partially buried, so watch carefully.

Features: Follow an historic Indian trail/wagon road/stage route. Visit the remains of Fort Piute and the Irwin Turkey Farm. Search for Indian petroglyphs around the ruins. Enjoy large Joshua trees and panoramic views. **Street-legal vehicles only once inside Mojave National Preserve.**

Time & Distance: This leg is just under 40 miles. Allow about 4 hours plus additional time for stops. Considerable travel time may be required to reach this trail and return home.

To Get There: Follow signs to the Avi Casino located at the southernmost tip of Nevada at the Colorado River. Head west from the casino on Aha Macav Parkway to Needles Hwy. Go north 2.5 miles to the Nevada State Line. Continue another 0.7 miles and turn left into a dry wash marked with a large cairn. (As a courtesy to the Mojave Indian Reservation, this starting point bypasses 3 miles of agricultural land on the reservation.)

Trail Description: Reset odometer at the start as you turn left off Needles Highway [01]. Head west in a wide, sandy wash, ignoring side roads. Bear right at 1.5 miles (02) following a line of telephone poles. The road is better defined and is soon marked with a sign post. Turn left away from the pole line at 3.0 then right at 3.4 miles. Bear left at 5.1 and right at 5.3. Continue straight at 5.7 miles where a larger power line service road crosses at a shallow angle. Do not follow the power line. Go straight again at 6.7 where another road crosses diagonally. Cross the California State Line at 7.9 miles (03). Continue straight at 8.0. Cross a ridge and descend into Piute Valley. Continue heading west ignoring side roads before reaching paved Hwy. 95 at 11.3 miles (04).

Cross over Hwy. 95 and continue heading west. Cross a cattle guard at 12.1 miles. Ignore several faint crossroads. Cross under major power lines at 18.6 miles (05) and continue west. You soon enter the Mojave National Preserve, administered by the National Park Service. This is a protected area. Stay on the road and obey national park rules. The road gets rockier and curves around the north side of Jed Smith Butte where several roads converge. Continue west before reaching a fenced area and remains of a stone cabin. This now defunct turkey farm was built in 1944 by the Irwin Family. Petroglyphs are scattered about the area. Fort Piute is reached at 20.5 miles. Turn around in a wide area just south of the Fort. Piute Gorge Hiking Trail continues up the rocky creek bottom. More petroglyphs can be seen along this trail.

Return east to the power lines at 22.5 miles (05) then turn right. Head south on a good road between the power lines, then turn right at 24.0 miles (06). After a straight section, the road meanders and climbs to the top of a ridge with great views of Lanfair Valley on the other side. After the road flattens out, cross a cattle guard and turn right at 28.0 miles. At 28.5 miles (07), the trail turns left. Before turning here, continue straight to visit an interesting corral just ahead. Turn around at the corral and return to the trail, then continue west. Cross a wide wash at 31.2 miles (08). Bear slightly left when the road forks at a water tank at 31.5. (Cairns always on right).

As you proceed, Joshua trees become more prevalent. A large road crosses at a shallow angle at 33.9 miles. The trail continues straight on the other side of the road. Cross another sandy wash at 34.7. Continue straight at 35.2 as you pass an old school bus. You must bear right at a fence at 36.0 miles (09). Bear left at 36.3 and follow the fence. At 37.3 miles (10), bear right away from the fence. The road is a bit washed out. Vehicles with less articulation will need momentum to get through. You'll join another road at 37.9 miles. Stay on this road for about 50 ft. then bear right. Continue straight across another road at 38.4. For good luck, tradition requires you put a penny in a can hanging from a Joshua tree at 39.3 miles. Add another can if it is full. The money is used for trail restoration. Mojave Road East (Trail #24) ends at Ivanpah Road at 39.8 miles (11).

Return Trip: You may continue on the Mojave Road (see Trail #25) or exit at this point. Head south on Ivanpah Road to Goffs. Left at Goffs takes you back to Needles via I-40. Right at Goffs takes you to Fenner at I-40.

Services: Nearest gas and food can be found at the I-40 interchange at Fenner, which is about 10 miles southwest of Goffs on Goffs Road. The Avi Casino has gas and a large RV campground.

Maps: Auto Club of So. California's map of the Mojave Preserve, Dennis Casebier book—*Mojave Road Guide*, DeLorme Atlas & Gazetteer.

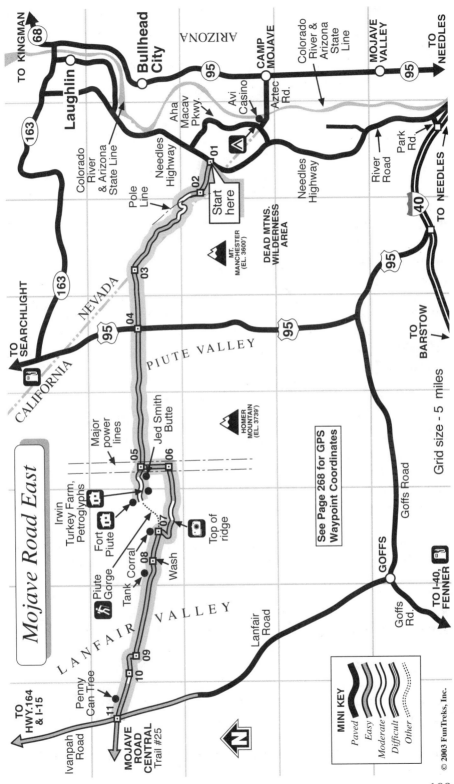

Mojave Road East

TO KINGMAN
68
Laughlin
163
Bullhead City
ARIZONA
95
CAMP MOJAVE
Avi Casino
Aztec Rd.
Aha Macav Pkwy.
Colorado River & Arizona State Line
MOJAVE VALLEY
95
TO NEEDLES

Colorado River & Arizona State Line
Needles Highway
Pole Line
01
02
Start here
Needles Highway
River Road
Park Rd.
95
40
TO NEEDLES
TO NEEDLES

MT. MANCHESTER (EL. 3600)
DEAD MTNS. WILDERNESS AREA

TO SEARCHLIGHT
163
NEVADA
03
04
95
95
PIUTE VALLEY
CALIFORNIA
TO BARSTOW

Major power lines
Jed Smith Butte
05
06
HOMER MOUNTAIN (EL. 3739')

Irwin
Turkey Farm, Petroglyphs
Fort Piute
07
Top of ridge
See Page 268 for GPS Waypoint Coordinates

Piute Gorge
Tank Corral
08
Wash
GOFFS
Goffs Road
TO I-40, FENNER

LANFAIR VALLEY
Lanfair Road
Goffs Rd.

Penny Can Tree
09
10
11

TO HWY. 164 & I-15
Ivanpah Road
MOJAVE ROAD CENTRAL Trail #25

N

MINI KEY
Paved
Easy
Moderate
Difficult
Other

Grid size - 5 miles

© 2003 FunTreks, Inc.

109

Steep hill at Watson Wash.

Bert Smith's cabin now owned by the National Park Service.

Rock Springs.

Windmill and water tank at Government Holes.

Register at mail box.

Clear water in cattle trough at Marl Springs.

Mojave Road Central

Location: The Mojave Road crosses the Mojave National Preserve between Bullhead City, AZ and Barstow, CA. The central part runs between Ivanpah Road and Kelbaker Road.

Difficulty: Moderate. When dry, this trail is mostly easy. One moderate section drops steeply into Watson Wash, which can be impassable during heavy rains. Don't underestimate the soft sand in Willow Wash; good 4-wheelers have gotten stuck here. You are a long way from services so carry plenty of water and gas. Dangerously hot in summer. Suitable for stock 4x4 SUVs with high ground clearance. Trail is marked with cairns (always on right).

Features: Hike a short distance to see historic Rock Springs and the Bert Smith stone cabin. Explore Marl Springs and Government Holes. Enjoy panoramic views of Kelso Sand Dunes and numerous mountain ranges. Camp overnight and relax in total solitude. Soak up the history of this once-important cross-country wagon route. **Street-legal vehicles only.**

Time & Distance: This leg is 44 miles. Allow about 5 hours plus additional time for stops. Considerable travel time may be required to reach this trail and return home.

To Get There: Drive the eastern portion of the Mojave Road (Trail #24). Or, from Goffs, head north on Lanfair Road 17.2 miles to the point Mojave Road crosses. This point is 0.8 miles north of Cedar Canyon Road.

Trail Description: Reset odometer at the start as you leave Ivanpah Road (01). Continue west where a road crosses at 1.9 miles. At 3.9 miles (02) continue west at an intersection with Caruthers Road. (If you have time, take a side trip here to Caruthers Canyon, which is located about 7.5 miles north. Beautiful rock formations and plenty of shade make this a popular picnic and camping spot. The road forks several times after New York Mountain Road. Bear right at each fork.)

Continuing west, the Mojave Road crosses a clearing at 6.0 miles. Then, at 6.7 miles, continue straight, avoiding a road that looks more like a ditch. Join well-maintained Cedar Canyon Road at 7.0 miles. At 7.4, bear left off Cedar Canyon Road at cairn. Mojave Road soon drops steeply into Watson Wash and heads northwest across the wash. Cairns may be displaced by heavy rains but the road is fairly obvioius. Cross the wash diagonally until reaching the barricaded mouth of Rock Spring Canyon. Turn right here and follow the wash. At 8.4 miles (03), you'll see a parking area on the left with a sign explaining the history of Rock Springs. Park here and take the short hike to Rock Springs.

After hiking, head north from the parking area and you'll reconnect with Cedar Canyon Road at 8.6 miles. Bear left uphill about 0.3 miles and turn left off Cedar Canyon Road at a cairn. The next crossroad goes left to Bert Smith's cabin. A short hike is required, but it's worth it. The cabin is in such great shape, you'd swear Bert was still living there. I found the back door unlocked. After visiting the cabin return to Mojave Road and continue (left).

Mojave Road heads in a west/southwest direction. Bear right when the road forks in less than a tenth of a mile. Cross over another road in about a mile then immediately bear left at the next fork. At 10.4 miles, the road curves around to the right to Government Holes, marked with a windmill and water tank at 10.5 miles (04). Continue downhill through the corral and bear slightly left as you come out. Immediately bear left again at the next road before reaching Cedar Canyon Road once again at 11.0 miles. Bear left and stay on this good road until you reach Kelso-Cima Road at 20.6 miles (05) just after the RR tracks. The Mojave Road continues across Kelso-Cima Road at the historical marker.

Continue west across remote, beautiful desert. The road is very sandy with continuous whoop-ti-dos. Proceed slowly. Continue straight at 25.3 miles as a road joins on the left. Make an important left turn at 25.9 miles (06). Bear slightly right at 26.8. There's a nice camping spot to the left. Cross under power lines then bear left into Marl Springs at 28.9. You can turn around at Lower Marl Springs at 29.0 miles (07). Head back out and continue left past Upper Marl Springs. Continue straight under more power lines at 30.6. A beautiful valley unfolds ahead. At 32.4 miles (08), stop and register at the Mail Box. Do your part to let the park service know how much this road is used. The road gets sandier and is mixed with black rock. Cross a bladed mine road at 37.5 miles (09). Stay right along the wall of black lava as the road splits in various directions. Keep up your speed so you don't get stuck. Bear right at 38.8 and go straight at 40.3. Continue running parallel to paved Kelbaker Road before reaching it at 44.0 miles (10).

Return Trip: Continue on Mojave Road West (Trail #26) across Kelbaker Road. Right on Kelbaker Road goes to Baker at Interstate 15 (about 15 miles). Left goes to Kelso then Interstate 40 (about 27 miles).

Services: Full services in Baker. Nothing in Kelso or at Interstate 40.

Maps: Automobile Club of Southern California's map of the Mojave National Preserve, Dennis Casebier book—*Mojave Road Guide*, DeLorme Atlas & Gazetteer.

112

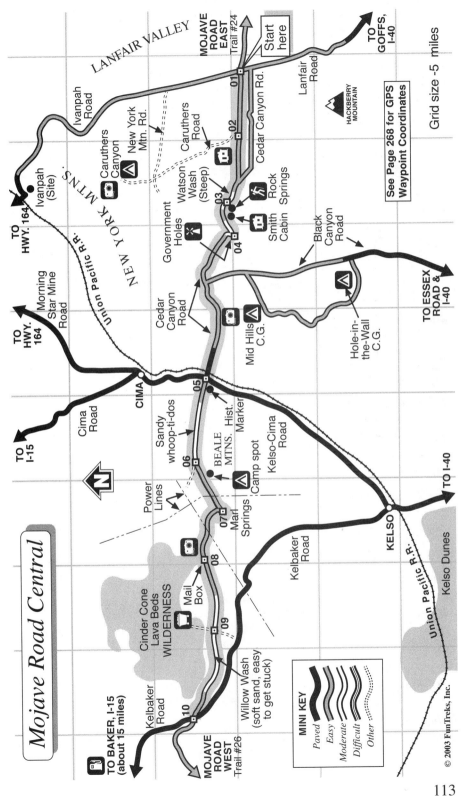

Mojave Road Central

LANFAIR VALLEY

MOJAVE ROAD EAST
Trail #24

Start here

TO GOFFS, I-40

01

Lanfair Road

Cedar Canyon Rd.

HACKBERRY MOUNTAIN

See Page 268 for GPS Waypoint Coordinates

Grid size - 5 miles

Ivanpah Road

New York Mtn. Rd.

Caruthers Road

02

Caruthers Canyon

Watson Wash (Steep)

03

Rock Springs

N E W   Y O R K   M T N S.

Ivanpah (Site)

TO HWY. 164

Morning Star Mine Road

Union Pacific R.R.

Government Holes

Smith Cabin

04

Black Canyon Road

TO HWY. 164

Cedar Canyon Road

Cedar Canyon Road

Hole-in-the-Wall C.G.

TO ESSEX ROAD & I-40

Cima Road

CIMA

05

Mid Hills C.G.

TO I-15

Sandy whoop-ti-dos

BEALE MTNS. Hist. Marker

Kelso-Cima Road

06

Camp spot

N

Power Lines

07

Marl Springs

Kelbaker Road

KELSO

TO I-40

Cinder Cone Lava Beds WILDERNESS

08

Mail Box

09

Union Pacific R.R.

Kelso Dunes

TO BAKER, I-15 (about 15 miles)

Kelbaker Road

10

Willow Wash (soft sand, easy to get stuck)

MOJAVE ROAD WEST Trail #26

MINI KEY
Paved
Easy
Moderate
Difficult
Other

© 2003 FunTreks, Inc.

113

Looking to get away from it all? How about this?

East side of Soda Dry Lake.

Mojave River in Afton Canyon. Stay out when water is deep.

Rocky road at Shaw Pass.

Afton Canyon.

Deep water in places.

Location: The Mojave Road crosses the Mojave National Preserve between Bullhead City, AZ and Barstow, CA. The western part runs between Kelbaker Road and Interstate 15.

Difficulty: Moderate. Most of this route is easy under dry conditions. The rockiest stretch is through Shaw Pass. Soft sand is encountered in many places. Soda Dry Lake and Afton Canyon can be impassable during periods of heavy rain. The end of this trip includes two water crossings that are mid-hubcap deep even during dry weather. You are a long way from services so carry plenty of water and gas. Dangerously hot in summer. Suitable for stock 4x4 SUVs with high ground clearance. Trail is marked with cairns most of the way. One exception is a sandy desert area below Shaw Pass where railroad ties point the way.

Features: Great scenery with a variety of trail conditions including a dry lake, a rocky pass, a sandy desert and several water crossings. Pick up a rock somewhere along the trail so you can place it on Traveler's Monument located on the west side of Soda Dry Lake. Join the fun and be counted. **Street-legal vehicles only except in nearby Rasor OHV Area.**

Time & Distance: This 40.2-mile leg takes about 5 hours to drive. Add time for stops. Considerable travel time required to reach trail and return home.

To Get There: Drive the central portion of the Mojave Road (Trail #25). Or, from Baker, head east, then south on Kelbaker Road about 15 miles. Watch for cairns for the Mojave Road on the right after Seventeenmile Point.

Trail Description: Reset odometer at the start at Kelbaker Road. [01]. Head north in a wash along the west side of Kelbaker Road. Bear left and circle around Seventeenmile Point until you begin heading in a southwest direction. Continue straight at 3.9 miles past Paymaster Road. You'll begin to see plastic pipe exposed along the road. Continue straight at a dilapidated metal water trough at 6.3 miles (02) at Jackass Canyon Road. Follow cairns and ignore many crossing roads. Remember cairns are always on the right. Bear left at an important fork at 10.2 miles (03) south of Little Cowhole Mountain. You will soon be able to see Baker and Interstate 15 far to the north. Pass through a fence at a cattle guard (Volunteer Gate) at 11.2 miles and start across Soda Dry Lake if conditions permit. (Make sure you travel with a second vehicle that can pull you out if you get stuck in the mud. If the lake

115

is too muddy, follow roads north along the east side of the lake to Baker. Head west on I-15 then south on Rasor Road back to Mojave Road.)

The Mojave Road cuts through wilderness as it crosses the lake so don't wander. A pile of rocks at 15.5 miles is called the *Traveler's Monument*. It was formed as each new passerby added a rock. A plaque on the monument reveals a secret that only Mojave Road travelers are to know. Hopefully, you picked up a rock to add to the pile. As you come off the lake, turn right at a large boulder field called the *Granites* and follow cairns north then west again. The area that follows is very soft sand. At 18.0 miles, you leave the Mojave National Preserve.

Continue straight across several roads at 19.0 miles (04). One of these roads is Rasor Road that goes north to the Rasor OHV Area and Interstate 15. Gradually, the terrain changes as you descend through Shaw Pass. Although not a dramatic pass, it is quite rocky. At 21.6 miles (05), make an important left turn at a crossroads. You'll head south then turn west again. The terrain is very sandy and the trail can be hard to find. Railroad ties begin to replace cairns as trail markers. Head southwest aiming to the left side of Cave Mountain, the tallest mountain on the horizon. You'll eventually run into the Mojave River, usually just a trickle. Keep going until you cross under a large railroad bridge at 31.2 miles (06).

The trail meanders up the Mojave River as it passes through beautiful Afton Canyon. The Bureau of Land Management has marked the trail. Don't enter the canyon if weather threatens. Flash floods are possible. Bear right at barricades at 34.8 miles (07) and follow the gravel road along the heavily-used railroad tracks. Pass through as quickly as possible; the road is very close to the tracks. After two fairly deep water crossings, you reach Afton Canyon Campgrounds. Continue west on the north side of the tracks. A road joins on the left at 36.6 miles (08). (This is a lesser-used portion of the Mojave Road and may be driven if you wish, but, no directions are provided here.) Continue north to reach I-15 at 40.2 miles (09).

Return Trip: At I-15, Barstow is 35 miles west; Baker is 24 miles east.

Services: Full services in Barstow and Baker. Toilets at Afton Canyon C.G.

Historical Highlights: The Mojave Road served as a major wagon road during a 25-year period before the railroads reached the area in 1883. For a complete history of the road, refer to Dennis Casebier book, the *Mojave Road Guide, An Adventure Through Time,* ISBN 0-914224-29-8.

Maps: Automobile Club of Southern California's map of the Mojave National Preserve, Dennis Casebier book—*Mojave Road Guide,* DeLorme Atlas & Gazetteer.

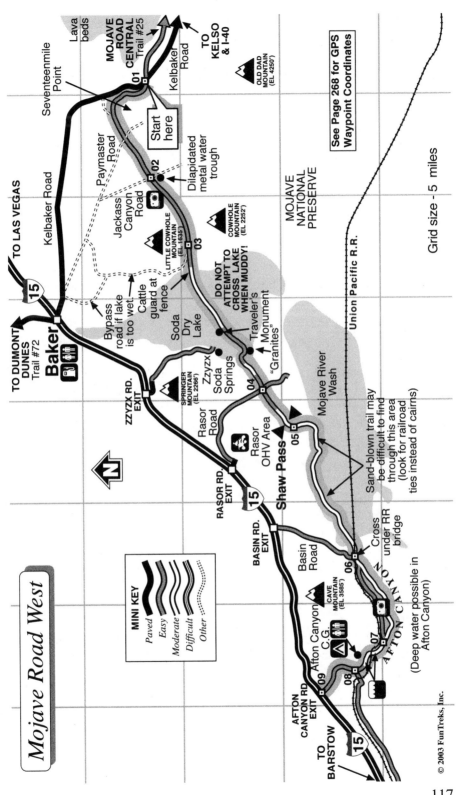

Mojave Road West

MINI KEY
- Paved
- Easy
- Moderate
- Difficult
- Other

See Page 268 for GPS Waypoint Coordinates

Grid size - 5 miles

MOJAVE ROAD CENTRAL Trail #25

TO KELSO & I-40

Kelbaker Road

OLD DAD MOUNTAIN (EL 4250')

Lava beds

Seventeenmile Point

Start here

Dilapidated metal water trough

Paymaster Road

Jackass Canyon Road

Kelbaker Road

TO LAS VEGAS

LITTLE COWHOLE MOUNTAIN (EL 1635')

COWHOLE MOUNTAIN (EL 2252')

MOJAVE NATIONAL PRESERVE

DO NOT ATTEMPT TO CROSS LAKE WHEN MUDDY!

Bypass road if lake is too wet.

Cattle guard at fence

Soda Dry Lake

Traveler's Monument

"Granites"

TO DUMONT DUNES Trail #72

Baker

ZZYZX RD. EXIT

SPRINGER MOUNTAIN (EL 2266')

Zzyzx Soda Springs

Rasor Road

Union Pacific R.R.

Mojave River Wash

Rasor OHV Area

RASOR RD. EXIT

Shaw Pass

Sand-blown trail may be difficult to find through this area (look for railroad ties instead of cairns)

BASIN RD. EXIT

Basin Road

Cross under RR bridge

CAVE MOUNTAIN (EL 3585')

Afton Canyon C.G.

AFTON CANYON

(Deep water possible in Afton Canyon)

AFTON CANYON RD. EXIT

TO BARSTOW

© 2003 FunTreks, Inc.

117

AREA 5

Inland Empire,
San Bernardino

27. Rincon-Shortcut Road
28. Cucamonga Big Tree Trail
29. Cleghorn Ridge
30. Pilot Rock Road
31. Santiago Peak

Inland Empire, San Bernardino

Finding worthy four-wheel-drive trails close to southern California's massive metropolitan areas is no easy task. Many trails in nearby national forests have been closed due to a combination of overuse and enforcement of strict environmental regulations. Still, California is a big place and not everything within a short drive is closed. Although none of the five trails selected here is difficult, each offers a unique experience. My favorite is *Cucamonga Big Tree Trail*. Located immediately northwest of San Bernardino, this trail provides a challenging adventure with minimal travel time. Another favorite is *Cleghorn Ridge*. It begins at the base of an Interstate 15 exit ramp and climbs steeply on a spectacular winding road. The trail also accesses difficult terrain. *Santiago Peak* starts easy but gradually gets rough as it climbs above 5,600 feet, providing outstanding views west towards Mission Viejo and east to Lake Elsinore. *Rincon-Shortcut Road* is located high in the beautiful San Gabriel Mountains above Azusa. Fewer people travel the road because of the extra time required to pick up the free permit and gate combination.

Easy but steep descent down Cleghorn Ridge (Trail #29) to Silverwood Lake.

119

Locked gate at both ends of trail requires free permit.

Switchbacks, switchbacks and more switchbacks.

San Gabriel Cyn. OHV Area.

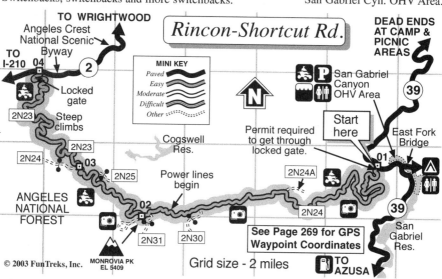

TO WRIGHTWOOD

Angeles Crest
National Scenic
Byway

DEAD ENDS
AT CAMP &
PICNIC
AREAS

TO
I-210 04

2

Rincon-Shortcut Rd.

Locked
gate

San Gabriel
Canyon
OHV Area

MINI KEY
Paved
Easy
Moderate
Difficult
Other

N

39

2N23

Steep
climbs

Start
here

East Fork
Bridge

2N23

Permit required
to get through
locked gate.

2N24

03

Cogswell
Res.

01

2N25

Power lines
begin

2N24A

ANGELES
NATIONAL
FOREST

02

39

2N24

San
Gabriel
Res.

2N31 2N30

**See Page 269 for GPS
Waypoint Coordinates**

© 2003 FunTreks, Inc.

MONROVIA PK
EL 5409

Grid size - 2 miles

TO
AZUSA

Rincon-Shortcut Road ㉗

Location: North of Azusa and Glendora, northeast of Pasadena.

Difficulty: Easy. First half of trip is a graded road but narrow in a few places. Last part of trip is rocky and steep in spots. Suitable for all stock SUVs with high ground clearance and low-range 4-wheel drive.

Features: Never-ending switchbacks at high elevation provide outstanding views. A free permit and gate combination are needed to drive the road. These can be picked up at the San Gabriel Canyon Forest Service Ranger District Office in Glendora or, on weekends, at the San Gabriel Canyon OHV Area on Hwy. 39 just before the trailhead. Vehicles parked on the trail must display a Forest Adventure Pass. An additional fee is charged for the small but popular OHV area. Mud play is the featured attraction.

Time & Distance: Although the finish is only 10 miles from the start as the crow flies, this twisting road measures 26.2 miles. Allow about 4 hours.

To Get There: Take Highway 39 north from Azusa (near Glendora). Turn left 0.8 miles after the East Fork Bridge onto F.S. 2N24. The OHV Area is 0.6 miles past the bridge.

Trail Description: Reset odometer at the start [01]. Use the lock combination that comes with the permit to open the lock. Small people may have trouble opening the very heavy gate. The road climbs rapidly up the mountain with great views of San Gabriel Canyon. Bear left at 7.8 miles. A wide spot at 9.7 miles has good views. Bear right at 10.8 where closed 2N30 goes left. You'll soon begin following power lines. Go right again at 12.9. Bear right on a narrowing road at a T at 13.3 miles (02). Go right again at 13.9 then left at 16.3. Bear right on 2N23 at 17.2 miles (03). The road is rougher now with several steep places. Bear left at 18.5 and 20.0. The trail ends at 26.2 miles (04) at Hwy. 2 at another heavy gate. The combination lock is the same.

Return Trip: Take Hwy. 2 west 43 miles to Interstate 210 near Pasadena.

Services: Full services in Azusa. Vault toilet at OHV area and parking area just east of East Fork Bridge. Commercial campgrounds on East Fork Road.

Maps: Angeles National Forest, USGS 100,000-scale map San Bernardino CA, N3400-W11700, Delorme Atlas & Gazetteer.

121

Side trip on F.S. 1N35.

The "Big Tree" at Joe Elliot Campground.

Falling rock can block trail at Calamity Canyon.

A cold fog settles in where trail crosses Day Canyon.

Native American "morteros."

Scenic switchbacks coming down San Sevaine Road.

122

Cucamonga Big Tree Trail

Location: North of Rancho Cucamonga. Northwest of San Bernardino in the San Bernardino National Forest.

Difficulty: Moderate. Generally this trail is suitable for high-clearance SUVs with low-range gearing and skid plates; however, the road is not maintained as you climb the western side up to Joe Elliott Campground. Rock slides can block the trail, especially at Calamity Canyon. Brush is tight in places. Don't drive this trail alone.

Features: A memorable and challenging drive with great views. Convenient for Inland Empire residents. Park and hike through beautiful Cucamonga Canyon where Cucamonga Creek flows all year. In the fall and winter (weather permitting), you can drive all the way to Lytle Creek. Gates control entry to the eastern half of the trail. They open the day after Labor Day and close with the first heavy snowfall or by March 1, whichever comes first. The portion of trail on the way to the campground is open all year. The trail is for day use only unless you are camping overnight at Joe Elliot Campground. It is best to make camping reservations and you'll need a permit to build a fire. Both are free. Contact the Cajon/Lytle Creek Ranger Station (see appendix). If you park anywhere along the trail, you must have a Forest Adventure Pass. (See page 14.)

Only licensed vehicles are allowed on this trail. This excludes all ATVs since they cannot be licensed. A very stiff fine discourages violators.

The local community sometimes tries to discourage people from using this trail by placing movable barricades on Skyline Drive leading up to the start. A San Bernardino Forest Ranger told me these barricades are illegal and you have every right to ignore them. However, don't confuse these movable barricades with legal forest service gates. Everyone using the trail should do so in a responsible way. Enter during daytime hours only.

Time & Distance: The entire trip is 23.7 miles. It's 12.1 miles to Joe Elliott Campground. Allow 2 to 3 hours to reach the campground and another 1 to 2 hours to reach Lytle Creek Road.

To Get There: Exit Interstate 210 at Carnelian Street in Rancho Cucamonga. Head north 1.3 miles and turn left on Hillside Road. Go west 0.5 miles to Sapphire Street and turn right. Go north another 0.5 miles to Almond Street and turn left. Within 100 feet, turn right and follow Skyline Drive uphill as the road narrows. A wide spot before a forest service gate marks the start of the trail in another 0.3 miles. If you stop here, be extremely careful. An unprotected cliff to the left is not obvious.

Trail Description: *Reset odometer at the start* [01]. Continue uphill as the road immediately gets rough. The road forks at 0.4 miles. Optional F.S. 1N35 goes left downhill 0.8 miles to a parking area for Cucamonga Canyon. Here you can hike along beautiful Cucamonga Creek. Follow 1N34 right to continue. Go straight at 1.1 miles as a narrow shelf road continues uphill with great views of the massive metropolitan area below. At 3.7 miles (02) stay on the main road through a flatter area as smaller roads branch away. This is a popular place for hang gliders to launch. Stay left at 4.1 and 5.3 miles. Cross a narrow, rocky shelf road at 6.1 miles (03) at Calamity Canyon. Watch for falling rock and possible blockage of the trail. Cross a rocky sluice at Day Canyon at 10.4 miles. This is a good lunch spot with great views. Unfortunately, the day I ran the trail, a thick fog bank moved in. I was told you could hike up Day Canyon about 10 minutes to a great water hole. Bear left at 12.1 miles (04) to reach Joe Elliot Campground.

To continue on the trail, bear right at the campground. A gate at 12.6 miles is open as described earlier. This is a very popular area for hunting in the fall, so be careful. Bear right at 16.1 where a gated road goes left. Watch for three large trees at 16.6 miles (05). An Indian village was once located here and many Indian grinding holes ("*morteros*") can be found in the area. Follow an improving road as it switchbacks impressively downhill. You pass under power lines before reaching the final gate at Lytle Creek Road at 23.7 miles (06).

Return Trip: Turn right to reach Interstate 15. Left takes you to the Cajon/Lytle Creek Ranger Station in a few miles.

Services: None along the trail.

Historical Highlights: A big fallen tree east of Joe Elliott Campground rests in a very strange position across its base. After the tree died, it began to deteriorate. People built fires inside the tree and it became unsafe. The forest service brought it down with dynamite but used a bit too much. The tree shot into the air and came to rest as you see it. Other trees nearby show signs of lightning strikes. You can see large grooves spiraling around their trunks.

Maps: San Bernardino National Forest, USGS 100,000-scale map San Bernardino CA, N3400-W11700, DeLorme Atlas & Gazetteer.

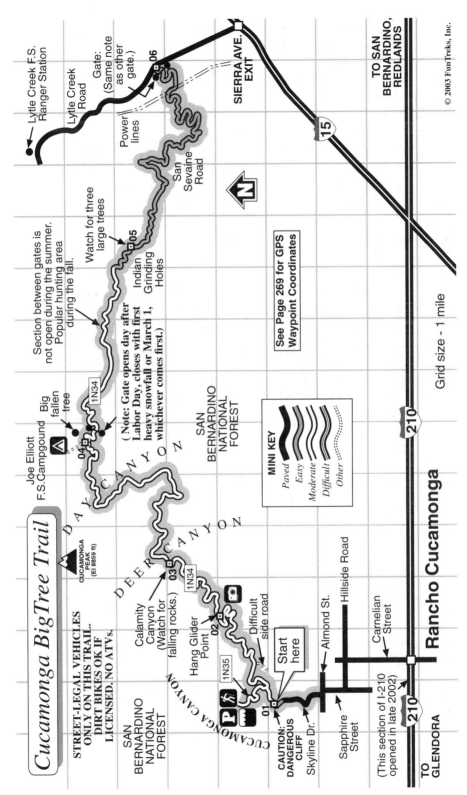

Cucamonga BigTree Trail

STREET-LEGAL VEHICLES ONLY ON THIS TRAIL. DIRT BIKES OK IF LICENSED. NO ATVs.

SAN BERNARDINO NATIONAL FOREST

CUCAMONGA PEAK (El 8859 ft)

Joe Elliott F.S. Campgound

Lytle Creek F.S. Ranger Station

Lytle Creek Road

Gate: (Same note as other gate.)

Power lines

Section between gates is not open during the summer. Popular hunting area during the fall.

Watch for three large trees

Big fallen tree

1N34

(Note: Gate opens day after Labor Day, closes with first heavy snowfall or March 1, whichever comes first.)

04

06

05

Indian Grinding Holes

San Sevaine Road

DAY CANYON

DEER CANYON

Calamity Canyon (Watch for falling rocks.)

03

1N34

02

Hang Glider Point

Difficult side road

1N35

01

Start here

CAUTION: DANGEROUS CLIFF

Skyline Dr.

CUCAMONGA CANYON

SAN BERNARDINO NATIONAL FOREST

MINI KEY
Paved
Easy
Moderate
Difficult
Other

See Page 269 for GPS Waypoint Coordinates

N

SIERRA AVE. EXIT

15

TO SAN BERNARDINO, REDLANDS

Almond St.

Sapphire Street

Hillside Road

Carnelian Street

Rancho Cucamonga

210

210

TO GLENDORA

(This section of I-210 opened in late 2002)

Grid size - 1 mile

© 2003 FunTreks, Inc.

125

Cleghorn Road splits many times. Optional routes are moderate to extremely difficult.

The east end of the trail provides fantastic views of Silverwood Lake State Recreation Area.

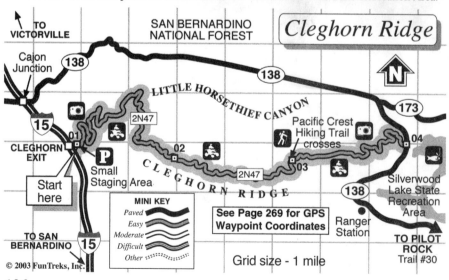

TO VICTORVILLE

SAN BERNARDINO NATIONAL FOREST

Cleghorn Ridge

Cajon Junction

138

138

N

LITTLE HORSETHIEF CANYON

173

2N47

01

Pacific Crest Hiking Trail crosses

04

CLEGHORN EXIT

P

02

03

CLEGHORN RIDGE

2N47

Start here

Small Staging Area

Silverwood Lake State Recreation Area

MINI KEY
Paved
Easy
Moderate
Difficult
Other

138

See Page 269 for GPS Waypoint Coordinates

Ranger Station

TO SAN BERNARDINO

15

TO PILOT ROCK
Trail #30

© 2003 FunTreks, Inc.

Grid size - 1 mile

Cleghorn Ridge ㉙

Location: North of San Bernardino, south of Victorville.

Difficulty: Easy. Steep and rutted in places. Many optional sideroads from moderate to very difficult. Suitable for stock 4x4 SUVs with high ground clearance and low range gearing, provided you take the easy choices.

Features: An exciting and scenic drive. An easy trail is intertwined with a difficult trail. Choose an easy or difficult route at almost every fork. Finish at beautiful Silverwood Lake State Recreation Area. Many other great roads in the area. If you park along the trail, you'll need a Forest Adventure Pass. A very popular area for ATVs and dirt bikes.

Time & Distance: This 15-mile drive takes less than 2 hours but you can spend much longer exploring other roads.

To Get There: The trail starts on the east side of Interstate 15 at the Cleghorn Exit which is just south of Cajon Junction.

Trail Description: Reset odometer at the start [01]. Read regulations posted at trailhead. Head east uphill on a steep, winding road. Bear right at 0.7 and 2.3 miles. At 3.9 miles continue straight on 2N47 where 3N22 crosses. Bear left at 5.1 and right at 5.5 miles. Continuing on the easy road, bear right at 5.9 miles. Stay straight on the main road at 7.0 miles [02] where another road crosses at a shallow angle. There is no right or wrong way; choose the best route for you. Bear left at 8.5 and 9.2 miles. At this point, you're above 5,300 ft. and the views are great. Bear left at 11.0 miles [03] where the Pacific Crest Hiking Trail crosses. A larger road joins on the right at 12.7 miles as you pass under power lines. A popular hardcore route descends steeply south of the main road. It branches off at various points. You won't be confused because it's obviously very difficult. Most people drive up it. You intersect with paved Highway 138 at about 15 miles [04].

Return Trip: Left on Highway 138 goes back to Interstate 15 at Cajon Junction (about 10 miles). Right continues on to Pilot Rock Trail #30.

Services: None along trail or at Interstate 15 Cleghorn Exit.

Maps: San Bernardino National Forest, USGS 100,000-scale map San Bernardino CA, N3400-W11700, DeLorme Atlas & Gazetteer.

Looking down on the south end of Silverwood Lake.

Ledge road winds uphill to great views.

First half of route is steep and rutted.

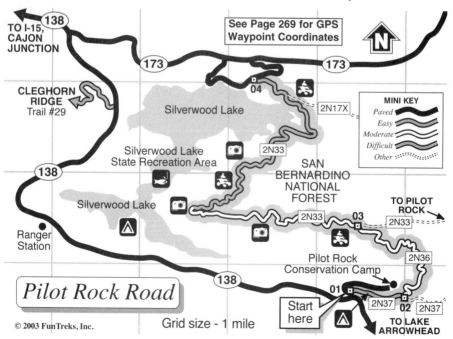

See Page 269 for GPS Waypoint Coordinates

TO I-15,
CAJON
JUNCTION

138

173

173

N

CLEGHORN
RIDGE
Trail #29

Silverwood Lake

04

2N17X

MINI KEY
Paved
Easy
Moderate
Difficult
Other

Silverwood Lake
State Recreation Area

2N33

SAN
BERNARDINO
NATIONAL
FOREST

138

Silverwood Lake

Ranger
Station

2N33

03

TO PILOT
ROCK

2N33

2N36

Pilot Rock
Conservation Camp

Pilot Rock Road

138

01

Start
here

02

2N37

2N37

TO LAKE
ARROWHEAD

© 2003 FunTreks, Inc.

Grid size - 1 mile

Pilot Rock Road

Location: North of San Bernardino, south of Victorville.

Difficulty: Moderate. The first half of the trip is mostly uphill and is steep and rutted in places. The last half is downhill and easy. Suitable for stock 4x4 SUVs with high ground clearance. Good for ATVs and dirt bikes.

Features: This route covers the most scenic part of F. S. Road 2N33, which actually starts farther east from a point northwest of Lake Arrowhead. The starting point described here is convenient for anyone completing Cleghorn Ridge (Trail #29). You can also run this route in the opposite direction and continue east on F.S. 2N33 to Pilot Rock near the Pinnacles. Those looking for a difficult trail can drive F.S. Road 2N17X which you'll pass as you complete this route. A Forest Adventure Pass is required if you stop to recreate.

Time & Distance: This 8.8-mile trip takes 1 to 2 hours.

To Get There: Take Hwy. 138 east about 16 miles from Interstate 15 at Cajon Junction. Turn left on a small paved road at a sign for Silverwood Lake State Recreation Area/Miller Canyon. Turn right almost immediately on F.S. 2N37. If you've driven Cleghorn Ridge first, take 138 right. The turn for Pilot Rock is 3.7 miles past the ranger station.

Trail Description: *Reset odometer at the start of 2N37* [01]. Head east through F.S. fee camping area. Cross a small paved section and turn left off of F.S. 2N37 at 0.7 miles [02]. Quickly make a right on F.S. 2N36. Pilot Rock Conservation Camp, on the left, is a minimum-security prison facility. After climbing steep switchbacks, turn left at a cluster of roads at 2.6 miles [03] then turn right at 2.7. Stay off the steep roads to the left. Turn right again at 3.1 and 3.9 miles. Stay left at 5.1 until you reach a scenic point where the trail swings east. After several more miles, you'll go by difficult 2N17X on the right before reaching a paved road at 8.8 miles [04].

Return Trip: Turn right and follow the paved road north to Hwy 173, then turn left. When you reach 138, turn right to reach I-15 at Cajon Junction.

Services: Several forest service campgrounds in the area.

Maps: San Bernardino National Forest, USGS 7.5-minute map of Silverwood Lake, DeLorme Atlas & Gazetteer.

It gets rockier and steeper towards the top.

Radio towers atop Santiago Peak in distance.

Santiago Peak

TO CORONA

Temescal Canyon Road

05

15

Check with Cleveland N.F. Trabuco R.D. in Corona to be sure this gate is open (See appendix)

Japanese Retreat

TO LAKE ELSINORE

SANTIAGO PEAK

04

5S01

Indian Truck Trail

CLEVELAND NATIONAL FOREST

03

3S04

CLEVELAND NATIONAL FOREST

6W11

3S04

6W04

N

See Page 269 for GPS Waypoint Coordinates

3S04

Deteriorated paved road

02

TO I-15, LAKE ELSINORE (11 miles)

MINI KEY
Paved
Easy
Moderate
Difficult
Other

Blue Jay Campground

6S05

Long Canyon Road

74

Start here

01

74

Grid size - 2 miles

© 2003 FunTreks, Inc.

Switchbacks-aplenty.

TO I-5, SAN JUAN CAPISTRANO

Santiago Peak 31

Location: West of Lake Elsinore, south of Corona.

Difficulty: Moderate. Most of the trip is easy, but closer to the top of the peak it gets steep and rocky. Suitable for stock 4x4 SUVs with high ground clearance.

Features: A fun, high-elevation drive with great views. Before you go, check with the Cleveland N.F., Trabuca R.D. to make sure gate at the bottom of the Indian Truck Trail is open (see appendix). You could also drive up Indian Truck Trail to check gate. (Gate is 1.8 miles from I-15.) Only licensed vehicles allowed on road. Forest Adventure Pass required if you stop to recreate.

Time & Distance: Allow 3 to 4 hours for this 27.6-mile trip.

To Get There: Take Highway 74 southwest from Lake Elsinore. Turn right 1.2 miles past the El Cariso Fire Station onto Long Canyon Road (not marked, watch for a sign to Los Pinos Camp.) If you are coming northeast on Hwy. 74, turn left 3.2 miles after the Upper San Juan Campground.

Trail Description: Reset odometer as you turn off Hwy. 74 [01]. Go north on paved Long Canyon Road. Bear right at 1.7 miles on lesser F.S. 6S05 (still Long Canyon Road). Pass Blue Jay Campground at 2.5. Turn left on hidden road at 3.4 miles (02). Pavement deteriorates to gravel then changes to attractive sandstone. Road climbs steeply then descends again. Bear left at 7.5 miles (03) when you intersect with Indian Truck Trail, F.S 5S01. You reach top of mountain at 15.5 miles (04) when road splits 3 ways. Right continues down other side of mountain. Great views to left. Turn around and go back down to Indian Truck Trail. *Reset odometer* and turn left (03). Great views as you descend many switchbacks. Pass through gate at 5.8. Go straight at 6.1 and 6.3 miles. You'll pass a Japanese Christian Retreat on your right. After passing through a junky area, bear right at 7.2 miles. You reach Interstate 15 at 7.6 miles (05).

Return Trip: Right on I-15 goes back to Lake Elsinore; left goes to Corona.

Services: Blue Jay Campground (see map). Full services in Lake Elsinore.

Maps: Cleveland National Forest, USGS 100,000 scale map Santa Ana, CA, DeLorme Atlas & Gazetteer.

AREA 6

Big Bear,
Lake
Arrowhead

32. Grapevine Canyon
33. Willow Creek Road
34. Dishpan Springs
35. Holcomb Creek
36. Butler Peak
37. John Bull Trail
38. Jacoby Canyon
39. Gold Mountain
40. Clarks Summit
41. Skyline Drive
42. Heartbreak Ridge
43. Rattlesnake Canyon

MINI KEY

Paved
Easy
Moderate
Difficult
Other

Grid size - 5 miles

© 2003 FunTreks, Inc.

EASY
MODERATE
DIFFICULT

N

TO YUCCA VALLEY

247

43

42

TO PIONEER-TOWN

TO BARSTOW

247

247

18

Lucerne Valley

18

18

TO APPLE VALLEY, VICTORVILLE

32

SAN BERNARDINO NATIONAL FOREST

3N14

3N16

3N16

3N14

3N16

37

39

38

18

18

Bear Valley

38

Big Bear Lake & Town

40

41

SAN BERNARDINO NATIONAL FOREST

38

38

38

Fawnskin

38

18

36

35

18

Green Valley

18

Rim of the World Scenic Byway

18

38

38

34

33

173

173

173

189

138

330

330

Lake Arrowhead

30

18

10

REDLANDS

San Bernardino

TO CLEGHORN RIDGE
Trail #29

TO PILOT ROCK
Trail #30

132

Big Bear, Lake Arrowhead

The forest and mountains around Big Bear and Arrowhead Lakes remind me of my home state of Colorado—beautiful drives mixed with some great rock crawling. Although private property around the lakes is densely developed, the surrounding San Bernardino National Forest remains unspoiled with relatively few people on the trails. But, if you plan to camp in a private or public campground between Memorial Day and Labor Day, make sure you make an advance reservation; this is an enormously popular place. What really impressed me about the area is the large number of open trails, all accurately rated and clearly marked by the forest service. Difficulty levels are posted on almost every trail for 4WD vehicles, ATVs and dirt bikes. Many trails have been adopted by local four-wheel-drive clubs who maintain and protect the trails. The most popular hardcore trails, *Dishpan Springs, Holcomb Creek* and *John Bull*, are fairly close together, making it possible to drive them all in one day. Make sure you take along a San Bernardino National Forest map in addition to this book. You'll need as much detail as possible to navigate this complex backcountry.

Trails are well marked and most are adopted by four-wheel-drive clubs.

Boulder outcrop before Grapevine Canyon.

Road narrows as it drops into canyon.

North of the N.F. boundary.

Willow Fire Restoration Area.

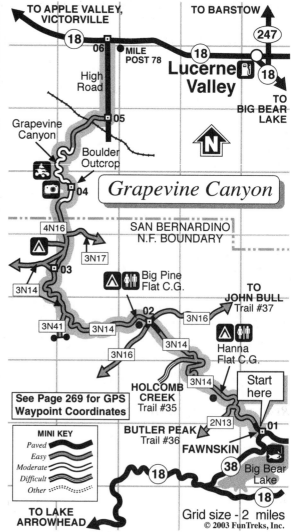

TO APPLE VALLEY,
VICTORVILLE

TO BARSTOW

247

18 06 MILE
POST 78

18 Lucerne
Valley 18

High
Road

TO
BIG BEAR
LAKE

N

05

Grapevine
Canyon

Boulder
Outcrop

04

Grapevine Canyon

4N16

SAN BERNARDINO
N.F. BOUNDARY

3N17

03

Big Pine
Flat C.G.

3N14

TO
JOHN BULL
Trail #37

3N16

02

3N41 3N14

3N14

Hanna
Flat C.G.

3N16

3N14

Start
here

See Page 269 for GPS
Waypoint Coordinates

HOLCOMB
CREEK
Trail #35

2N13

01

MINI KEY

Paved
Easy
Moderate
Difficult
Other

BUTLER PEAK
Trail #36

FAWNSKIN

38 Big Bear
Lake

18

TO LAKE
ARROWHEAD

Grid size - 2 miles
© 2003 FunTreks, Inc.

Grapevine Canyon 32

Location: Connects Big Bear Lake with Hwy. 18 west of Lucerne Valley.

Difficulty: Moderate. The road surface is easy but switchbacks descending through Grapevine Canyon are narrow and steep. Soft sand makes them susceptible to erosion. Suitable for stock 4x4 SUVs.

Features: Pass through charred forest before descending into dramatic Grapevine Canyon. Forest Adventure Pass required if you stop to recreate.

Time & Distance: Allow 2 to 3 hours for this 22.8-mile trip.

To Get There: Take Hwy. 38 to the little town of Fawnskin on the north side of Big Bear Lake. You'll see three fawn statues where you turn.

Trail Description: Reset odometer as you turn off Hwy. 38 onto Rim of the World Drive [01]. As you head northwest, the pavement changes to gravel and the road becomes F.S. 3N14. Bear right at 1.3 and 2.0 miles. Continue straight at 2.4 and 4.3. Go straight again at 6.8 miles (02) as you cross F.S. 3N16. Continue past the Big Pine Flat Campground. You'll enter Willow Fire burn area. Stay right at 10.3 miles where closed 3N41 goes left. Bear right at 12.3 miles (03) following sign to Lucerne Valley. Go by entrance to Horse Spring Campground. Stay north on 4N16 until you exit the forest.

   The road winds through a small valley then forks at a dramatic boulder outcropping at 15.6 miles (04). This is a good place to stop for lunch and take some photos. Continue downhill to the left as you drop into dramatic Grapevine Canyon. Be careful of possible washouts of the soft road surface. Continue downhill on a narrow road as you pass under power lines. Bear right downhill at a cattle guard at 17.4. Bear left at 18.4 then left again across railroad tracks at 19.6. Go straight at 19.8 then immediately bear right. Turn left on paved "High Road" at 20.3 miles (05). You reach Hwy. 18 at 22.8 miles (06) between mile posts 78 and 79.

Return Trip: Left on Hwy. 18 goes to Victorville, right to Lucerne Valley.

Services: Several large Forest Service Campgrounds along the trail. Full services in Big Bear Lake and Lucerne Valley.

Maps: San Bernardino National Forest, USGS 250,000 scale map San Bernardino, CA, DeLorme Atlas & Gazetteer.

Much of road is wide and easy.

Willow Creek can get deeper than this.

Pinnacles Staging Area has vault toilet and picnic tables.

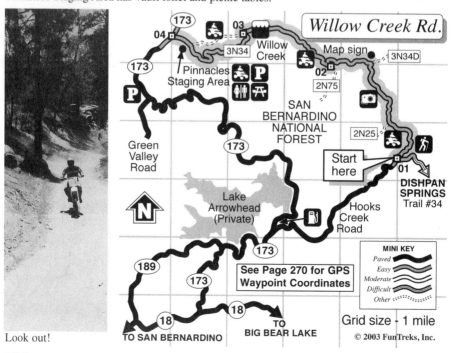

Willow Creek Rd.

173

04

03

3N34

Willow Creek

Map sign — 3N34D

173

Pinnacles Staging Area

P

02

2N75

SAN BERNARDINO NATIONAL FOREST

2N25

Green Valley Road

173

Start here

01

DISHPAN SPRINGS
Trail #34

N

Lake Arrowhead (Private)

Hooks Creek Road

173

189

173

See Page 270 for GPS Waypoint Coordinates

18

18

MINI KEY
Paved
Easy
Moderate
Difficult
Other

Grid size - 1 mile

189

173

18

TO SAN BERNARDINO

18

TO BIG BEAR LAKE

© 2003 FunTreks, Inc.

Look out!

136

Willow Creek Road ㉝

Location: North of Lake Arrowhead, east of Highway 173.

Difficulty: Easy. Gentle grades suitable for all SUVs. Willow Creek can be deep after heavy rains. Watch for speeding dirt bikes and ATVs.

Features: Pass through dense forest and open meadows on this fun drive. Accesses more difficult Jeep trails as well as ATV and dirt bike trails of the Pinnacles OHV Area. Adventure Pass required if you stop to recreate.

Time & Distance: This 7.4-mile cruiser takes 1 to 2 hours.

To Get There: From Highway 18 near mile marker 24.5, go north on Highway 173 to Lake Arrowhead. Hwy. 173 turns right after 1.5 miles. After 3.2 miles, turn right on Hooks Creek Road at small gas station. After another 3.2 miles downhill, turn left at fork just after pavement ends. This fork has a large white sign with a forest map showing routes in the area.

Trail Description: Reset odometer as you turn left at sign [01]. Bear left at 0.1 miles and climb through forest. Stay right on main road at 0.4. Bear right at 0.5 where difficult 2N27Y goes left. Stay on 3N34 as smaller trails branch off. Stay right at 1.0 miles where 2N25 goes left. Cross over a high meadow at 1.7. At 2.3 miles, bear left at another map sign. Bear left again at 2.5. Bear right at 2.8 where moderate trail 2N28Y goes left. At 3.1 miles, bear left where 3N38 joins on right. Make a hard right at 3.3 miles [02] where 2N75 goes left. Bear right uphill at 4.0 staying on 3N34 as the road twists and climbs more steeply. Cross Willow Creek at 5.0 miles. Road 3N34 splits at 5.2 miles [03]. Right is more difficult. I went left. The roads come back together at the Pinnacle Staging Area at 7.0 miles. Continue straight to Highway 173 at 7.4 miles [04].

Return Trip: Bear left on Hwy. 173 and follow it back to Hwy. 18 through Lake Arrowhead. It starts as a dirt road but soon becomes paved. (Right on Hwy. 173 takes a northern route back to Silverwood Lake.)

Services: Vault toilet and picnic tables at the Pinnacle Staging Area. Full services in Lake Arrowhead.

Maps: San Bernardino National Forest, USGS 7.5-minute map of Lake Arrowhead, Sidekick Map Arrowhead, DeLorme Atlas & Gazetteer.

Crossing Deep Creek is much easier than it used to be, but it still gets deeper than this.

Boulder field as you come out of creek.

Be careful at this steep, rocky spot.

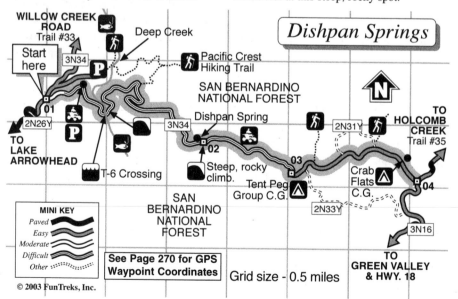

WILLOW CREEK ROAD
Trail #33

Deep Creek

Start here

3N34

Pacific Crest Hiking Trail

Dishpan Springs

SAN BERNARDINO NATIONAL FOREST

Dishpan Spring

01

2N26Y

3N34

02

TO LAKE ARROWHEAD

T-6 Crossing

Steep, rocky climb.

Tent Peg Group C.G.

2N31Y

03

TO HOLCOMB CREEK
Trail #35

Crab Flats C.G.

04

2N33Y

3N16

SAN BERNARDINO NATIONAL FOREST

MINI KEY
Paved
Easy
Moderate
Difficult
Other

See Page 270 for GPS
Waypoint Coordinates

Grid size - 0.5 miles

TO GREEN VALLEY
& HWY. 18

© 2003 FunTreks, Inc.

138

Dishpan Springs ◆34◆

Location: East of Lake Arrowhead and Cedar Glen.

Difficulty: Difficult. Large boulders and steep rocky climbs. Crossing Deep Creek is no longer as difficult as it once was since the forest service laid concrete on the creek bottom.

Features: This trail is more commonly called *The Deep Creek Trail.* Although short, it's a great hardcore trail. A very popular area for ATVs and dirt bikes. Great hiking and fishing in the area. Forest Adventure Pass required if you stop to recreate.

Time & Distance: About 3.5 miles of this 4.8-mile trail is difficult. Allow 1 to 2 hours depending on size of group and vehicle capability.

To Get There: From Highway 18 near mile marker 24.5, go north on Highway 173 to Lake Arrowhead. Hwy. 173 turns right after 1.5 miles. After 3.2 miles, turn right on Hooks Creek Road at small gas station. After another 3.2 miles downhill, turn right at a fork just after pavement ends. This fork has a large white sign with a forest map showing routes in the area. Another way to reach this trail is to drive Willow Creek Road (Trail #33) in the opposite direction starting from the Pinnacles Staging Area.

Trail Description: Reset your odometer when you turn right at the sign (01). The trail quickly gets rough as you drop downhill and go by a small parking area on the left. Cross Deep Creek at 0.7 miles and negotiate a tough boulder field on left as you come out. A dangerous, tippy side hill of loose granite follows. Be careful climbing a steep, rocky section at 2.4 miles (02). Bear left when you reach the end of the trail at 3.5 miles (03). Go straight at 4.0, left at 4.2 and straight at 4.3. You'll go by Crab Flats Campground at 4.6 before reaching F.S. 3N16 at 4.8 miles (04).

Return Trip: Left takes you to the start of Holcomb Creek (Trail #35) in 2.8 miles. Right takes you back to Hwy. 18 on F.S 3N16. (See map for Holcomb Creek, Trail #35.)

Services: None along trail. Full services in Lake Arrowhead.

Maps: San Bernardino National Forest, USGS 100,000 scale map San Bernardino, Sidekick Map Arrowhead, DeLorme Atlas & Gazetteer.

The Rock Garden at the start of trail.

Wet boulders for a bit more challenge.

Deep moguls test articulation.

Last crossing of Holcomb Creek.

Holcomb Creek ◆35◆

Location: Northwest of Big Bear Lake between Green Valley and Fawnskin.

Difficulty: Difficult. No single obstacle stands out on this trail; it's just one challenging boulder field after another. Narrow and tippy in places. Wet tires add to the difficulty as the trail crosses tributaries to Holcomb Creek. You can also increase difficulty by choosing a more aggressive line through the boulders. This trail is not recommended for stock vehicles. Lockers, high ground clearance and undercarriage protection recommended.

Features: An interesting hardcore trail that winds along Holcomb Creek. The Rock Garden begins the trail and sets the stage for what's ahead. You can explore a difficult side trail through Lower Largo Flats (F.S. 2N06X, not described in this book). There are many ATV and dirt bike trails in the area but green sticker vehicles not allowed on many main forest roads. A Forest Adventure Pass is required if you stop to recreate.

Time & Distance: Just under 6 miles. Allow 2 to 3 hours depending upon size of group and capability of vehicles. Add more time for 2N06X.

To Get There: Go north on Green Valley Lake Road from Highway 18 just northeast of Arrowbear Lake near mile marker 34.5. Green Valley Lake Road is marked with a small street sign and is easy to miss. After 2.6 miles, turn left on wide dirt road F.S. 3N16. Follow signs to Crab Flats Campground. After a couple of miles, you'll go by a small staging area for 2N12X, a green-sticker trail. Ignore lesser side roads that branch off. The road to Crab Flats Campground goes left soon after the paved section begins. This also takes you to Dishpan Springs, Trail #34. To reach Holcomb Creek, bear right and go another 2.8 miles. Look for small signs on the right along a paved section when it turns sharply left.

    You can also reach Holcomb Creek after completing Dishpan Springs, Trail #34. Just turn left on F.S. 3N16 shortly after you go by Crab Flats Campground.

Trail Description: Reset your odometer at the start (01). Maneuver through the Rock Garden. Cross small side creeks at 1.3 and 2.3 miles. Turn right downhill at 2.9 miles or take a bypass on the left. Pass through another challenging stretch of boulders at 3.3 miles. F.S. Road 2N06X goes left to Lower Largo Flats at 3.9 miles (02). Signs indicate no green-sticker vehicles are allowed on this side trail. At 4.8 miles, descend short but steep Root

141

Hill, a good place to get jammed up if you are not careful. Bear left at 5.2 miles down some nasty moguls that will test your articulation. Immediately cross Holcomb Creek, which can be deep after a period of heavy rain. After the creek, bear right as the road follows the creek to F.S. 3N14 reached at 5.9 miles (03).

Return Trip: Right on 3N14 goes downhill to Fawnskin on Highway 38 along the north rim of Big Bear Lake. As you go downhill, watch for 2N13 which goes right to Butler Peak, Trail #36.

Left on 3N14 goes uphill to major Forest Road 3N16. If you turn right on 3N16 it will eventually take you to difficult John Bull Trail #37. You can also reach John Bull from the other end of 3N16 by accessing it from Highway 18. (See John Bull trail description.)

There is a shortcut to 3N16 which makes the trip to John Bull more interesting. It shortens the trip but is a bit complicated. The route is border-line moderate. You'll need a forest service map because I have not mapped it in this book. The description is as follows:

When you finish Holcomb Creek, turn left on 3N14. Go uphill less than a tenth of a mile and turn right on a smaller road. Although signs are confusing, this is F.S. 3N08. *Reset your odometer.* Continue straight at 0.4 when a road joins on the right. You can see Holcomb Creek below on the right and beaver ponds. Bear right staying on 3N08 at 2.2 miles. Bear right again at 2.4 where 3N89 goes left. You are still on 3N08 but it is not marked very well. Bear left uphill at 3.3. Bear right at 3.7. At first, you may not notice the road that goes left. Go straight at 3.8 as a road joins on the right. Drop down into a steep gully and climb out the other side. To your left is a large rock wall of a strip mine. You reach F.S. 3N16 at 4.6 miles. Turn right and go east 5.5 miles to reach John Bull.

Services: None along trail. Hanna Flat Campground located on 3N14 south of the exit point of Holcomb Creek. This is a large, popular campground and is usually full on summer weekends. Some services in Fawnskin. Full services in town of Big Bear Lake.

Maps: San Bernardino National Forest, USGS 7.5 minute map Butler Peak, CA, NIMA 2552 I SE-SERIES V895, Sidekick Map Big Bear Lake, DeLorme Atlas & Gazetteer.

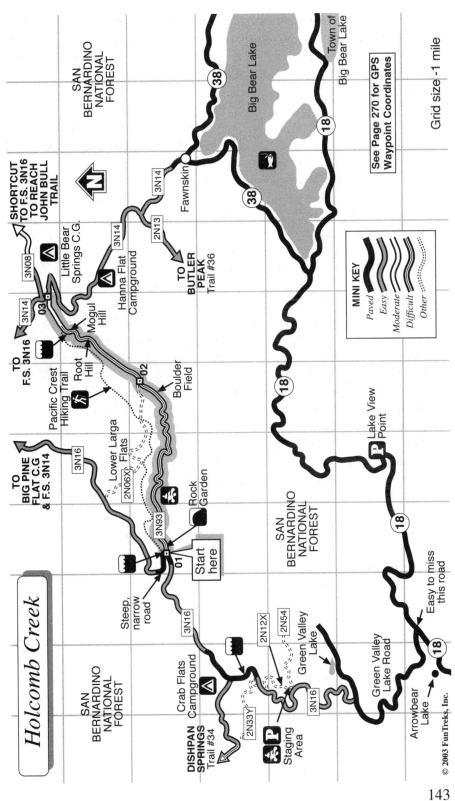

Holcomb Creek

SAN BERNARDINO NATIONAL FOREST

SAN BERNARDINO NATIONAL FOREST

SAN BERNARDINO NATIONAL FOREST

SHORTCUT
TO F.S. 3N16
TO REACH
JOHN BULL
TRAIL

3N08

TO
F.S. 3N16

3N14

3N14

Little Bear
Springs C.G.

03

Mogul
Hill

Root
Hill

Hanna Flat
Campground

3N14

2N13

TO
BUTLER
PEAK
Trail #36

Fawnskin

38

18

Big Bear Lake

Town of
Big Bear Lake

See Page 270 for GPS
Waypoint Coordinates

Grid size - 1 mile

N

Pacific Crest
Hiking Trail

02

Boulder
Field

Lower Larga
Flats

2N06X

3N93

Rock
Garden

TO
BIG PINE
FLAT C.G
& F.S. 3N14

3N16

01

Start
here

Steep,
narrow
road

3N16

Crab Flats
Campground

DISHPAN
SPRINGS
Trail #34

2N33Y

P
Staging
Area

2N12X

2N54

Green Valley
Lake

3N16

MINI KEY
Paved
Easy
Moderate
Difficult
Other

18

18

Lake View
Point

P

18

Green Valley
Lake Road

Arrowbear
Lake

18

Easy to miss
this road

© 2003 FunTreks, Inc.

143

Big Bear Lake seen in distance from tower.

Rocky hike up to lookout tower.

Road gets narrow and steep at the top.

Spotted this fawn early in the morning.

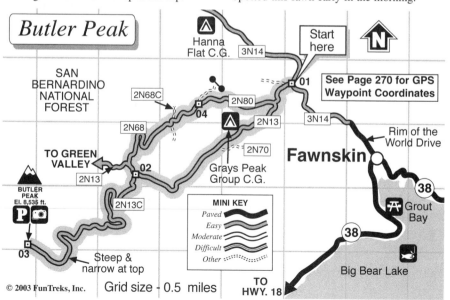

Butler Peak

Hanna Flat C.G. 3N14

Start here

N

SAN BERNARDINO NATIONAL FOREST

2N68C

2N80

01

See Page 270 for GPS Waypoint Coordinates

04

2N68

2N13

3N14

Rim of the World Drive

TO GREEN VALLEY

02

2N13

2N70

Grays Peak Group C.G.

Fawnskin

BUTLER PEAK El. 8,535 ft.

2N13C

38

Grout Bay

MINI KEY
Paved
Easy
Moderate
Difficult
Other

38

03

Steep & narrow at top

Big Bear Lake

© 2003 FunTreks, Inc.   Grid size - 0.5 miles

TO HWY. 18

Butler Peak 36

Location: West of Big Bear Lake and Fawnskin.

Difficulty: Easy. A steep, narrow shelf road as you near the top of Butler Peak but suitable for all SUVs if not snow covered or icy.

Features: An unforgettable drive that climbs above 8,400 ft. Park and take a short, steep hike to the lookout tower with spectacular 360-degree views. Forest Adventure Pass required if you stop to recreate.

Time & Distance: It is 4.8 miles one-way to the peak. Alternate return route is slightly longer. Allow about an hour to reach the top.

To Get There: From Highway 38 at Fawnskin on the north shore of Big Bear Lake, head northwest from three fawn statues on Rim of the World Drive. Pavement changes to dirt and the road becomes F.S. 3N14. After 1.3 miles, turn left on F.S. 2N13.

Trail Description: Reset odometer as you turn left off 3N14 (01). Head west on 2N13. At 0.1 miles, stay left where a lesser road goes right at a clearing. Bear right at 1.0 where 2N70 goes left. Turn left on 2N13C at 2.2 miles (02). A small sign with tower symbol marks this turn. You will climb to about 8400 ft. before reaching a small parking area below the lookout tower at 4.8 miles (03). Climb a rocky footpath starting near a propane tank. You are permitted to climb up the lookout tower at your own risk. The steps are extremely steep. The tower was unmanned when I was there.

Return the way you came. When you reach the sign with the tower symbol, you can go right the way you came up or take an alternate route. *Reset your odometer for the alternate route and turn left.* Turn right at 0.1 miles on 2N68 (not marked). Bear left at 0.9, then, within 50 feet, turn right staying on 2N68. Bear right at 1.3 miles (04) on 2N80. Make a left at 1.5 and 2.1 before reaching the original starting point at 2.5 miles (01).

Return Trip: Bear right on 3N14 and head downhill to Fawnskin.

Services: None on trail. Some services in Fawnskin. Full services in the town of Big Bear Lake located on the southeast shoreline.

Maps: San Bernardino National Forest, USGS 7.5 minute map Butler Peak, CA, NIMA 2552 I SE-SERIES V895, DeLorme Atlas & Gazetteer.

Tight and tippy in places.

Most drivers don't come for the scenery.

Expect cooler temperatures on this trail as it climbs to about 8,000 feet.

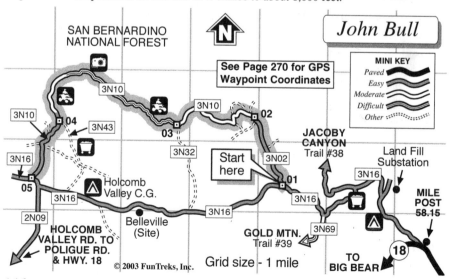

SAN BERNARDINO
NATIONAL FOREST

N

John Bull

See Page 270 for GPS
Waypoint Coordinates

MINI KEY
Paved
Easy
Moderate
Difficult
Other

3N10

3N10

3N10

02

3N10

04

3N43

03

3N32

JACOBY
CANYON
Trail #38

Land Fill
Substation

3N16

3N16

Start
here

3N02

01

3N16

05

3N16

Holcomb
Valley C.G.

3N16

MILE
POST
58.15

2N09

Belleville
(Site)

3N16

GOLD MTN.
Trail #39

3N69

18

**HOLCOMB
VALLEY RD. TO
POLIGUE RD.
& HWY. 18**

© 2003 FunTreks, Inc.

Grid size - 1 mile

**TO
BIG BEAR**

John Bull Trail ◆37◆

Location: North/northeast of Big Bear Lake.

Difficulty: Difficult. Large boulders and steep climbs. Lockers and very high ground clearance required. Not for stock SUVs.

Features: Considered the toughest trail in the Big Bear area. The tough part is fairly short. Hike a short distance for views of Lucerne Valley. Forest Adventure Pass required if you stop to recreate.

Time & Distance: Total trip is 6.7 miles. Difficult portion is 2.2 miles. Allow about 2 hours for well-equipped vehicles.

To Get There: From Highway 18 east of Big Bear Lake, follow signs to Big Bear Landfill, heading northwest from mile post 58. Turn left before the substation and follow F.S. 3N16 uphill 2.2 miles to F.S. 3N02 on the right. You can also drive Gold Mountain (Trail #39) first, then turn left on 3N16 and go 0.9 miles to 3N02.

Trail Description: Reset your odometer as you turn off 3N16 (01). Follow 3N02 north on an easy road. Turn left on 3N10 after 1.1 miles (02). The road gradually gets rougher as you wind tightly through the trees. You climb to about 7,800 feet before descending. A clearing at 2.7 miles (03) marks the official start of John Bull. *Reset your odometer* and continue west on 3N10 following signs. Bear left at 0.1 miles. A large boulder field set in loose soil looms directly ahead. At 0.5 miles, you reach the highest point on the trail with good views through the trees. More boulder fields follow with good camping spots along the way. There's an especially good spot at 2.1 miles. A few challenges remain as you gradually descend. A sign marks the end of the trail at 2.2 miles. Bear left at 2.3 miles around a pit. Bear right at 2.9. Bear right again at 3.0 miles (04) where 3N43 goes left. Bear left at 3.5 staying on 3N10. You reach major F.S. Road 3N16 at 4.0 miles (05).

Return Trip: Go east 0.2 miles on 3N16. Turn right on larger Holcomb Valley Road 2N09. Bear left in 2.4 miles when 2N09 becomes Poligue Rd.

Services: None along trail. Return to Big Bear Lake.

Maps: San Bernardino National Forest, USGS 100,000 scale map Big Bear Lake, CA, Sidekick Map Big Bear Lake, DeLorme Atlas & Gazetteer.

Primitive camping at boulder outcroppings along northern leg of trail. Great views.

Most of the trail is just one lane. Suitable for stock 4x4 SUVs with high ground clearance.

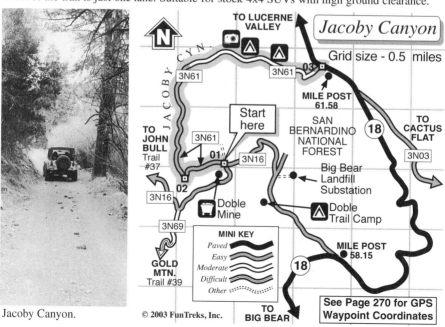

Jacoby Canyon.

Jacoby Canyon

TO LUCERNE VALLEY

Grid size - 0.5 miles

3N61

3N61

03

MILE POST 61.58

SAN BERNARDINO NATIONAL FOREST

TO CACTUS FLAT

18

3N03

Start here

TO JOHN BULL Trail #37

3N61

01

3N16

02

Big Bear Landfill Substation

3N16

Doble Mine

Doble Trail Camp

3N69

MINI KEY

Paved
Easy
Moderate
Difficult
Other

MILE POST 58.15

18

GOLD MTN. Trail #39

© 2003 FunTreks, Inc.

TO BIG BEAR

See Page 270 for GPS Waypoint Coordinates

148

Jacoby Canyon 38

Location: Northeast of Big Bear Lake.

Difficulty: Moderate. Mostly easy but a bit steep and narrow in places. Suitable for stock 4x4 SUVs with high ground clearance. Slightly more difficult when driven in the opposite direction.

Features: Many people mistakenly overlook this short but enjoyable trip. The road drops steeply into narrow Jacoby Canyon then winds its way back to Highway 18. On the way out, you pass several boulder outcroppings which serve as outstanding primitive camping spots. Only licensed vehicles allowed on this road. Forest Adventure Pass required if you stop to recreate.

Time & Distance: Only 2.9 miles. You can drive it in less than an hour, but add time to explore the area around the scenic boulder outcroppings.

To Get There: From Highway 18 east of Big Bear Lake, follow signs to Big Bear Landfill, heading northwest from mile post 58. Turn left before the substation and follow F.S. 3N16 uphill 0.7 miles to F.S. 3N61 on the right. Before you head down the trail, take a few minutes to explore the Lucky Baldwin Mine (Doble Mine) just ahead on 3N16.

Trail Description: Reset odometer as you turn off 3N16 [01]. Head downhill on 3N61. Continue straight at 0.1 miles past a mine on the left. The road swings right down the canyon at 0.4 miles (02). It follows the canyon then turns east. The only real challenge comes at 1.8 miles on a short, steep hill with some small moguls. Watch for two good camp spots at 1.9 and 2.3 miles. Highway 18 is reached at 2.9 miles (03).
    Reverse Directions: From Highway 18 near mile post 61.58, head southwest on a dirt road. Bear right immediately and follow sign for 3N61. Nice camping spot on right at 0.6 and 1.0. Descend steep hill at 1.1. Follow trail south then east uphill to 3N16.

Return Trip: Right on Highway 18 goes back to Big Bear Lake. Left goes to Lucerne Valley and Barstow.

Services: None along trail. Services in Big Bear Lake or Lucerne Valley.

Maps: San Bernardino National Forest, USGS 7.5-minute map of Big Bear City, Sidekick Map Big Bear Lake, DeLorme Atlas & Gazetteer.

Great views as you climb many switchbacks.

Talus slope on alternate route 3N69A.

Steep, sharp rock in places.

Vertical mine shaft near trail.

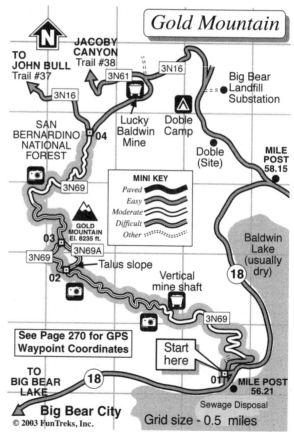

Gold Mountain

N

TO
JOHN BULL
Trail #37

3N16

JACOBY CANYON
Trail #38

3N61

3N16

Big Bear
Landfill
Substation

SAN
BERNARDINO
NATIONAL
FOREST

04

Lucky
Baldwin
Mine

Doble
Camp

Doble
(Site)

**MILE POST
58.15**

3N69

MINI KEY
Paved
Easy
Moderate
Difficult
Other

**GOLD
MOUNTAIN**
El. 8235 ft.

03

3N69A

3N69

Talus slope

02

Baldwin
Lake
(usually
dry)

Vertical
mine shaft

18

3N69

See Page 270 for GPS
Waypoint Coordinates

Start
here

TO
BIG BEAR
LAKE

18

01

**MILE POST
56.21**

Sewage Disposal

Big Bear City

© 2003 FunTreks, Inc.

Grid size - 0.5 miles

150

Gold Mountain ◆39◆

Location: Northeast of Big Bear Lake, north of Big Bear City.

Difficulty: Difficult. A few sharp rock ledges require that this trail be rated difficult, but most of the trail is moderate. Suitable for some aggressive stock SUVs. Good articulation and skid plates recommended. Watch for a dangerous open vertical mine shaft near the trail.

Features: Zigzag uphill to the top of 8,235-foot Gold Mountain with improving views at every turn. The route passes through historic gold mining country. No Green Sticker vehicles are allowed. Forest Adventure Pass required if you stop to recreate.

Time & Distance: Total of 4.5 miles. Allow 1 to 2 hours.

To Get There: From the north side of Big Bear Lake, head east on Highway 18. Turn left (north) uphill on a small road near mile post 56.21. This point is less than two miles out of town.

Trail Description: Reset your odometer at the start (01). Stay on the lower road through a clearing as it swings east past signs marking the trail. Bear left uphill after 0.2 miles and begin a series of steep switchbacks. Drive up and over a mound at 1.4 miles. This is a tailings pile for a large vertical mine shaft on the right. A series of sharp rock ledges follows. Bear left at 2.5 miles (02) on the main trail. (A more challenging alternate route goes right on 3N69A. It crosses a massive talus slope.) Bear left again at 2.9 miles (03) where 3N69A returns to main trail. You reach the top of Gold Mountain at 3.0 miles and begin to descend. Going down the north slope is a bit easier and more forested. Forest Road 3N16 is reached at 4.5 miles (04).

Return Trip: Turn right on 3N16 and follow it 2.3 miles downhill to Highway 18. You'll pass remains of a stamp mill from the Lucky Baldwin (Doble) Mine. In 1876, over 200 miners worked here. You'll also pass the entrance to Jacoby Canyon, Trail #38. If you turn left on 3N16 when you complete Gold Mtn., the entrance to John Bull, Trail #37, is 0.9 miles west.

Services: None along trail. Return to Big Bear Lake.

Maps: San Bernardino National Forest, USGS 7.5-minute map of Big Bear City, Sidekick Map Big Bear Lake, DeLorme Atlas & Gazetteer.

Near the top of F.S. 2N06 on eastern side.

Typical conditions below Clarks Summit.

Starting down Clarks Grade.

A wide spot on F.S. 1N54 (Clarks Grade).

Clarks Summit 40

Location: South of Big Bear Lake, north of Highway 38.

Difficulty: Moderate. Steep and narrow in places, especially on the descent from Clarks Summit. A couple of spots are so narrow there is barely enough room to get out of your vehicle. Full-size vehicles may get brush marks. Also, on the western portion, the soil is soft, increasing the possibility of boulders breaking loose and rolling onto the trail. You might even be forced to back up and turn around. Despite these unlikely situations, most stock 4x4 SUVs with good ground clearance and skid plates can handle the trail. Route-finding is complicated but roads are well marked. Don't drive this trail if you are squeamish about heights.

Features: Explore the lesser traveled back side of Bear Mountain Ski Area. The upper portion of Clarks Summit shares the same road as easier Skyline Drive, Trail #41. Enjoy outstanding views to the south from higher elevations. For those unaccustomed to narrow shelf roads, the descent from Clarks Summit will be exhilarating. Street-legal vehicles only, no Green Sticker vehicles. Adventure Pass required if you stop to recreate.

Time & Distance: Allow 4 to 5 hours for this 30.1-mile trip.

To Get There: Take Hwy. 38 east from San Bernardino or south from Big Bear Lake to F.S. Road 1N04 at mile marker 30.97. If you are starting from Big Bear Lake, an alternative way to drive this trail would be to go up Skyline Drive, then head downhill on the western portion of Clarks Summit to Highway 38.

Trail Description: *Reset odometer at Hwy. 38 and 1N04* [01]. Head northwest uphill past a small parking area. Bear right at 2.2 and 2.4 miles. Better 1N45 merges with 1N04 for a short distance. Bear right uphill at 2.6 miles on 1N04. Continue straight at 3.3, 3.5 and 5.3 miles. Avoid the urge to turn uphill too soon. A larger road crosses at 6.0 miles; continue straight following 1N04 as it heads diagonally left. (A hard left here would take you back to Hwy. 38.) Finally, at 6.2 miles (02) turn right uphill on larger 2N06 (Radford Truck Trail). This starts a long drive up the mountainside. The road narrows and gets a bit rougher as it climbs. Pass through a seasonal forest gate at 10.8 miles. This gate is likely closed when it snows. Bear left at 11.3 miles as 2N21 joins 2N06. Continue straight at 11.6 and 11.7. At 12.0 miles (03), you meet F.S. 2N10. This is Skyline Drive, Trail #41.

Turn left on 2N10 and head west across a ridge. The road is now 2 lanes. Continue straight at 12.3 where 2N10D joins on the right. Bear left at 13.2 and 13.3. Continue straight at 14.4 on a road marked Grandview Loop. At 15.4 bear left following sign to Lodgepole Pine. Slow down as you approach blind curves. Drive as if a fast-moving car is coming from the opposite direction. You might want to take a break here and hike to Grand View Point about 1/4 mile. It has great views of the valley you will soon be descending.

At 17.1 miles (04), turn left on a much lesser road marked 1N54 (Clarks Grade). This starts the descent from Clarks Summit. *Reset your odometer*. A gate here is closed during the winter. Bear left at 0.2 where 1N54A goes right. This is an interesting side trip but eventually ends as the road narrows to nothing. The low-profile shrubbery through this area is very pretty, especially during the spring when the shrubs are flowering. You'll soon want to shift into low range so you can move slowly under total control. The road becomes quite narrow in places and you may have to maneuver around fallen rocks. Be careful if you get out of your vehicle. The edge of the road is very soft, and the slope is extremely steep. The drive downhill is long with countless switchbacks.

Continue straight at 5.8 miles (05) where 1N64 goes right. Bear left at 6.8 where 1N94 goes right (I didn't see this road as I drove by but I saw it on my map later). Bear right downhill at 7.0 miles where 1N04 goes left. Bear left at 7.6 miles. At 7.8 miles (06), turn left on paved Seven Oaks Road and follow it east quite a distance. Turn right at 10.7 miles on Glass Road before reaching Highway 38 at 13.0 miles (07). You're at mile marker 26.5.

Return Trip: Left on Highway 38 goes back to Big Bear Lake in 29 miles. Right goes to Redlands in 25 miles. The original starting point of the trail is about 4.5 miles to the left.

Services: No services along the trail. Full services in Redlands, Big Bear Valley and Big Bear Lake. Three Forest Service Campgrounds along Highway 38 near entrance and exit points.

Maps: San Bernardino National Forest, USGS 100,000 scale map Big Bear Lake, CA, DeLorme Atlas & Gazetteer.

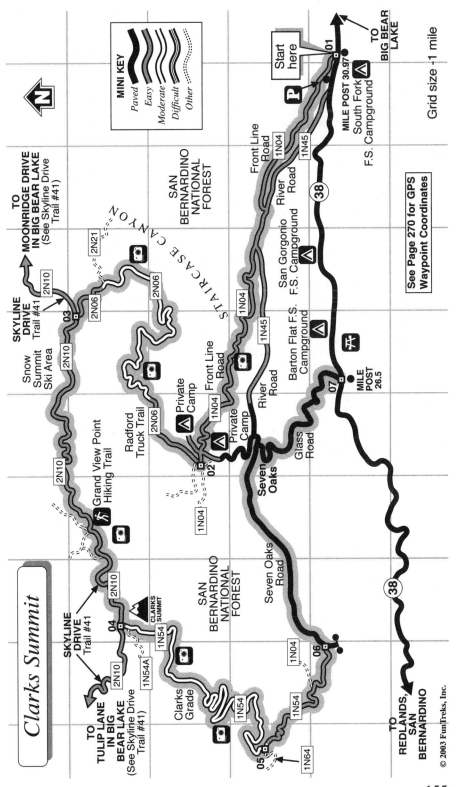

Clarks Summit

© 2003 FunTreks, Inc.

Grid size -1 mile

See Page 270 for GPS Waypoint Coordinates

MINI KEY

Paved
Easy
Moderate
Difficult
Other

Road suitable for any SUV.

One of many short hikes off Skyline Drive.

Aspen Glen Picnic Area. Park, relax or take a hike.

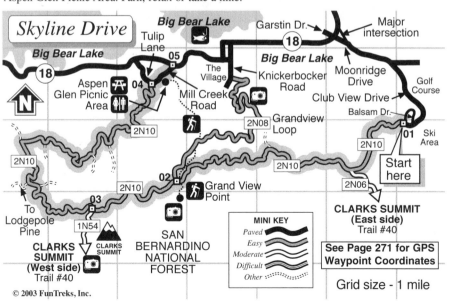

Skyline Drive

Big Bear Lake

Tulip Lane

Big Bear Lake

18

Garstin Dr.

Major intersection

18

Big Bear Lake

The Village

Knickerbocker Road

Moonridge Drive

Golf Course

Aspen Glen Picnic Area

05

04

Mill Creek Road

Club View Drive

Balsam Dr.

N

2N10

2N08

Grandview Loop

2N10

01

Ski Area

2N10

2N10

2N10

Start here

2N06

02

Grand View Point

03

CLARKS SUMMIT (East side)
Trail #40

To Lodgepole Pine

1N54

CLARKS SUMMIT

CLARKS SUMMIT (West side)
Trail #40

SAN BERNARDINO NATIONAL FOREST

MINI KEY
Paved
Easy
Moderate
Difficult
Other

See Page 271 for GPS Waypoint Coordinates

Grid size - 1 mile

© 2003 FunTreks, Inc.

156

Skyline Drive **41**

Location: Directly south of Big Bear Lake.

Difficulty: Easy. Suitable for any SUV. Slow down at blind curves.

Features: Don't skip this trip because you think it's too easy. The drive is fun and the scenery is great. Forest Adventure Pass required if you stop to recreate. No Green Sticker vehicles.

Time & Distance: Allow 2 hours for this 13-mile trip. Many great side roads.

To Get There: From Highway 18 on the southeastern end of Big Bear Lake, head southeast on Moonridge Drive. Bear right after one mile on Club View Drive. Continue straight uphill past Balsam Drive to the start at 2.2 miles.

Trail Description: Reset odometer at the start [01]. Follow signs for F.S. 2N10 uphill. Bear right at 0.7 miles, ignoring an incorrect sign. Continue straight at 1.2 miles [02] following sign to Lodgepole Pine. Continue straight at 1.6, 2.4, 2.6 and 3.7 miles. You follow part of Grandview Loop for a short distance. Continue straight at 4.6 miles. (Before proceeding, consider taking the short, scenic hike to Grand View Point on the left.) At 6.4 miles [03], the western portion of Clarks Summit, Trail #40, goes left on 1N54. Continue right on 2N10. Bear right at 8.1 not following signs to Lodgepole Pine. Go straight at 8.4 and right at 8.8 miles. Bear left at 10.3, 10.8 and 11.0. Pass through a large forest service gate at 11.8 miles [04] and immediately turn right on paved Mill Creek Road. Intersect with Tulip Lane at 12.5 miles. Left will take you to Hwy. 18 if you're heading west. Right continues on Mill Creek Road to Hwy. 18, which is reached at 13.0 miles [05]. This way takes you past Aspen Glen Picnic Area, a nice place to stop for lunch. People park here to take the 3-mile hike up to Grand View Point.

    Now that you've see the basic trail, you might like to try some of the many side roads that you passed. I drove the Grandview Loop. It was narrower and tighter than Skyline Drive but still easy. To start at the bottom of Grandview Loop, head south from Hwy. 18 on Knickerbocker Road past the Middle School. Follow signs for 2N08.

Services: Toilets at Aspen Glen Picnic Area.

Maps: San Bernardino National Forest, USGS 7.5 minute map Big Bear Lake, CA, DeLorme Atlas & Gazetteer.

Getting through *The Squeeze*.　　　Pick a difficult line or something easier.

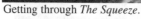

Remains of arrastra near Round Valley Group Campground.

This Cherokee has a few modifications.　　Watch for dangerous open mine shafts.

Heartbreak Ridge ◆42◆

Location: Between Big Bear Lake and Yucca Valley.

Difficulty: Difficult. Trail includes narrow canyons, steep shelf roads, large boulders and sharp rock. Lockers, skid plates and high ground clearance recommended. Not super difficult but fairly tough. Some aggressive stock vehicles with good articulation might get through, but tow-strap assistance will likely be necessary and body damage is possible. Route-finding is complex so follow directions carefully. Remote location. Don't drive alone.

Features: Travel on easy forest roads to remote canyons in search of rock-crawling challenges. Not a scenic trail. Many old mines in the area. Some roads allow green-sticker vehicles, others do not. ATVs and dirt bikes should access the area from Cactus Flat Staging Area on F.S. Road 3N03, one of the exit routes for this trail. Fifty-inch wide trails are for green-sticker vehicles only. Adventure Pass required if you stop to recreate.

Time & Distance: A total of 16.4 miles as described here. Allow 3 to 4 hours depending upon vehicle capability and size of group. Allow plenty of travel time.

To Get There: Head southeast from Big Bear Lake or northeast from San Bernardino on Highway 38. Turn east on F.S. 2N01 near mile marker 41.

Trail Description: Reset your odometer at the start (01). Head downhill on a a road that changes from pavement to gravel. At 2.3 miles, continue straight as 2N04 and 2N64Y branch off. Turn right at 6.3 miles (02) on 2N89Y and head uphill on a rougher road. Continue straight at 6.6 miles as the road changes to 2N61Y. (Road 2N89Y goes right to Round Valley Group Campground. It has an interesting arrastra, a crude grinding machine pulled by mules. The campground also has spring water, picnic tables and a primitive pit toilet. Reservations are required to camp.) Negotiate a tougher section at 7.9 miles. Bear left at 8.1 miles where a lesser road to the right goes up to an old mine and abandoned truck.

Make a right at 8.3 miles (03) and begin a more difficult section. You will return to this spot later. The trail winds tightly through low trees and passes by an old Pontiac. Driver's choice at 8.9 miles; right is easier. Pass through *The Squeeze* at 9.0 miles. This section does not have a bypass but other obstacles do. Bear right at 9.2 miles (04) and begin a difficult climb. The trail loops around and returns to this spot. Going up the left side is

159

easier. At 9.8 miles, it flattens out at the top of Heartbreak Ridge. We stopped here for lunch. There are vertical mine shafts in the area, so keep an eye on the kids. Bear left at 10.0 and head back down the loop. Turn right at 10.6 and go back out the way you came in.

At 11.5 miles (03), you finish the part you've already driven. Turn right and continue. Bear left at 11.6; right dead ends at a mine. The trail goes downhill and gets easier. Bear left at 12.8 miles. You should now be back on 2N61Y. At 13.3 miles (05), make a sharp left, almost reversing direction on larger 2N02.

Turn left downhill on 2N70Y at 13.7 miles. Driver's choice at 13.9; right is harder. Weave through a shady area with low-hanging cottonwood trees at 14.8 miles. Continue straight as a road joins on the right before reconnecting with 2N02 at 15.1 miles (06). Bear left at 2N02. At 16.1 miles you pass through the Rose Mine Area identified by distinctive red soil.

Return Trip: At 16.4 miles (07), select from three possible return routes:

Return to Highway 18 via 2N02. Continue straight (northwest) on 2N02. The road forks at the top of a small hill after about 1.2 miles. Bear left staying on 2N02 all the way back to Baldwin Lake Road in about 7 miles. Right on Baldwin Lake Road takes you back to Highway 18. This is the shortest and most scenic way back to Big Bear Lake.

Return to Highway 18 via 3N03. Continue straight (northwest) on 2N02. The road forks at the top of a small hill after about 1.2 miles. Bear right on 3N03. It takes you back to Highway 18 in about 7.8 miles. The Cactus Flat Staging Area will be on the left after about 6 miles. This is the shortest way to Lucerne Valley.

Return the way you came. Turn left on 2N01. A road will join on your right and you'll pass the start of 2N89Y on the left. You should now recognize 2N01 as the road on which you originally started. It will take you back to Highway 18 in 6.3 miles. This is the shortest way back to San Bernardino and Redlands.

Services: Several group campgrounds in the area have primitive pit toilets. Return to Big Bear Lake or Redlands for all other services.

Maps: San Bernardino National Forest, USGS 7.5-minute map of Onyx Peak, CA NIMA 2652 II NW-Series V895, DeLorme Atlas & Gazetteer.

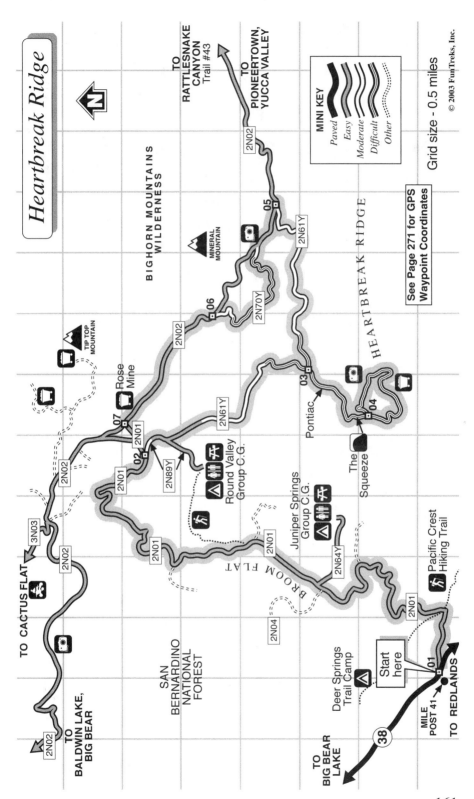

Heartbreak Ridge

TO
RATTLESNAKE
CANYON
Trail #43

TO
PIONEERTOWN,
YUCCA VALLEY

2N02

BIGHORN MOUNTAINS
WILDERNESS

05

MINERAL
MOUNTAIN

2N61Y

06

2N70Y

2N02

H E A R T B R E A K   R I D G E

TIP TOP
MOUNTAIN

Rose
Mine

07

2N02

2N01

02

2N89Y

2N01

03

2N61Y

Pontiac

04

The
Squeeze

Round Valley
Group C.G.

3N03

2N02

2N01

Juniper Springs
Group C.G.

2N01

2N64Y

Pacific Crest
Hiking Trail

2N01

B R O O M   F L A T

2N04

TO CACTUS FLAT

SAN
BERNARDINO
NATIONAL
FOREST

Deer Springs
Trail Camp

Start
here

01

TO
BALDWIN LAKE,
BIG BEAR

2N02

MILE
POST 41

TO REDLANDS

38

TO
BIG BEAR
LAKE

N

Flash floods possible in Rattlesnake Canyon.

Saloon and Bath House in Pioneertown.

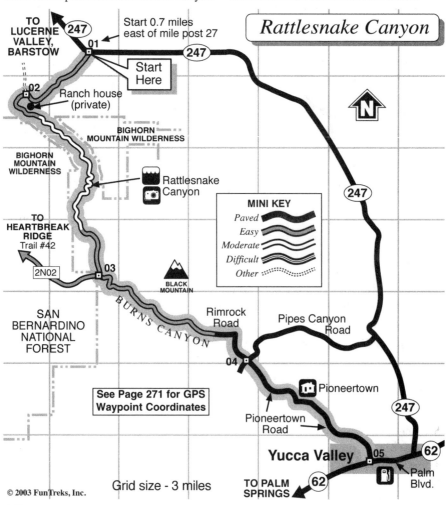

Rattlesnake Canyon

TO LUCERNE VALLEY, BARSTOW 247

01 Start 0.7 miles east of mile post 27

247

Start Here

02 Ranch house (private)

BIGHORN MOUNTAIN WILDERNESS

BIGHORN MOUNTAIN WILDERNESS

Rattlesnake Canyon

N

MINI KEY
Paved
Easy
Moderate
Difficult
Other

TO HEARTBREAK RIDGE Trail #42

2N02 03

BURNS CANYON

BLACK MOUNTAIN

247

SAN BERNARDINO NATIONAL FOREST

Rimrock Road

Pipes Canyon Road

04

See Page 271 for GPS Waypoint Coordinates

Pioneertown

Pioneertown Road

247

Yucca Valley 05

62

Palm Blvd.

© 2003 FunTreks, Inc.

Grid size - 3 miles

TO PALM SPRINGS 62

162

Rattlesnake Canyon 43

Location: Between Lucerne Valley and Yucca Valley.

Difficulty: Moderate. Soft sandy soil through a narrow canyon susceptible to flash flood damage. Stay out if rain is expected.

Features: A remote and little-known trail that passes through a non-wilderness corridor of the Bighorn Mountain Wilderness Area. Exit route goes by Pioneertown, built in 1946 as a movie set for countless western classics.

Time & Distance: Allow about 4 hours for this 32.3-mile trip.

To Get There: Head east from Lucerne Valley or north from Yucca Valley on Hwy. 247. Turn south on a dirt road 0.7 miles east of mile marker 27.

Trail Description: Reset odometer at the start [01]. Head southwest on a sandy road. Ignore lesser roads for a few miles then bear right at 3.1, 3.4 and 3.5 miles. You gradually end up heading in a northwest direction as you pass a ranch house. At 3.8 miles (02), turn left in a wash as another road joins on the right. The wash takes you into Rattlesnake Canyon. Watch for wandering range cattle. All side roads are off limits as you pass through the wilderness. Cross over a high-tech cattle guard at 9.4 miles. The narrowest part of the canyon will likely have some water at the surface. Cross another cattle guard at 12.1. Bear left at 13.0, 13.4 and 13.9 as you exit the canyon on an improving road. Go straight at 14.9 and 15.9 miles before intersecting with Burns Canyon Road at 16.1 miles (03).
  Reset your odometer and turn left on Burns Canyon Road. Bear right at 4-way intersection at 0.4 miles and follow a narrow dirt road through scenic Burns Canyon. Continue straight at 6.4 miles on paved Rimrock Road. Bear right at 7.3. Continue straight when you hit larger Pioneertown Road at 8.7 miles (04). Pioneertown is reached at 11.9 miles. Follow Pioneertown Road into Yucca Valley and Hwy. 62 at 16.2 miles (05).

Return Trip: Turn left on Hwy. 62 to reach Hwy. 247 in 1.8 miles. Left on 247 goes to Lucerne Valley and Barstow.

Services: None along trail. Full services in Yucca Valley.

Maps: San Bernardino National Forest, USGS 250,000 scale map of San Bernardino, CA, DeLorme Atlas & Gazetteer.

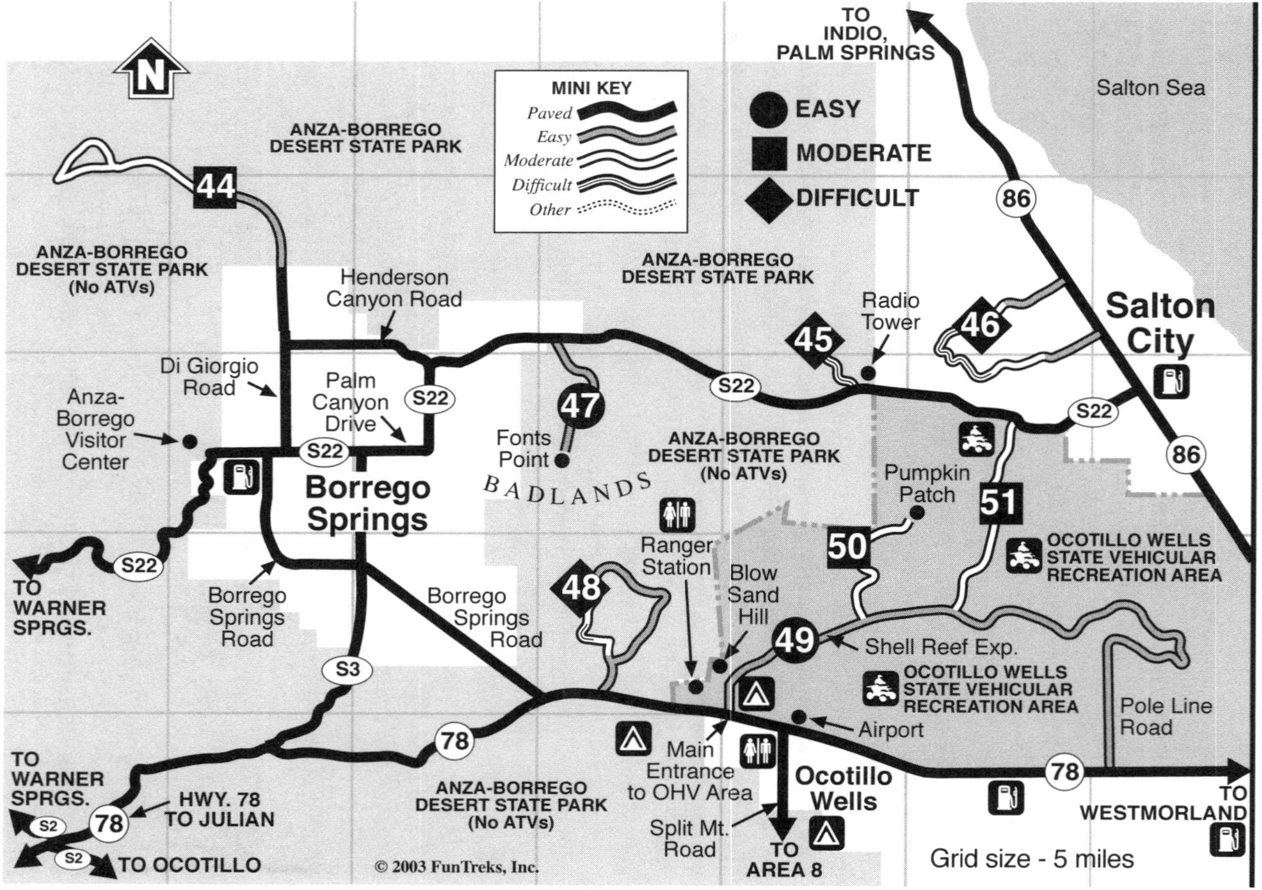

AREA 7

Anza-Borrego Desert, Ocotillo Wells, Truckhaven

44. Lower Coyote Canyon
45. Calcite Mine
46. Truckhaven
47. Fonts Point
48. The Slot
49. Ocotillo Wells SVRA
50. Pumpkin Patch
51. Cross Over Trail

© 2003 FunTreks, Inc.

Grid size - 5 miles

Anza-Borrego Desert, Ocotillo Wells, Truckhaven

Covering 600,000 acres, Anza-Borrego Desert State Park is one of the largest state parks in North America. Just the northern portion of the park is covered in Area 7. Some of the park is designated wilderness and closed to motorized recreation, but many unique and exciting backroads remain open to explore. Although a few of the trails are difficult, most are perfect for the average SUV. You must stay on designated routes and only street-legal vehicles are allowed. Those looking for offroad travel need look no further than adjacent Ocotillo Wells State Vehicular Recreation Area. Although this 70,000-acre park has many established trails, the western three-fourths of the park allows offroad travel. The moonscape terrain is enormously popular with owners of ATVs, dirt bikes, Jeeps and SUVs. Campgrounds, ramadas and modern vault toilets are strategically positioned throughout the park. Those looking for ultimate challenge can test their suspension and lockers at nearby Truckhaven. Early in March, thousands of avid four wheelers flock to the area to enjoy the annual Tierra Del Sol Desert Safari, perhaps the largest four-wheel-drive event in the world.

Roads can be seen winding through the Borrego Badlands. View from Fonts Point, Trail #47.

165

Second water crossing is the deepest.

Campground in Sheep Canyon.

Top of ridge before entering Collins Valley.

Open range, watch for wild horses.

Toughest part of trail.

Salvador Canyon

Historical Marker

Rocky climb

Sheep Canyon

Lower Coyote Canyon

N

03

Collins Valley

04

Desert Gardens

Gate: Closed June 1 to Sept. 30

Indian Canyon

02

Start here

ANZA-BORREGO DESERT STATE PARK

BOUNDARY

PARK

01

MINI KEY
Paved
Easy
Moderate
Difficult
Other

Henderson Canyon Road to S-22

See Page 271 for GPS Waypoint Coordinates

Di Giorgio Road to Borrego Springs

Grid size - 1 mile

© 2003 FunTreks, Inc.

166

Lower Coyote Canyon 44

Location: Northwest of Borrego Springs.

Difficulty: Moderate. Soft sand, a tough rocky climb and potentially deep water. High ground clearance and skid plates recommended. This trail can change from year to year from summer flooding.

Features: Follow scenic Coyote Creek, usually dry but potentially deep after a rain. Climb a rocky ridge to a secluded campground. Watch for bighorn sheep and wild horses. Must return the way you came. Trail closed June 1 through Sept. 30. Street-legal vehicles only; no ATVs.

Time & Distance: About 9.5 miles one-way to campground. Allow 3 to 4 hours for round trip plus additional time to explore other legal roads.

To Get There: North of Borrego Springs, from intersection of Di Giorgio Rd. and Henderson Canyon Rd., go north 1.7 miles to park boundary.

Trail Description: Reset odometer at park boundary [01]. Continue north on an easy sandy road (when dry). Pass hiking trail to Alcoholic Pass at 2.5 miles. Go by Desert Gardens then drop into a dry trench at 3.4 miles. I found dry the first marked water crossing at 3.5 miles. However, the second water crossing at 4.0 miles [02] had water mid-hubcap deep (late January). Once in the water, you turn right, cutting through tall reeds. This water could be very deep during the rainy season. Pass through gate at 5.2, cross water then bear left at 5.5 miles. Begin a rough, rocky climb at 5.6 miles— some real four-wheeling. Stack rocks if necessary to avoid body damage. Rocks end by 6.2 at top of ridge. Great views of Collins Valley ahead. Bear left at 6.6 miles. Right is short spur to interesting historical marker. Bear left at 7.3 miles [03]. Bear right at 9.2 for Sheep Canyon before reaching campground ramada at 9.5 miles [04]. Campground has several loops.

Return Trip: You can explore a few other open roads in the area but you eventually must return the way you came.

Services: Picnic tables, a ramada and primitive, roofless pit toilets at campground. Full services in Borrego Springs.

Maps: Anza-Borrego Desert Region Recreation Map, USGS 100,000 scale map of Borrego Valley, CA, DeLorme Atlas & Gazetteer.

Looking down from mine.

Toughest part of trail.

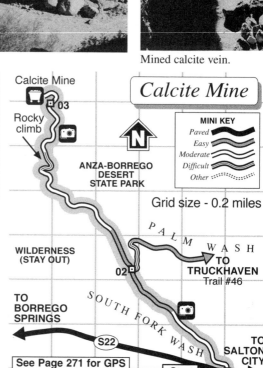
Mined calcite vein.

Trail is deeply rutted in places.

Calcite Mine

Calcite Mine

03

Rocky climb

N

ANZA-BORREGO DESERT STATE PARK

MINI KEY
Paved
Easy
Moderate
Difficult
Other

Grid size - 0.2 miles

P A L M   W A S H
TO **TRUCKHAVEN**
Trail #46

WILDERNESS (STAY OUT)

02

S O U T H   F O R K   W A S H

TO BORREGO SPRINGS

S22

TO SALTON CITY

See Page 271 for GPS Waypoint Coordinates

Start here

01

© 2003 FunTreks, Inc.

168

Calcite Mine 45

Location: West of Salton City, north of Ocotillo Wells State Vehiclular Recreation Area.

Difficulty: Difficult. Rating based on one short, rocky climb. Most of trail is moderate. Conditions can change quickly after rains. Stay out when wet. Aggressive stock SUVs can get through. Skid plates recommended.

Features: Although short, this is a fun drive. Just enough challenge to make it interesting but not overwhelming. Extend trip by following Palm Wash east to Salton City. Stay out of wilderness north and west of mine.

Time & Distance: Takes about an hour to reach the mine. Only 1.9 miles from Highway S22. Many side canyons to explore east along Palm Wash.

To Get There: Located on the north side of Highway S22 between mile markers 38 and 39 just west of the large microwave tower. Across the road from the historic Truckhaven Trail (not the same as Truckhaven, Trail #46).

Trail Description: Reset your odometer at the start (01). Head downhill at information board. When you reach the bottom of the wash, bear left slightly and follow sign uphill on other side of wash. Trail can be washed out and tippy in places. By 0.3 miles, it flattens out. Bear left at 0.6 miles (02). (Right drops down into Palm Wash on a steep, rocky road. This is a good alternate exit route after you've been to the mine.) The road gets steep and rough again at 0.9. This stretch could be impassable if wet. Great views behind you. At 1.4 miles, drop into a narrow wash and climb out the other side on a steep, rocky ledge. This is the only difficult spot on the trail. Vehicles with good articulation and high ground clearance will not have a problem. Climb a narrow shelf road that is tippy in places before reaching the mine at 1.9 miles (03). Great photo opportunities at the highest point.

Return Trip: Return the way you came or exit east via Palm Wash.

Services: None along trail. Gas and food in Salton City and Borrego Springs.

Historical Highlights: Calcite crystals were once used in the manufacturing of optical equipment. During WWII, the Polaroid Corporation sent 30 miners to this location to extract calcite that was used to make gunsights.

Maps: Anza-Borrego Desert Region Recreation Map, USGS 7.5-minute map Seventeen Palms, CA, DeLorme Atlas & Gazetteer.

169

Can you find the Fireplug?

An extreme test of articulation.

The area looks very different during the Tierra Del Sol Desert Safari.

Short wheel base is helpful.

Guides are provided during the Tierra Del Sol event.

Truckhaven 46

Location: Directly west of Salton City.

Difficulty: Difficult. The area is a maze of deeply cut trenches and sharp ridges. Extremely narrow with tight turns, near-vertical climbs and cliff-like descents. Articulation is severely tested for the average hardcore vehicle. Short wheel-based vehicles have a distinct advantage. Lockers are necessary, preferably front and rear. It is nearly impossible to follow an exact route without a guide; however, you can't really get lost for long. Just head east in any of the main washes to return to Highway 86. Slick and dangerous if wet. Don't go alone. Vehicle damage possible.

Features: The route described here has no particular significance other than to introduce you to the area. Even with directions, it will be difficult to follow this exact route; the area is simply too confusing. Try to find the fireplug located on a high plateau. From there, you can get a better view of the area. A compass or GPS unit will assist you in finding your way. Make sure you have adequate water and supplies. You can find easy and moderate routes in the area, but one wrong turn can lead to trouble. The best way to learn the area is to go with someone who's been there many times. Another way is to attend the Tierra Del Sol Desert Safari held annually in early March. At that time, trails are marked and guides are provided. Unfortunately, it gets very crowded and progress is slow. You can wait hours in line if someone breaks down.

It is very important to pack out your own trash. If you see trash left by someone else, try to pick it up as well. Much of the land in the area is private property including the area along the paved road as you enter. During the Tierra Del Sol, this area becomes a city of campers and motor homes. The sponsor of the event is the Tierra Del Sol 4WD Club out of San Diego. Although most of the trash is not from four-wheelers, the club has regular cleanup runs.

Do not confuse the historic Truckhaven Trail with the route described here. The historic trail generally follows the path of Highway S22; however, just bits and pieces of it remain on each side of the road. The trail is described on a sign just across from the entrance to Calcite Mine, Trail #45. The historic Truckhaven Trail is not covered in this book but you can drive it at various points where it is marked along S22.

Time & Distance: While the route described here is 11.8 miles, your mileage will vary. I drove the route in about 3 hours with the help of an expert guide. Plan to spend at least a day in the area.

To Get There: From Highway 86 west of Salton City, find North Marina Drive located about 2 miles north of Highway S22.

Trail Description: *Reset your odometer as you turn off Highway 86* (01). Head southwest on paved North Marina Drive. Pass through an area of deteriorated paved roads. On the right is Palm Wash, a major wash you can follow all the way to the Calcite Mine, Trail #45. The pavement ends after a mile. Continue west until 1.4 miles and bear left at a fork. You'll head south briefly and cross Anza Ditch. Bear right at 1.6 miles on a single-lane road. This area (02) is the approximate location where the vendors set up for the Tierra Del Sol event. Bear right at 1.7 miles and head north, crossing several small washes before you reach Palm Wash at 2.2 miles. Turn left and follow the wash west.

Reset your odometer at 2.2 miles (03) and turn right into a lesser wash. It starts easy but gradually worsens. Stay in the bottom of the wash until 2.0 miles (04) when you climb a ridge and things get more confusing. Bear right after the first ridge. Hopefully, a few tracks remain to show the way, but, if not, try to head generally northwest. These trenches get extremely narrow, testing your articulation to the maximum. At approximately 2.9 miles, you head northeast climbing to the top of a small plateau.

On top of the plateau, you'll find a fireplug at 3.1 miles (05). This was built by the Tierra Del Sol club just for fun. Chained to the fireplug is a metal box. You can take one item out of the box if you replace it with another item. Don't leave anything outside the box.

Reset your odometer and head north from the fireplug. The trail is still very squirrelly, but watch for cairns which ostensibly show you the way out. You'll zigzag downhill, eventually heading in a northeast direction until you reach Grave Wash at 0.8 miles (06). Turn right and follow Grave Wash east to Highway 86 at 5.2 miles (07).

Return Trip: Left on Highway 86 goes to Indio and Palm Springs, right goes to Brawley and El Centro. Salton City, a residential community, is east of the highway.

Services: None along trail. There's a small store with gas and several small restaurants at Hwy. 86 and S22. Westmoreland, north of Brawley, has a major 24-hour gas station if you can't get gas in Salton City.

Maps: USGS 7.5-minute map of Seventeen Palms, N3315-W11600, DeLorme Atlas & Gazetteer.

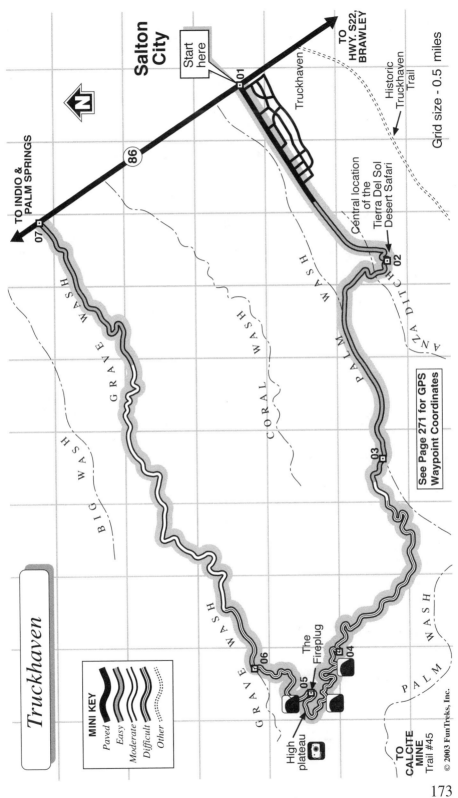

Truckhaven

MINI KEY
Paved
Easy
Moderate
Difficult
Other

Salton City

Start here

01

TO HWY. S22, BRAWLEY

Truckhaven

Historic Truckhaven Trail

Grid size - 0.5 miles

86

TO INDIO & PALM SPRINGS

07

Central location of the Tierra Del Sol Desert Safari

02

ANZA DITCH

03

PALM WASH

CORAL WASH

GRAVE WASH

BIG WASH

See Page 271 for GPS Waypoint Coordinates

The Fireplug

04

05

06

High plateau

PALM WASH

TO CALCITE MINE Trail #45

© 2003 FunTreks, Inc.

173

Fonts Point above Borrego Badlands.

Park and hike a short distance.

Wash is very wide at the start. Avoid the soft sand along the outer edges of the wash.

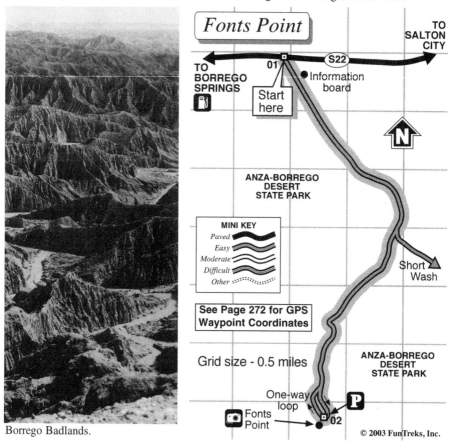

Fonts Point

TO SALTON CITY

S22

TO BORREGO SPRINGS

01 Start here

Information board

N

ANZA-BORREGO DESERT STATE PARK

MINI KEY
Paved
Easy
Moderate
Difficult
Other

See Page 272 for GPS Waypoint Coordinates

Short Wash

Grid size - 0.5 miles

ANZA-BORREGO DESERT STATE PARK

One-way loop

P

Fonts Point 02

Borrego Badlands.

© 2003 FunTreks, Inc.

174

Fonts Point 47

Location: East of Borrego Springs.

Difficulty: Easy. This trip can be done in a two-wheel-drive, high-clearance vehicle as long as you stay in the center of the wash where the sand is hard packed. However, it's a good idea to stay in four-wheel drive all the time in case you wander into the soft sand. Keep up your speed in case you begin to bog down. Check at Anza-Borrego Park Visitor Center for road conditions.

Features: A short drive in a wide sandy wash culminating with a truly outstanding view of Borrego Badlands. Don't skip this trip.

Time & Distance: Just under 4 miles from Highway S22 to Fonts Point. Takes about 20 minutes one way. You can add to the trip by exploring Short Wash that goes left at 1.9 miles. It connects to Palo Verde Wash, which runs south all the way to the Ocotillo Wells State Vehicular Recreation Area and eventually to Highway 78.

To Get There: Take Highway S22 east from Borrego Springs. Turn south 0.4 miles east of mile marker 29. A large information board marks the start.

Trail Description: Reset odometer at the start [01]. Head south in a wide, sandy wash. The wash is well packed in the center with some washboard sections. Stay right 1.9 miles where Short Wash goes left. After 3 miles, the trail narrows significantly with more curves. Be careful, the sand is very soft along the side of the trail through this section. The trail forks at 3.6 miles and begins a one-way loop. Follow arrows to the left, not right. Park at 3.9 miles [02] and hike uphill a short distance to the viewpoint. Make sure you take a camera; it's an awesome sight.

Return Trip: Return the way you came.

Services: None on trail. Gas and food in Borrego Springs. The Anza-Borrego Visitor Center is located on the west end of Borrego Springs. Stop and check out their large book section to learn more about the history and geology of the park.

Maps: Anza-Borrego Desert Region Recreation Map, USGS 7.5-minute map Fonts Point, CA, N3315-W11607, DeLorme Atlas & Gazetteer.

Sand hill is very steep.

Moderate portion of trail below sand hill.

Part way into The Slot.

176

Grid size - 0.5 miles

© 2003 FunTreks, Inc.

The Slot ◀48▶

Location: West of the Ocotillo Wells State Vehicular Recreation Area.

Difficulty: Difficult. One very steep sand hill gives this trail its difficult rating. Some moderate rock crawling, but most of the route is easy. If you drive trail in opposite direction, you can avoid the difficult sand hill. Do not attempt to drive up the sand hill because this causes unnecessary erosion.

Features: Kids will love this trip. Drive, then hike into narrow canyon. Descend extremely steep sand hill. Explore other roads in the area.

Time & Distance: Takes about an hour one-way before you must park and hike. Loop as described here is 11.7 miles. Add 15 minutes for short hike.

To Get There: Follow signs for Buttes Pass located on Hwy. 78 about 3 miles west of the Ranger Station at Ocotillo Wells SVRA. From points west, turn left 1.5 miles east of Borrego Springs Road near mile post 87.

Trail Description: Reset your odometer at the start (01). Head north on a wide single-lane, sandy road. At 0.9 miles (02) bear left at fork. Turn left at T at 1.8 miles. Follow along the top of a ridge as the trail swings north. It appears to end at an overlook at 2.8 miles, however, a difficult, steep sand hill continues east. It is one-way for obvious reasons. Turn around if you have no experience in sand. At the bottom of the hill at 2.9 miles (03), turn right. Follow the canyon until it's too narrow to continue. I stopped at 3.5 miles. Hike in as far as you like, then return to the bottom of the sand hill.

    Reset your odometer at the bottom of the sand hill (03) and continue north through a moderate rocky area as you exit via Borrego Mountain Wash. Turn left at 1.0 miles after a peculiar-looking rock. Bear right at 2.3 miles (04) in San Felipe Wash. Turn right again at 4.1 miles (05) at sign for Buttes Pass. Stay on widest part of trail as you climb. Bear left at 5.9 and right at 6.3 before reconnecting with the original road at 6.7 miles (02). Bear left to return to Highway 78.

Return Trip: At Hwy. 78, right goes to Borrego Spgs., left to Ocotillo Wells.

Services: None along trail. Closest gas located at Blu-In Park about 6 miles east of Ocotillo Wells on Hwy. 78. (Open seasonally, closed Mondays.)

Maps: Anza-Borrego Desert Region Recreation Map, USGS 7.5-minute map Borrego Mountain, CA, DeLorme Atlas & Gazetteer.

Narrow wash at mile 15.4.

Hillsides east of Shell Reef.

Cahuilla Trail.

Gas Domes look like bubbling mud pots.

Blowing sand can hide trail.

Artesian well.

You can't always rely on signs to show you the way.

Ocotillo Wells SVRA 49

Location: East of Borrego Springs, southwest of Salton City.

Difficulty: Easy. (Rating does not apply to entire Recreation Area.) Gentle grades and mostly wide dirt roads. The section between the Gas Domes and the Artesian Well follows a narrow twisting wash that changes with every rain. Winds can blow sand across the trail, changing conditions and making route-finding more difficult. Dangerously hot in the summer.

Features: The route selected here is one of hundreds since you can go almost anywhere in the western two-thirds of the area. This route was selected to give you a quick tour. Many moderate and difficult trails are scattered throughout the area, including popular Blow Sand Hill and Devil's Slide. Stop at the ranger station on the western tip of the park and pick up a full-color, detailed map of the area. It explains regulations and all of the unique features that Ocotillo Wells has to offer. The park is open 24 hours a day, 7 days a week, and no fees are charged. All types of vehicles use the area including ATVs, dirt bikes, sand rails and four-wheel-drive vehicles from hardcore to stock SUVs. All vehicles must be licensed or have a "green sticker."

The map on the next page differentiates roads from washes; however, there is often no distinction between the two. Sometimes the washes are wider and smoother than the roads. Other times, they can be extremely narrow or even impassable. Both roads and major washes are marked with signs, but they are sometimes damaged or removed. An absence of major landmarks makes route-finding very difficult in this vast, 70,000-acre OHV wonderland. The free map provided at the ranger station is complete with a latitude and longitude grid, allowing you to easily determine your position with a simple GPS unit. A compass can also be very helpful.

To learn about the area, consider attending the *MDA Off Road for Hope* event held annually in early February. It's open to anyone with an ATV, dirt bike, sand rail or four-wheel-drive vehicle. Everyone has fun and proceeds go to a good cause.

Time & Distance: Allow about 3 hours for this 21.8-mile route. You can spend many days exploring the area.

To Get There: Take Highway 78 to well-marked Ranger Station Road about 2 miles west of Ocotillo Wells near mile post 91. Ocotillo Wells is about halfway between Borrego Springs and Highway 86 southwest of the Salton Sea.

179

Trail Description: *Reset odometer as you turn off Highway 78 on Ranger Station Road* [01]. Head north and turn right on Quarry Road within 0.1 miles. Continue straight past camping areas as Main Street joins on the right at 1.3 miles. Bear right at sign for Shell Reef Expressway at 1.7. Stay on this wide road as it heads northeast crossing many other marked roads and washes. Pass the Devil's Slide at 4.1 miles. Bank Wash crosses at 5.7 miles (02) as Wolfe Well Road joins on the right. (Pumpkin Patch, Trail #50, goes left here.) Continue straight passing Shell Reef at 6.4 miles. Shell Reef is fenced off but just ahead is a moonlike landscape perfect for ATVs and dirt bikes. The road is hard to see through this area. Just continue to head east and it becomes defined again. Make a right at 7.8 miles (03) staying on Shell Reef Expressway. (Straight here would take you to Cross Over Trail, Trail #51.) The road is rougher and poorly defined as Tarantula Wash crosses through this area. Continue heading southeast until you run into Cahuilla Trail at 8.9 miles (04).

Bear left on Cahuilla Trail. It heads north briefly then turns east. Continue straight at 10.9 where a lesser road goes left. At 11.5 miles (05), turn left on Gas Dome Trail. Cross Pole Line Road at 12.8 miles. (East of Pole Line Road you must stay on established routes.) Gas Dome Trail curves around and heads southeast. You climb gradually before reaching the gas domes at 14.8 miles. Again they are fenced off and easy to spot. Past the gas domes, the trail drops into a narrow wash at 15.4 miles. This is a fun section to drive as the wash meanders south. You reach an artesian well marked by a tiny palm tree at 16.1 miles (06). Turn right at the well and head west on Cahuilla Trail. This was an interesting drive for me as wind blew sand across the trail nearly covering it up. At 18.3 miles (07) you connect with Pole Line Road again. Left takes you to Highway 78 at 21.8 miles (08).

Return Trip: Left on Highway 78 takes you to Highway 86, right goes back to where you started at Ocotillo Wells.

Services: Ocotillo Wells SVRA has several campgrounds (see map) with ramadas, picnic tables and modern vault toilets. The Ranger Station has flush toilets and showers. Ocotillo Wells has several small restaurants, ATV rentals and full-hookup campgrounds. At the time of this writing, gas was not available in Ocotillo Wells. You must head east about 6 miles to Blu-In Park. It has gas (not cheap), a small eating place and a few supplies. It is closed Mondays and may close unexpectedly at other times. Salton City has gas but they sometimes run out. Westmoreland, south on Highway 86, has a reliable 24-hour gas station but it's a long drive. Borrego Springs also has gas, but stations are not open all the time.

Maps: Ocotillo Wells SVRA map, DeLorme Atlas & Gazetteer.

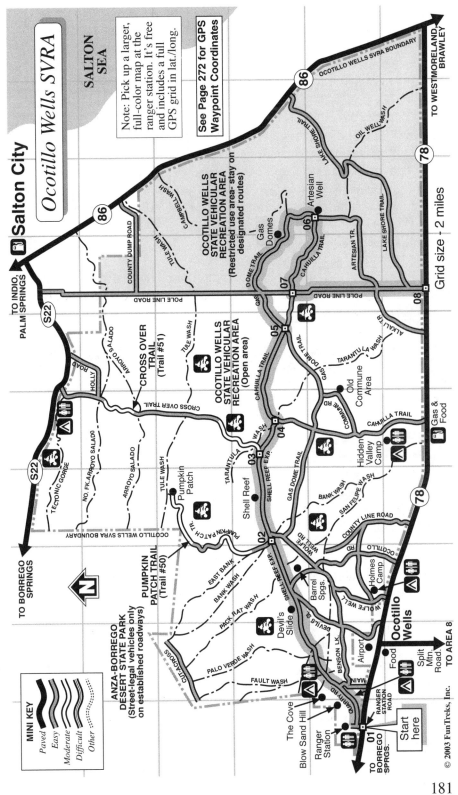

Salton City

Ocotillo Wells SVRA

SALTON SEA

Note: Pick up a larger, full-color map at the ranger station. It's free and includes a full GPS grid in lat./long.

See Page 272 for GPS Waypoint Coordinates

TO WESTMORELAND, BRAWLEY

OCOTILLO WELLS SVRA BOUNDARY

OIL WELL WASH

LAKE SHORE TRAIL

86

78

Grid size - 2 miles

TO INDIO, PALM SPRINGS

S22

COUNTY DUMP ROAD

CAMPBELL WASH

TULE WASH

OCOTILLO WELLS STATE VEHICULAR RECREATION AREA (Restricted use area- stay on designated routes)

Gas Domes

Artesian Well

06

CAHUILLA TRAIL

ARTESIAN TR.

LAKE SHORE TRAIL

DOME TRAIL

07

POLE LINE ROAD

POLE LINE ROAD

08

ARROYO SALADO

HOLLY

CROSS OVER TRAIL (Trail #51)

TULE WASH

CROSS OVER TRAIL

OCOTILLO WELLS STATE VEHICULAR RECREATION AREA (Open area)

05

GAS DOME TRAIL

DOME TRAIL

GREEN

CAHUILLA TRAIL

TARANTU LA WASH

ALKALI TR.

ROAD

NO. FK. ARROYO SALADO

ARROYO SALADO

TECTONIC GORGE

S22

TULE WASH

Pumpkin Patch

PUMPKIN PATCH TR.

TARANTULA

WASH

03

04

Old Commune Area

COMMUNE RD

CAHUILLA TRAIL

Gas & Food

TO BORREGO SPRINGS

N

OCOTILLO WELLS SVRA BOUNDARY

Shell Reef

SHELL REEF EXP.

GAS DOME TRAIL

02

BANK WASH

SAN FELIPE WASH

Hidden Valley Camp

COUNTY LINE ROAD

78

PUMPKIN PATCH TRAIL (Trail #50)

EAST BANK

BANK WASH

PACK RAT WASH

CUT ACROSS

PALO VERDE WASH

SHELL REEF EXP.

WOLFE WELL RD

WOLFE WELL

Barrel Spgs.

Holmes Camp

OCOTILLO RD

ANZA-BORREGO DESERT STATE PARK (Street-legal vehicles only on established roadways)

Devil's Slide

DEVIL'S S.

BENSON LK.

Airport

Food

Split Mtn. Road

TO AREA 8

Ocotillo Wells

FAULT WASH

COUNTRY RD

MAIN

RANGER STATION ROAD

Start here

01

TO BORREGO SPRGS.

The Cove

Blow Sand Hill

Ranger Station

MINI KEY

Paved

Easy

Moderate

Difficult

Other

© 2003 FunTreks, Inc.

181

Part of trail follows rocky wash. Conditions in wash can change quickly.

Optional difficult side hills.

Undulating hilly area is fun to drive.

The Pumpkin Patch.

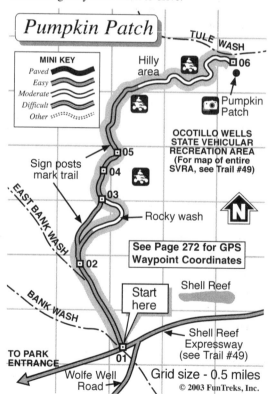

Pumpkin Patch

TULE WASH

MINI KEY
Paved
Easy
Moderate
Difficult
Other

Hilly area

06

Pumpkin Patch

OCOTILLO WELLS STATE VEHICULAR RECREATION AREA
(For map of entire SVRA, see Trail #49)

Sign posts mark trail

05
04
03

Rocky wash

EAST BANK WASH

See Page 272 for GPS Waypoint Coordinates

02

Start here

Shell Reef

BANK WASH

Shell Reef Expressway (see Trail #49)

TO PARK ENTRANCE

01

Wolfe Well Road

Grid size - 0.5 miles

© 2003 FunTreks, Inc.

Pumpkin Patch 50

Location: Northeast of Ocotillo Wells, southwest of Salton City. Inside Ocotillo Wells State Vehicular Recreation Area.

Difficulty: Moderate. One rocky wash and some tight undulating hills. Potentially impassable if wet. Route-finding can be very confusing if sign posts are missing. Difficult side roads branch off, so be careful.

Features: Crosses a fun, hilly area inside the park and ends at a curious geologic feature. Great for ATVs and dirt bikes too.

Time & Distance: Just 4.4 miles one way. Takes about an hour if you don't make any wrong turns. Allow time to reach start of trail and return.

To Get There: Follow directions for previous trail, Ocotillo Wells SVRA, Trail #49. Per those directions, proceed to Bank Wash, reached at 5.7 miles.

Trail Description: *Reset odometer as you leave Shell Reef Expressway* [01]. Head north at sign for Bank Wash. East Bank Wash also converges here, so stay right in East Bank Wash. Turn right at 0.9 miles (02) at small sign for Pumpkin Patch. Follow a narrowing wash as it curves east then back to the west. (You can avoid this wash by following sign posts across a flat area just west of the wash. It's not as much fun and hard to find.) Continue straight at 1.9 miles (03) as a road joins on left. Head north following brown carsonite sign posts spaced several hundred feet apart. Bear left at 2.2 miles (04) then immediately left again. Make a hard left at 2.4 miles (05). Terrain changes to small hills and whoop-ti-dos by 2.6 miles. Interesting side hills are great for ATVs and dirt bikes. Road becomes better defined by 3.3 miles as hills get bigger. You come out of the hills heading east parallel to Tule Wash before reaching the Pumpkin Patch at 4.4 miles (06).

Return Trip: You can return the way you came or take Tule Wash east to Cross Over Trail #51 or Pole Line Road. Tule Wash is usually a fun, easy route; however, conditions vary. There are several more difficult trails to explore around the Pumpkin Patch but it's easy to get lost.

Services: None on trail. See complete list of services described in Trail #49.

Maps: Ocotillo Wells SVRA map, USGS 7.5-minute map of Shell Reef, CA, N3307.5-11600/7.5, DeLorme Atlas & Gazetteer.

Winding trail encountered after first ridge.

Markers confirm location.

Many choices for those who wish to try side trails. A great ATV and dirt bike area.

Moonscape-like terrain.

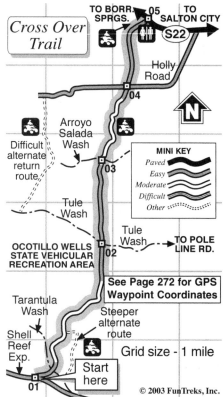

Cross Over Trail

TO BORR. SPRGS.

05

TO SALTON CITY

S22

Holly Road

04

Arroyo Salada Wash

Difficult alternate return route

03

MINI KEY

Paved
Easy
Moderate
Difficult
Other

Tule Wash

Tule Wash

TO POLE LINE RD.

OCOTILLO WELLS STATE VEHICULAR RECREATION AREA

02

See Page 272 for GPS Waypoint Coordinates

Tarantula Wash

Steeper alternate route

Shell Reef Exp.

Grid size - 1 mile

Start here

01

© 2003 FunTreks, Inc.

Cross Over Trail 51

Location: Northeast of Ocotillo Wells, southwest of Salton City. Inside Ocotillo Wells State Vehicular Recreation Area.

Difficulty: Moderate. Steep climbs and tight turns. Suitable for high clearance stock SUVs. Stay off trail if wet. Route-finding is challenging.

Features: Primary north/south route through Ocotillo Wells SVRA. A fun drive with many alternate routes of varying difficulty. Accesses great terrain for ATVs and dirt bikes. If looking for more challenge, try alternate routes shown on map.

Time & Distance: About 6.7 miles from Shell Reef Expressway to Hwy. S22. Allow about 2 hours as described here.

To Get There: Follow directions for Ocotillo Wells SVRA, Trail #49. Per those directions, proceed 7.8 miles and go straight rather than turn right.

Trail Description: Reset odometer as you leave Shell Reef Expressway [01]. Continue east a short distance then bear left at 0.2 miles. Cross Tarantula Wash then climb up and over a steep ridge. Continue north as the trail weaves down the other side. At 2.2, stay down the middle as the trail splits. Cross a wide unidentified wash at 2.4 before reaching Tule Wash at 2.8 miles [02]. (Left here would take you to the Pumpkin Patch; right goes to Pole Line Road.) Continue north on parallel roads, all with serious whoop-ti-dos. Cross another small wash and dirt hills before reaching Arroyo Salada at 4.3 miles [03]. You reach a high point at 4.5 with good views of the area. The road weaves north but is well-defined. Cross another wide wash before intersecting with Holly Road at 5.4 miles [04]. (A right turn here is the quickest way to S22). Continue north as multiple roads make route-finding confusing. At 6.4 miles, swing right through another popular hilly area. Pass trash dumpsters and portable toilets before reaching S22 at 6.7 miles [05].

Return Trip: Right on S22 to Salton City, left to Borrego Springs. Or, try more difficult alternate return route shown on map.

Services: None on trail. See complete list of services described in Trail #49.

Maps: Ocotillo Wells SVRA map, USGS 7.5-minute map of Shell Reef, CA, N3307.5-11600/7.5, DeLorme Atlas & Gazetteer.

AREA 8

Anza-Borrego Desert, Corral Canyon, Ocotillo

52. Oriflamme Canyon
53. Blair Valley
54. Pinyon Mountain Rd.
55. Sandstone Canyon
56. Canyon Sin Nombre
57. Mud Caves, Diablo Dropoff
58. Mortero Wash

59. Los Pinos Lookout
60. Bronco Peak
61. Sidewinder
62. McCain Valley
63. Table Mountain
64. Smugglers Cave/ Elliot Mine

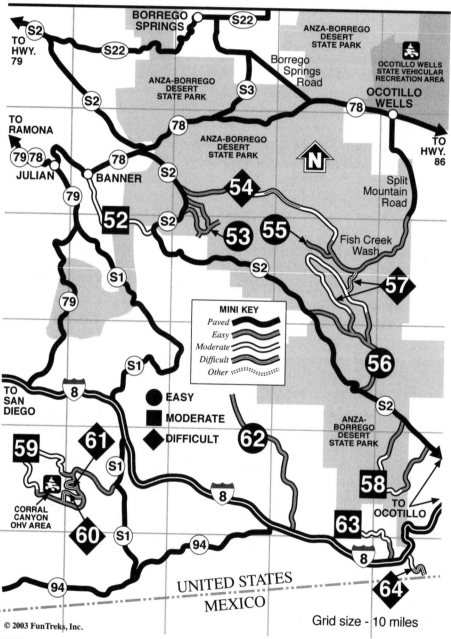

MINI KEY
Paved
Easy
Moderate
Difficult
Other

● EASY
■ MODERATE
◆ DIFFICULT

© 2003 FunTreks, Inc.

Grid size - 10 miles

UNITED STATES
MEXICO

Anza-Borrego Desert, Corral Canyon, Ocotillo

Area 8 includes some of the most remote backcountry in California, including the southern portion of Anza-Borrego Desert State Park. Trails are a long way from towns and services. *Smugglers Cave/Elliot Mine* literally stops at the Mexican border. It's possible to encounter illegal immigrants on the southernmost trails, so you'll appreciate the dominant presence of the U.S. Border Patrol. As mentioned earlier, you must remain on designated routes inside Anza-Borrego Park and all vehicles must be street legal. If this sounds too tame, think again. Several trails offer significant challenge including *Pinyon Mountain Road* where you'll find *The Squeeze*. Here you'll learn why fold-in mirrors were invented. Farther south, in Corral Canyon OHV Area, *Sidewinder* and *Bronco Peak* trails offer serious rock crawling for the hardcore enthusiast. The area also has plenty of open space for ATVs and dirt bikes. Stock SUV drivers won't be disappointed either; moderate *Los Pinos Lookout* starts at the park, heads north to a manned lookout tower, then circles back around the perimeter of the OHV area. Finally, when you've had enough of the hot desert, head uphill to the beautiful little mountain town of Julian.

Crowd gathers at *The Squeeze* on difficult *Pinyon Mountain Trail #54.*

Dramatic switchbacks climb out of Oriflamme Canyon.

Some snow at the top in early February.

Chariot Canyon is partially shaded.

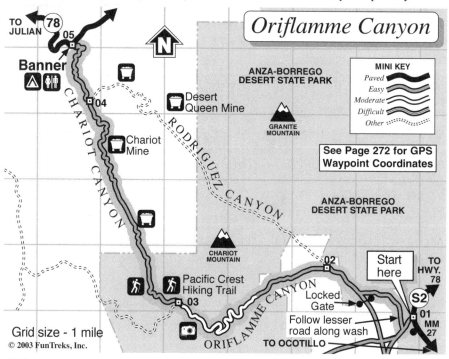

Oriflamme Canyon

TO JULIAN **(78)** 05

Banner

ANZA-BORREGO DESERT STATE PARK

MINI KEY
Paved
Easy
Moderate
Difficult
Other

04

Desert Queen Mine

GRANITE MOUNTAIN

See Page 272 for GPS Waypoint Coordinates

C H A R I O T   C A N Y O N

Chariot Mine

R O D R I G U E Z   C A N Y O N

CHARIOT MOUNTAIN

ANZA-BORREGO DESERT STATE PARK

02

Start here

TO HWY. 78

Pacific Crest Hiking Trail

03

Locked Gate

S2

01 MM 27

Follow lesser road along wash

O R I F L A M M E   C A N Y O N

TO OCOTILLO

Grid size - 1 mile

© 2003 FunTreks, Inc.

188

Oriflamme Canyon 52

Location: Southeast of Julian and Banner, southwest of Borrego Springs.

Difficulty: Moderate. Mildly rocky with steep, narrow switchbacks. Suitable for stock 4x4 SUVs with high ground clearance. Possible snow during the winter months at higher elevations.

Features: Heart-pumping scenic drive through remote canyon. Can be driven in either direction. Return via difficult Rodriguez Canyon to make a loop. Many historic mines and buildings. Excellent spring wildflowers.

Time & Distance: Allow about 1-1/2 hours one-way for this 11.1-mile drive.

To Get There: Turn west just north of mile post 27 from Hwy. S2 about 10 miles south of Hwy. 78. The road is well marked. To drive trail in opposite direction, head southeast from Banner on dirt road near Banner Store.

Trail Description: Reset odometer as you turn off Hwy. S2 [01]. Head southwest <u>less than</u> 0.2 miles and turn right on a lesser road alongside a wash. (Don't turn on the better road that forks just ahead at 0.2.) Stay close to the wash but not in it until that's your only choice. Bear right on a better road at 1.4 miles as you exit the wash. A gate stops you from going left. Rodriguez Canyon goes right at 2.0 miles (02), you go left. Bear right at 2.4 and 3.0. You enter Anza-Borrego State Park at 3.3 and begin to climb more steeply. The road is narrow with very tight switchbacks until you reach the top at about 5.5 miles. Bear right at 5.7 miles (03) where a major road goes left. Go by the Pacific Crest Hiking Trail on the right about 6.0. Cattle guard at 6.9 marks point where you leave park. You'll pass through a shady wooded area with active mines and private cabins. Do not trespass on any private property or risk a shotgun in your face. Stay left at 8.3. Bear left where Rodriguez Canyon Road goes right at 9.8 miles (04). The road winds downhill to the little town of Banner and paved Highway 78 reached at 11.1 miles (05).

Return Trip: From Banner, head northeast for Ocotillo Wells and Borrego Springs. Head west for Julian.

Services: Nothing on trail. Banner is a small resort community with a country store and a commercial RV campground.

Maps: Anza-Borrego Desert Region Recreation Map, USGS 100,000-scale map of Borrego Valley, CA, DeLorme Atlas & Gazetteer.

First part of trip heads into Little Blair Valley the back way.

Parking at Pictograph Hiking Trailhead.

High point of Pictograph Hiking Trail.

Look for this boulder with pictographs.

Entire route suitable for stock SUVs.

190

Blair Valley 53

Location: South of Borrego Springs between Julian and Ocotillo Wells.

Difficulty: Easy. Most of this trip is a single-lane, sandy road with gentle grades. Suitable for all SUVs when dry.

Features: A relaxing drive through two beautiful valleys. See Native American pictographs at the end of beautiful Pictograph Hiking Trail. Visit the site of an old Indian village. Hike to the top of Ghost Mountain to see the Marshal South Home. At Foot and Walker Pass, see a monument for historic Butterfield Stage Route that crosses southward through the area. Enjoy primitive camping in a pristine setting. Permit required for large groups.

Time & Distance: Covers 11.2 miles as described here with two side trips. Allow about 2 hours driving time. Allow an additional 40 minutes for the 2-mile, round-trip hike to the pictographs.

To Get There: From Scissors Crossing at Highways 78 and S2, drive south 5.3 miles on Hwy. S2. Look for a small sign on the left for Little Blair Valley.

Trail Description: Reset your odometer as you turn left off Hwy. S2 (01). Follow a single-lane road as it parallels S2 for a short distance then departs more southeast. The sandy road is narrow with an occasional rough spot. You'll see several good camping spots along the road. After a mile, the road swings to the left and follows along the base of a ridge on the right. Stay left at 1.2. Bear right at 1.8 miles (02) at a sign for Little Blair Valley which appears as you gradually descend. I turned right at 2.3 miles to follow a more interesting path closer to the boulder-strewn ridge on the right. Excellent camping spots in this area. This route bypasses a dry lake bed. The trail is marked with tiny pictograph signs. Continue southeast avoiding lesser turnoffs until you rejoin the original trail at 3.1 and continue south.

Turn left at 4.1 miles (03) and follow a twisting sandy road to a parking area for the Pictograph Hiking Trail at 5.5 miles. If you can't hike all the way to the pictographs (about a mile one-way), at least hike part way up the trail. It's a very enjoyable hike as it climbs between interesting boulders.

Reset your odometer at the parking area and return to the main trail. Continue straight a short distance to the Morteros Hiking Trail on the left. This short, easy hike leads to a spot that was once an Indian Village. Look for grinding holes, called "morteros" that can be found in the boulders. An interpretive panel explains the history of the area.

Continue southwest on an improving road as you climb a short distance and then descend into Blair Valley. Ghost mountain is on the left. An optional side road goes left at 2.0 miles (04). It leads to an interpretive sign and parking area for a hiking trail that goes up to the Marshal South Home (Yaquitepec). The one-mile hike is very steep.

Reset your odometer when you return to the main trail (04) and continue north. At 0.2 a road joins on the right. This is an alternate route into the parking area for the Marshal South Home. At 1.8 miles, a road goes right to a group camping area. Continue straight as several roads cross the area. I stayed to the right near the bluffs. At 2.6 miles, you cross a road that was the original Butterfield Stage Route. To the right is Foot and Walker Pass where you can hike to a monument for the stage route. Turn right into campground at 3.1 miles. Paved Highway S2 is just ahead at 3.2 miles (05).

Return Trip: Right on Highway S2 goes back to Scissors Crossing at Highway 78. Left goes to Oriflamme Canyon, Trail #52, and eventually to Ocotillo on Interstate 8.

Services: Vault toilets at primary campground near Highway S2. Full services in Borrego Springs and Julian. Banner has RV camping and a country store.

Historical Highlights: The Indian village on the Morteros Hiking Trail was seasonally occupied by the nomadic Kumeyaay Indian Tribe for nearly 1,000 years. *Morteros* were created by Kumeyaay women as they crushed seeds to make meal.

Marshal South lived with his wife and three children on Ghost Mountain for 16 years in the 1930s and 40s. They built an adobe home they called *Yaquitepec*. A talented writer and poet, he supported his family in part by writing monthly articles for *Desert Magazine*. These controversial stories of his hard life in the desert captivated some readers and disgusted others. The experiment ended when his wife divorced him around 1947.

The Butterfield Stage Route was built in the late 1850s by John Butterfield and his 800 employees. The 2,800-mile trip from Missouri to San Francisco took about 25 days. Foot and Walker pass required passengers get out and walk and sometimes help push the stage. It is this situation that gave the pass its name.

Maps: Anza-Borrego Desert Region Recreation Map, USGS 100,000-scale map of Borrego Valley, DeLorme Atlas & Gazetteer.

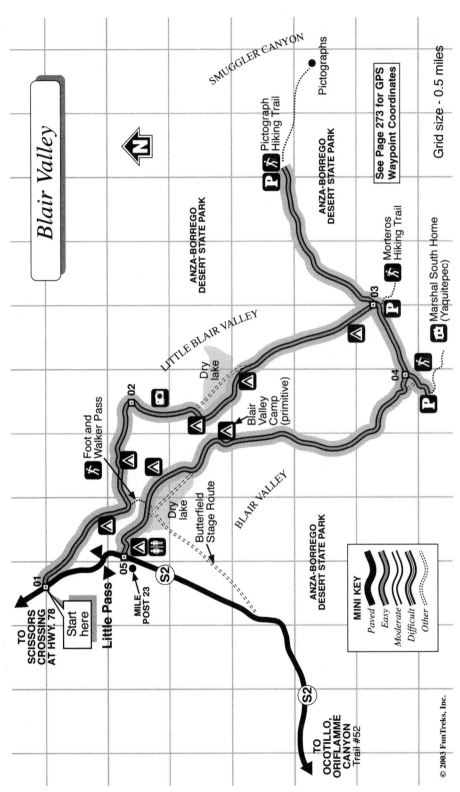

Blair Valley

N

SMUGGLER CANYON

Pictographs

Pictograph Hiking Trail

Pictographs

P 🥾

See Page 273 for GPS Waypoint Coordinates

Grid size - 0.5 miles

ANZA-BORREGO DESERT STATE PARK

ANZA-BORREGO DESERT STATE PARK

LITTLE BLAIR VALLEY

Dry lake

Morteros Hiking Trail

🥾

03

P

Marshal South Home (Yaquitepec)

🏠

Foot and Walker Pass

🥾

02

📷

◁

◁

◁

◁

04

🥾

◁

Blair Valley Camp (primitive)

P

◁

◁

Dry lake

Butterfield Stage Route

BLAIR VALLEY

ANZA-BORREGO DESERT STATE PARK

◁

01

◁

🚻

05

S2

MILE POST 23

TO SCISSORS CROSSING AT HWY. 78

Start here

Little Pass

MINI KEY

Paved
Easy
Moderate
Difficult
Other

S2

TO OCOTILLO, ORIFLAMME CANYON Trail #52

© 2003 FunTreks, Inc.

193

Fold-in mirrors are handy at *The Squeeze*.   Left side of *Pinyon Dropoff*.

View from high in the Vallecito Mountains   Crowd gathers to watch the fun.

Damage to full-size vehicle at *The Squeeze*.   Right side of *Pinyon Dropoff*.

Pinyon Mountain Road ◆54◆

Location: South of Borrego Springs, southwest of Ocotillo Wells.

Difficulty: Difficult. Trail passes through a narrow canyon with steep hills and one extremely steep descent. Not recommended for stock or full-size vehicles. For experienced drivers only. Lockers will make the trip easier. Do not drive this trail if heavy rain is expected. You would not want to be in Fish Creek Canyon during a flash flood. Don't go alone.

Features: This trail is worth the drive just for the scenery, but the main attractions are *The Squeeze* and *Pinyon Dropoff*. Neither obstacle has a bypass. The photo of the Toyota Tundra on the opposite page shows what can happen to a full-size vehicle at *The Squeeze*. Excellent driving skills are needed to descend extremely steep *Pinyon Dropoff*, a.k.a. *Heart Attack Hill*. You should consider this a one-way trip since you can't turn back after *The Squeeze*. The last part of the trip is easy as you exit through Fish Creek Wash and spectacular Split Mountain. No ATVs are allowed on trail, but street-legal dirt bikes are permitted provided they stay on designated routes.

Time & Distance: This trip measures 30.5 miles from Highway S2 to paved Split Mountain Road. Under normal circumstances, allow 4 to 5 hours driving time. (I drove this trail with a large group of vehicles while attending the *MDA Offroad for Hope* event held in early February at Ocotillo Wells State Vehicular Recreation Area. We started on the trail about 9:30 A.M. and returned to Ocotillo Wells about 4 P.M.)

To Get There: From Scissors Crossing at Highway 78, head south 4.4 miles on Highway S2. When you reach the boundary to Anza-Borrego Desert State Park, look for a sign for Pinyon Canyon on the left near mile post 22.

Trail Description: *Reset your odometer as you turn left off of Highway S2* (01). Head east a short distance until North Pinyon Mountain Road goes left. Continue straight on Pinyon Mountain Road as it swings in a southeast direction. You'll pass through several miles of Desert Creosote and Cholla before approaching the foothills of the Vallecito Mountains. Bear right at 3.5 and 3.9 miles where lesser roads go left. Bear left at 4.2. Roads converge at 4.3 miles. Bear right, then in just 20 feet, go straight. You should be able to see the road in the distance as it climbs east. Go straight at 5.7 then right at 5.8. Continue straight at 6.3 where a road goes right.

You begin to descend into Pinyon Canyon about 6.6 miles before reaching *The Squeeze* at 7.0. Stay to the left side as you pass through but be careful not to go too high up the wall. After an easy stretch, make a sharp right turn out of the canyon at 7.6 miles (02). Some good rock crawling follows as you climb to the top of a small ridge. After a small dropoff, you reach the larger *Pinyon Dropoff* at 7.9 miles. The left side is easier but both sides are very difficult. Before you start down, make sure your vehicle is square to the hill. Back up if necessary to get in the proper position. Try to descend smoothly without slamming on your brakes. You may have to put rocks in some of the larger holes.

Several smaller challenges follow after the *Pinyon Dropoff* as you continue downhill. Bear right at a T at 8.9 miles (03) following signs to Fish Creek. A steep, rocky hill at 9.5 miles should be approached cautiously. It has a large depression that must be straddled; otherwise, a rollover is possible. After this point the trail gets easier as you follow the sandy bottom of Fish Creek Wash. Bear right at 12.7 then continue straight at 13.8 where a road joins on the left. Bear left at 17.3 where a road joins on the right. You'll go by the entrance to Sandstone Canyon, Trail #55, on the right at 18.0 miles (04). At 20.9 miles (05), the exit point of Mud Caves/Diablo Dropoff, Trail #57, joins on the right.

Reset your odometer and continue east in Fish Creek Wash. Bear right at 0.9 miles (06) and right again at 2.7 miles. Stay to the right at 5.4 miles (07) where North Fork Fish Creek Wash goes left. In this same area, on the right, is a small sign for the Wind Caves Hiking Trail. This short, steep hike is worth the time. Soon the towering walls of Split Mountain loom above as you weave out of the canyon. You'll pass Fish Creek Camp on the right before reaching paved Split Mountain Road at 9.6 miles (08).

Return Trip: Left goes into Ocotillo Wells and Highway 78 in about 8 miles.

Services: None along trail. Several restaurants and full hook-up campgrounds in Ocotillo Wells. Closest gas is 6 miles east of Ocotillo Wells on Hwy. 78.

Maps: Anza-Borrego Desert Region Recreation Map, USGS 250,000-scale map Santa Ana, CA, DeLorme Atlas & Gazetteer.

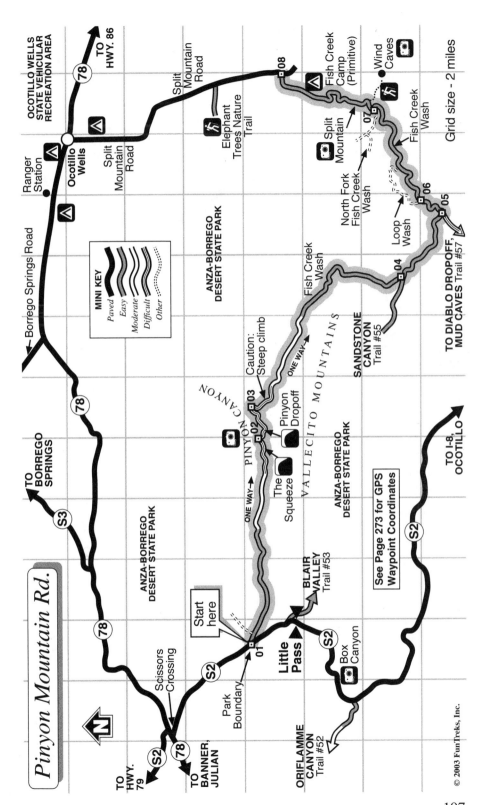

Pinyon Mountain Rd.

OCOTILLO WELLS
STATE VEHICULAR
RECREATION AREA

TO HWY. 86

78

Split Mountain Road

Ranger Station

Ocotillo Wells

Split Mountain Road

Borrego Springs Road

78

TO BORREGO SPRINGS

S3

78

Scissors Crossing

S2

TO HWY. 79

S2

78

TO BANNER, JULIAN

N

Elephant Trees Nature Trail

Split Mountain Road

ANZA-BORREGO DESERT STATE PARK

MINI KEY
Paved
Easy
Moderate
Difficult
Other

PINYON CANYON

Caution: Steep climb

03

02

The Squeeze

Pinyon Dropoff

ONE WAY

ONE WAY

VALLECITO MOUNTAINS

ANZA-BORREGO DESERT STATE PARK

Fish Creek Wash

Start here

01

Park Boundary

S2

BLAIR VALLEY Trail #53

Little Pass

S2

Box Canyon

ORIFLAMME CANYON Trail #52

See Page 273 for GPS Waypoint Coordinates

S2

TO I-8, OCOTILLO

08

Fish Creek Camp (Primitive)

Wind Caves

Split Mountain

07

Fish Creek Wash

North Fork Fish Creek Wash

Loop Wash

06

05

04

SANDSTONE CANYON Trail #55

Fish Creek Wash

TO DIABLO DROPOFF, MUD CAVES Trail #57

Grid size - 2 miles

© 2003 FunTreks, Inc.

197

Exiting Sandstone Canyon.

Fish Creek Canyon.

Entering Split Mountain

It's a short but steep hike to the Wind Caves

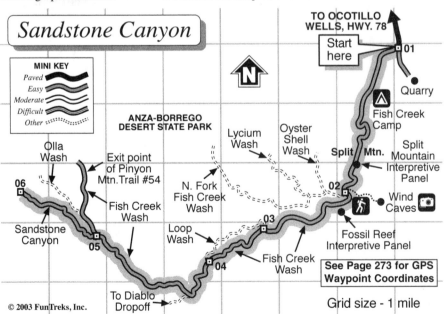

Sandstone Canyon

MINI KEY
Paved
Easy
Moderate
Difficult
Other

N

ANZA-BORREGO DESERT STATE PARK

TO OCOTILLO WELLS, HWY. 78

Start here

01

Quarry

Fish Creek Camp

Lycium Wash

Oyster Shell Wash

Split   Mtn.

Split Mountain Interpretive Panel

Olla Wash

Exit point of Pinyon Mtn. Trail #54

N. Fork Fish Creek Wash

02

Wind Caves

06

Fish Creek Wash

Sandstone Canyon

05

Loop Wash

03

Fossil Reef Interpretive Panel

04

Fish Creek Wash

See Page 273 for GPS Waypoint Coordinates

© 2003 FunTreks, Inc.

To Diablo Dropoff

Grid size - 1 mile

198

Sandstone Canyon ⑤⑤

Location: Southwest of Ocotillo Wells.

Difficulty: Easy. Sandy wash bottom suitable for most stock 4x4 SUVs. Conditions can worsen after storms. Dangerous flash floods possible.

Features: Lengthy drive through massive Fish Creek Canyon ends at dramatic Sandstone Canyon. See geologic wonders including Split Mountain, the Wind Caves and Fossil Reef. Explore more difficult side canyons.

Time & Distance: It's 15 miles one way to the end of Sandstone Canyon. Allow 3 to 4 hours for round trip plus time for hikes and side trips.

To Get There: From Ocotillo Wells, drive south 8 miles on Split Mountain Road. Turn right at sign for Fish Creek Canyon when pavement ends.

Trail Description: Reset odometer as you enter Fish Creek Canyon [01]. Head west in wide wash. You'll see Fish Creek Camp on the left as massive canyon walls begin to rise above you. Interpretive panel at 3.7 miles explains how Split Mountain was created. Bear left at 4.3 miles (02) where lesser canyon goes right. Also note small sign for Wind Caves Hiking Trail on the left. The hike is steep but not too long. Another interpretive panel on left at 4.6 miles explains Fossil Reef. Bear left at 6.9 miles (03) where alternate Loop Wash goes right. It rejoins the main wash at 8.7 miles (04). (Consider going this way on your return trip.) Stay right at 9.7 miles where a lesser canyon goes left. This difficult route goes up to Diablo Dropoff described in Mud Caves/Diablo Dropoff Trail #57. Bear left into Sandstone Canyon at 12.5 miles (05). A large sign clearly identifies this turn. The canyon gradually narrows as high vertical walls close in. I stopped at 15.0 miles (06) where it became too narrow to continue. I hiked from this point. The narrow section soon ends and the canyon widens again. You can continue to hike, but driving any farther is not allowed.

Return Trip: Return the way you came or take alternate Loop Wash.

Services: A couple of restaurants and campgrounds in Ocotillo Wells. Gas is available about 6 miles east of Ocotillo Wells on Highway 78.

Maps: Anza-Borrego Desert Region Recreation Map, USGS 100,000 scale map El Cajon, CA, DeLorme Atlas & Gazetteer.

Folded rock layers of sedimentary sandstone.

Canyon Sin Nombre.

Vallecito Wash at the corner of Hollywood & Vine.

Camping in side canyon.

200

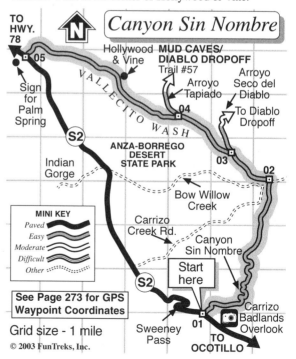

Canyon Sin Nombre

TO HWY. 78

05

Sign for Palm Spring

S2

Indian Gorge

Hollywood & Vine

VALLECITO WASH

MUD CAVES/ DIABLO DROPOFF
Trail #57

Arroyo Tapiado

04

Arroyo Seco del Diablo

To Diablo Dropoff

ANZA-BORREGO DESERT STATE PARK

03

02

Bow Willow Creek

MINI KEY
Paved
Easy
Moderate
Difficult
Other

Carrizo Creek Rd.

Canyon Sin Nombre

Start here

S2

See Page 273 for GPS Waypoint Coordinates

Grid size - 1 mile

© 2003 FunTreks, Inc.

Sweeney Pass

01

Carrizo Badlands Overlook

TO OCOTILLO

Canyon Sin Nombre 56

Location: Northwest of Ocotillo, southwest of Ocotillo Wells.

Difficulty: Easy. Route follows mostly sandy wash bottom. Suitable for stock 4x4 SUVs. Don't park or camp near steep embankments. This is one of three major earthquake fault zones in southern California.

Features: A geologic wonderland that cuts through striking Carrizo Badlands. Follows Butterfield Stage Route through Vallecito Valley.

Time & Distance: Allow 1 1/2 to 2 hours for this 11.6-mile drive.

To Get There: Trail starts from Highway S2 between Sweeney Pass and the Carrizo Badlands Overlook approximately 13 miles northwest of Ocotillo.

Trail Description: *Reset odometer as you turn off Highway S2* [01]. Head northeast downhill. As you cut through the Carrizo Badlands you'll see a mixture of solid granite and folded sedimentary sandstone. Some of this rock is over 100 million years old and contains fossils from a time when the Colorado River flowed through the area. Note distinctive rock fold at 1.9 miles (see photo opposite page). Continue straight past a slot canyon tributary at 2.4 miles. People like to camp in these protected areas but they would be unsafe if an earthquake or flash flood were to occur. You exit Canyon Sin Nombre after 2.8 miles and begin following a wide, poorly defined, smoke-tree wash. By 3.7, massive Vallecito Valley can be seen ahead. Bear left at 4.0 before reaching Vallecito Wash at 4.3 miles (02). A hard left turn here would take you back out Carrizo Creek Road. Turn slightly left to follow Vallecito Wash. Stay to the right side of this very wide wash. Go straight at 5.5 miles (03) where Arroyo Seco del Diablo goes right. Stay right at 6.2. Continue straight again at 7.1 miles (04) where Arroyo Tapiado goes right. This is where you turn for Mud Caves/ Diablo Dropoff Trail #57. Continue straight past Hollywood and Vine sign at 9.0 and Palm Spring at 10.6. Road swings left at 11.3 before reaching Hwy. S2 at 11.6 miles (05).

Return Trip: Left goes to Ocotillo, right to Scissors Crossing at Hwy. 78.

Services: None along trail. Gas and food in Ocotillo near Interstate 8.

Maps: Anza-Borrego Desert Region Recreation Map, USGS 100,000 scale map El Cajon, CA, DeLorme Atlas & Gazetteer.

Large mud cave can be seen from main trail. Diablo Dropoff is steeper than photo shows.

Toughest part of trail is over this last ridge of the Diablo Dropoff. You can't turn around.

Typical rough spot. Collapsed wall partially blocks Arroyo Seco del Diablo.

Mud Caves/Diablo Dropoff ◆57◆

Location: Northwest of Ocotillo, southwest of Ocotillo Wells.

Difficulty: Difficult. This rating is primarily applied to the Diablo Dropoff. This stretch is steep and badly eroded with soft sand at the top. Above the the dropoff, the trail loops through two deeply cut washes of moderate difficulty. Canyon walls can collapse, however, partially or totally blocking the trail. This typically occurs after heavy rains and earthquakes. This area is an active earthquake fault zone. Don't stop, camp or picnic near steep cliffs or under overhangs. Stock 4x4 SUVs with high ground clearance should be able to complete this trail under normal conditions. This is potentially a dangerous area. Only you can determine if it is safe to proceed.

Features: The mud cave network in Anza-Borrego Desert State Park may be one of the largest in the world. At least 22 caves have been counted, some up to 1,000 feet long and 80 feet high. Thousands of people come here to explore the caves, even organized Boy Scout Troops. The park does not discourage visitors, but vehicles must park on the dirt road. When hiking in the caves, walk on cave bottoms only. Picnic outside the caves and pack out all trash.

Time & Distance: It is 11.3 miles from the start of Arroyo Tapiado to Fish Creek Wash and another 18 miles to Ocotillo Wells. Combined, Arroyo Tapiado and Arroyo Seco del Diablo measure 17.6 miles. Add time to reach the trail, explore the caves and return home. This usually adds up to at least a full day. You can also camp overnight and spend a weekend in the area.

To Get There: To reach the start as described here, follow directions to Canyon Sin Nombre, Trail #56. Turn right after 7.1 miles into Arroyo Tapiado Wash.

If you are coming from Julian or Borrego Springs on Highway 78, follow Highway S2 south about 27 miles and turn left at sign for Palm Spring near mile post 43. The road swings right after 0.3 miles and follows Vallecito Wash another 4.2 miles to Arroyo Tapiado on the left.

If you have a hardcore vehicle with lockers, you can drive to the Mud Caves from Fish Creek Wash. This requires that you drive up difficult Diablo Dropoff. Follow directions for Sandstone Canyon, Trail #55.

Trail Description: Reset your odometer at the start of Arroyo Tapiado (01). Head north in a wide wash. Bear right at 1.2 miles (02) following cairns. The road enters mud hills and becomes better defined. I ran into several vehicles parked along the road at 2.3 miles (03). Stop here and explore the area on foot. Several of the larger mud caves are located in this area.

After checking out the caves, continue north. I reached a point at 3.2 miles where the canyon wall collapsed and partially blocked the road. Enough people had gotten through to make it passable. Bear right at 6.0 where a lesser wash goes left. Bear right and climb out of the main wash at 6.4 miles (04) at a sign marked Arroyo Diablo Turnoff. A road curves around and heads south across Middle Mesa. Turn right at 8.7 miles into the Arroyo Seco del Diablo. At 8.9 miles (05), you must decide whether to continue south back to Vallecito Wash or turn left and go down the Diablo Dropoff to Fish Creek.

To reach Fish Creek: Turn left out of Diablo Wash. A small sign marked this turn. Head north across Middle Mesa. Continue straight past an overlook at 9.8 before reaching the dropoff at 10.3 miles (06). Don't descend the dropoff unless your destination is Ocotillo Wells. Getting back up is very difficult. Sandy moguls at the top are not too bad going down. The tough part is closer to the bottom where a steep ridge must be descended. It's very rutted and washed out. Good ground clearance is needed to get down. After you get through this spot, you drop into a rocky wash and turn right. The wash is not wide enough to pass another vehicle so check ahead. Fish Creek Wash is reached at 11.3 miles (07). Turn right and follow directions in the last paragraph of the trail description for Pinyon Mountain Road, Trail #54.

To complete Arroyo Seco del Diablo: *Reset your odometer* and continue south in the wash. The wash is narrow in places with several collapsed spots. I spotted what appeared to be more mud caves at 2.2 miles. Bear left at 3.3. The canyon begins to widen at 4.5 miles before reaching Vallecito Wash at 6.3 miles (08).

Return Trip: Left takes you through Canyon Sin Nombre, Trail #56 (in reverse direction) and is the shortest way to Ocotillo near Interstate 8. Right follows Vallecito Wash back to Hwy. S2 near the sign for Palm Spring (use directions for Canyon Sin Nombre). This is the shortest way to Julian and Borrego Springs.

Services: None along trail. Gas is available in Ocotillo, Julian, Borrego Springs and 6 miles east of Ocotillo Wells on Hwy. 78.

Maps: Anza-Borrego Desert Region Recreation Map, USGS 100,000-scale map El Cajon, CA, DeLorme Atlas & Gazetteer.

Mud Caves/Diablo Dropoff

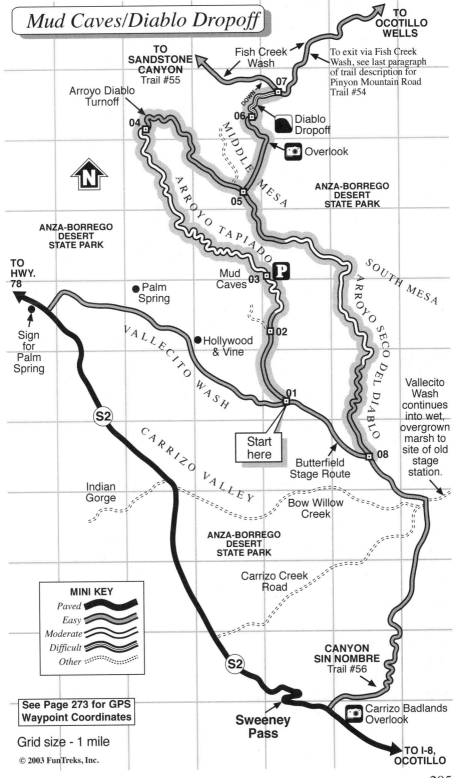

TO OCOTILLO WELLS

TO SANDSTONE CANYON
Trail #55

Fish Creek Wash

To exit via Fish Creek Wash, see last paragraph of trail description for Pinyon Mountain Road Trail #54

07

DOWN

Arroyo Diablo Turnoff

04

06

Diablo Dropoff

Overlook

MIDDLE MESA

ANZA-BORREGO DESERT STATE PARK

N

05

ARROYO TAPIADO

ANZA-BORREGO DESERT STATE PARK

SOUTH MESA

TO HWY. 78

Palm Spring

Mud Caves

03

P

ARROYO SECO DEL DIABLO

02

Sign for Palm Spring

Hollywood & Vine

VALLECITO WASH

S2

01

Start here

Butterfield Stage Route

08

Vallecito Wash continues into wet, overgrown marsh to site of old stage station.

CARRIZO VALLEY

Indian Gorge

Bow Willow Creek

ANZA-BORREGO DESERT STATE PARK

Carrizo Creek Road

MINI KEY

Paved
Easy
Moderate
Difficult
Other

CANYON SIN NOMBRE
Trail #56

S2

See Page 273 for GPS Waypoint Coordinates

Sweeney Pass

Carrizo Badlands Overlook

Grid size - 1 mile

© 2003 FunTreks, Inc.

TO I-8, OCOTILLO

205

Piedras Grandes looms over Dos Cabezas.

Water tower at Dos Cabezas station.

Stock SUV climbs over rock ledge.

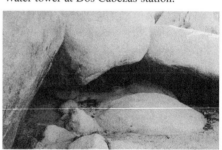
Boulder-sheltered camp spot.

One of 21 tunnels through Carrizo Gorge.

Goat Canyon Trestle.

Mortero Wash 58

Location: West of Ocotillo.

Difficulty: Moderate. One rocky ledge requires high ground clearance and four-wheel drive. Unpredictable conditions where trail climbs in and out of rutted, sandy washes. Deep, soft sand has stranded many motorists. Most of trail is easy and suitable for stock 4x4 SUVs. Dangerously hot in summer. Watch for illegal immigrants and don't leave your vehicle unattended.

Features: A remote drive into rugged desert backcountry. See remains of an historic railroad station. Take a short hike to Indian Hill, one of the oldest Native American campsites in Anza-Borrego Desert State Park. Here you'll find outstanding pictographs in fire-blackened caves. Serious hikers can depart from Mortero Palms to remote Carrizo Gorge and Goat Canyon to see one of the highest, curved wooden trestles in the world. Do not camp or build fires near pictographs. Art has been damaged by illegal fires.

Time & Distance: Just under 18 miles as described here. Allow about 3 hours driving time. Add time for stops, side trips and hikes.

To Get There: At a sign for Mortero Wash, turn south off Highway S2 about 0.2 miles west of mile post 56. This point is about 8 miles northwest of Ocotillo at Interstate 8.

Trail Description: Reset odometer as you leave Highway S2 [01]. Head south on a graded washboard road. Signage restricting entry to side roads helps keep you on the correct route. After a couple of miles, follow a sandy wash through Mortero Canyon. The road winds through a mixture of rock and sand and soon the water tower can be seen ahead. As you near the tower, a road from the Cabezas Mine joins on the right at 4.0 miles. Bear left to the water tower when the road forks at 4.1 miles (02).

After taking a few minutes to check out the area, turn around and head west alongside the railroad tracks. Cross a sandy wash spanned by a trestle. Continue straight at 4.5 miles as the road from Cabezas Mine joins on the right. Continue alongside the tracks ignoring side roads. The road ends where it drops into a wash at 6.4 miles (03). If you have someone to watch your car, you can park here and hike to Indian Hill about a mile. Details of this hike can be found in *Afoot and Afield in San Diego County* by Jerry Schad (see appendix). It is illegal to hike along the railroad tracks. Watch for illegal immigrants using tracks as escape route from Mexico.

Return to the water tank, bear right and cross the tracks. Head south 1.2 miles from the water tank where an optional side trip goes right to an area called Piedras Grandes (meaning large rocks). An interesting boulder outcrop is just 0.2 miles down this side road. Shade and wind protection make this a good place to take a break. Native Americans also found this place appealing. Evidence of this can be found in the form of pictographs and morteros scattered around the area. Do not build fires or camp near pictographs. You can continue down this side road but it eventually dead ends.

Reset your odometer when you return to the main trail. Turn right and continue south. Continue to bear right as roads join on the left. At one point, you'll climb over a small rock ledge. Several roads converge at 1.0 miles (04). Right goes to Mortero Palms, straight goes to Dos Cabezas Spring and left continues to Hayden Spring. (Mortero Palms is a departure point for a hiking trail to Goat Canyon Trestle. It's an all-day adventure, quite difficult and easy to get lost. For detailed information, once again, refer to Jerry Schad's book. See appendix.)

Continue east following signs to Hayden Spring. Continue straight at 1.9, then bear left at 2.6 where Hayden Spring goes right. Bear left at 3.5 miles (05). Cross tracks at 3.9 and head north on a less-distinct road that parallels the tracks. You will not cross the tracks again. You eventually join a larger road that heads east around the north side of the tracks as they curve right. Bear left off this larger road at 6.2 miles (06) and head northeast. Go straight at 7.7 before reaching Highway S2 at 8.0 miles (07).

Return Trip: Right on S2 goes to Ocotillo and Interstate 8 (about 6 miles).

Services: None on trail. All camp spots primitive. Gas and food in Ocotillo.

Historical Highlights: Dubbed "The Impossible Railroad," The San Diego & Arizona Eastern Railroad (later San Diego & Imperial Valley) took an incredible 12 years to build. A super-human effort was required to complete the 11-mile stretch through hellish Carrizo Gorge. Twenty-one tunnels and 14 trestles were constructed through this section. The railroad finally opened in 1919 and stayed in operation over 50 years despite numerous major setbacks. In 1976, flash floods from tropical storm Kathleen destroyed dozens of trestles, effectively dooming the railroad. It opened briefly before finally closing in 1983. The tracks are still in excellent shape.

Maps: Anza-Borrego Desert Region Recreation Map, USGS 100,000-scale map El Cajon, CA, DeLorme Atlas & Gazetteer.

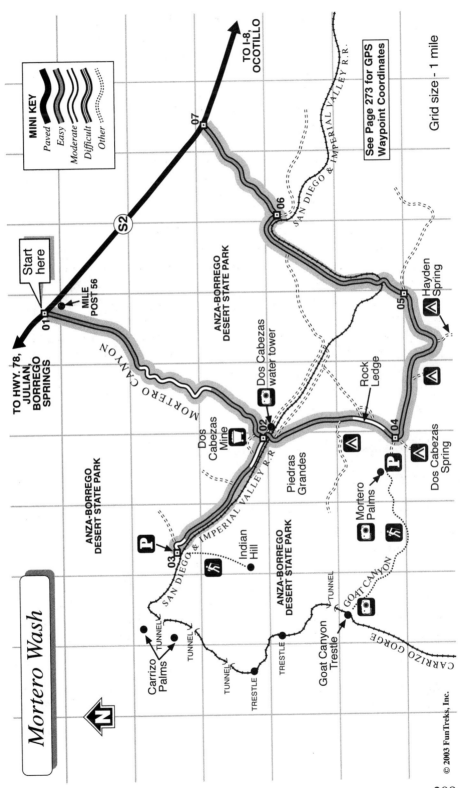

Mortero Wash

MINI KEY
Paved
Easy
Moderate
Difficult
Other

See Page 273 for GPS Waypoint Coordinates

Grid size - 1 mile

TO I-8, OCOTILLO

Start here

MILE POST 56

TO HWY. 78, JULIAN, BORREGO SPRINGS

S2

07

06

05

04

02

03

N

ANZA-BORREGO DESERT STATE PARK

ANZA-BORREGO DESERT STATE PARK

ANZA-BORREGO DESERT STATE PARK

MORTERO CANYON

SAN DIEGO & IMPERIAL VALLEY R.R.

SAN DIEGO & IMPERIAL VALLEY R.R.

Dos Cabezas water tower

Dos Cabezas Mine

Piedras Grandes

Rock Ledge

Mortero Palms

Dos Cabezas Spring

Hayden Spring

Indian Hill

Carrizo Palms

TUNNEL

TUNNEL

TUNNEL

TUNNEL

TRESTLE

TRESTLE

TRESTLE

Goat Canyon Trestle

GOAT CANYON

CARRIZO GORGE

© 2003 FunTreks, Inc.

209

Lookout tower barely visible atop Los Pinos Mountain.

Looking back at Corral Canyon from tower.

Tough spot on Espinosa Trail.

This clearing on Espinosa Trail is a good place to stop for lunch.

Los Pinos Lookout 59

Location: About 50 miles east of San Diego and south of Interstate 8 at Buckman Springs exit. Follow signs to Corral Canyon OHV Area.

Difficulty: Moderate. Climbs a rough shelf road to the top of Los Pinos Mountain. This section gets very muddy and slippery when it rains. The toughest part of route descends Espinosa Trail which follows a narrow, rough ravine. Suitable for aggressive stock 4x4 SUVs with high ground clearance, skid plates and good articulation. Tight brush in places. Very hot in the summer.

Features: Visit Los Pinos Mountain Lookout Tower. If the gate is open, rangers will usually allow you to climb the tower. Explore remote and challenging backcountry as you make a large loop around Corral Canyon OHV Area. Camp at established campgrounds while trying other nearby trails. This is a great area for ATVs and dirt bikes. The Cleveland National Forest has detailed maps of the OHV area which show dirt bike and ATV routes. Maps are available at the Descanso Ranger Station in Alpine (see appendix). Maps are also posted on large information panels at Four Corners Trailhead and the two campgrounds.

Make sure you stay on the designated trail while driving the Los Pinos route. Most of the land outside the loop is either wilderness or private. All offroad travel must be done within the boundary of the OHV open area. Two play areas are also available (see map). Follow all posted regulations.

Lake Morena County Park is located just east of Corral Canyon. Although the northern portion of the park was closed due to low water at the time of this writing, the southern portion (not shown on map) remains open. The 3,250-acre park offers fishing, small boat rentals, campgrounds with water and electric hookups, hiking and picnicking. To reach the southern portion of the park continue south on Buckman Springs Road.

Time & Distance: Allow about 3 hours driving time for this 19.7-mile trip. Add time to visit the lookout tower and explore the OHV area.

To Get There: Take Interstate 8 to the Buckman Springs exit. This exit has a rest stop. Head south on Buckman Springs Road 3.3 miles to Corral Canyon Road. Turn right and go 5.8 miles west to a parking area near a paved 4-way intersection called Four Corners.

Trail Description: *Reset odometer at Four Corners* [01]. Turn right following sign (Los Pinos 16S17). Head uphill on a rough dirt road. Turn right at 2.3 miles to reach the lookout tower. Return to the trail and proceed down the back side of Los Pinos Mountain. The trail narrows as it passes through sparse evergreens. At 4.6 miles (02), (counting the mileage to the lookout tower), turn left onto a lesser road marked with an adopt-a-trail sign. The road drops into a wooded ravine. Several places are steep with good size boulders. Go by water storage tanks at 5.4. A clearing at 6.5 is a good place to stop for lunch. Continue straight at 7.0 at what appears to be a road joining on the left.

Turn left when you reach a better road at 7.7 miles (03). The road climbs in places and is deeply rutted. Bear left at 8.6. Bear left at 10.1 miles (04) where roads converge. Avoid the temptation to go right here. Bear right at 11.4 and 11.7 miles. Bear left at a T at 11.8 miles (05). You should now be on Skye Valley Road. Go right where Corral Canyon Road goes left at 13.7 miles (06). Continue straight at 15.7 where Bronco Flats joins on the left. (Bronco Flats is the second part of Bronco Peak Trail #60.) Bear left at a curve at 16.6. You reach Bobcat Meadow Campground at 18.7 miles. From here, the road is paved as it returns to the original starting point at 19.7 miles (01).

Return Trip: Return via Corral Canyon Road the way you came in.

Services: Vault toilets at Bobcat Meadow and Corral Canyon Campgrounds. Gas is available north on I-8 at Pine Valley, south on Buckman Springs Road at Campo and east on I-8 at the Golden Acorn Casino at the Crestwood/ Live Oak Springs exit.

Maps: Corral Canyon OHV Area map (available at the Descanso Ranger District Office in Alpine), Cleveland National Forest, USGS 100,000-scale map of El Cajon, CA, DeLorme Atlas & Gazetteer.

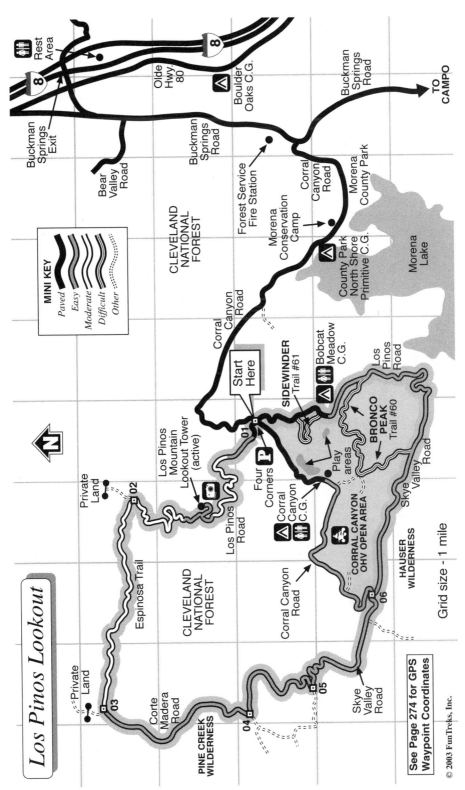

Los Pinos Lookout

MINI KEY
Paved
Easy
Moderate
Difficult
Other

N

Rest Area

8

8

Buckman Springs Exit

Bear Valley Road

Olde Hwy. 80

Buckman Springs Road

Buckman Springs Road

Boulder Oaks C.G.

Buckman Springs Road

TO CAMPO

Forest Service Fire Station

Morena Conservation Camp

Corral Canyon Road

Morena County Park

CLEVELAND NATIONAL FOREST

Corral Canyon Road

County Park North Shore Primitive C.G.

Morena Lake

Start Here

SIDEWINDER Trail #61

Bobcat Meadow C.G.

Los Pinos Road

01

Los Pinos Mountain Lookout Tower (active)

Four Corners

P

Corral Canyon C.G.

Play areas

BRONCO PEAK Trail #60

Skye Valley Road

Private Land

02

Espinosa Trail

CLEVELAND NATIONAL FOREST

Los Pinos Road

CORRAL CANYON OHV OPEN AREA

HAUSER WILDERNESS

Corral Canyon Road

06

Grid size - 1 mile

Private Land

03

Corte Madera Road

PINE CREEK WILDERNESS

04

05

Skye Valley Road

See Page 274 for GPS Waypoint Coordinates

© 2003 FunTreks, Inc.

Starting down from Bronco Peak.

Typical terrain.

Toughest obstacle.

214

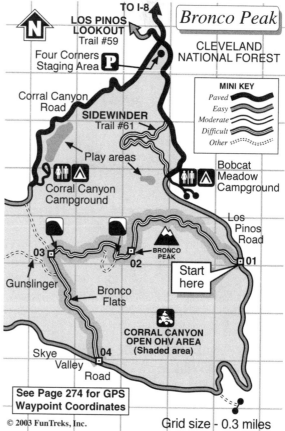

Bronco Peak

TO I-8

LOS PINOS LOOKOUT
Trail #59

CLEVELAND NATIONAL FOREST

Four Corners Staging Area P

Corral Canyon Road

SIDEWINDER
Trail #61

MINI KEY
Paved
Easy
Moderate
Difficult
Other

Play areas

Bobcat Meadow Campground

Corral Canyon Campground

Los Pinos Road

BRONCO PEAK

Start here

03 Gunslinger

02

01

Bronco Flats

CORRAL CANYON OPEN OHV AREA
(Shaded area)

Skye Valley Road

04

See Page 274 for GPS Waypoint Coordinates

© 2003 FunTreks, Inc.

Grid size - 0.3 miles

Bronco Peak ◆60◆

Location: About 50 miles east of San Diego and south of Interstate 8 at Buckman Springs exit. Inside Corral Canyon OHV Area.

Difficulty: Difficult. A nasty hardcore trail that climbs up and down gnarly Bronco Peak. Very steep with tight brush and large boulders. Several places are steep enough to cause a rollover if driver is not careful. Front and rear lockers recommended. Hot in the summer. Watch for snakes and poison oak.

Features: A fun, rock-crawling challenge. Rapidly climbs to an elevation above 4100 feet then quickly drops 700 feet into a canyon.

Time & Distance: Allow 1 to 2 hours for this 2.7-mile challenge. With large groups or marginally equipped vehicles, add more time.

To Get There: Follow directions to Corral Canyon OHV Area as described in Los Pinos Lookout Trail #59. When you reach the Four Corners parking area, bear left heading south on a narrow, paved road. Once you reach Bobcat Meadow Campground, continue another 0.8 miles, after the road turns to dirt, to an unmarked trail on the right.

Trail Description: Reset your odometer at the start (01). Head west uphill on a road that quickly deteriorates. At 0.7 miles, a dirt bike/ATV trail crosses at a shallow angle. Bear left then immediately right as you cross the other trail. Watch for speeding dirt bikes. Cross over the top of Bronco Peak at 1.1 miles (02). At 1.3 miles, the main trail appears to go downhill. You turn right uphill on lesser tracks. A difficult downhill section follows immediately. Vehicles have rolled here so be careful. The toughest spot is reached at 1.9 miles (03) just before you intersect with Bronco Flats Trail. Turn left (right is extremely difficult). Stay left at 2.0 where Gunslinger Trail intersects. Continue to bear left until you reach the main road at 2.7 miles (04).

Return Trip: Head east, then north to get back to Bobcat Meadow Campground. From there, go out the way you came in.

Services: Vault toilets at campgrounds. Gas available north at Pine Valley, south at Campo and east on I-8 at the Crestwood/ Live Oak Springs exit.

Maps: Corral Canyon OHV Area map, Cleveland National Forest, USGS 7.5-minute map of Morena Reservoir, CA, DeLorme Atlas & Gazetteer.

Make sure everything inside is tied down.   Last obstacle is a tough one.

Getting advice on tire placement.   Lunch break at Bobcat Meadow Campground.

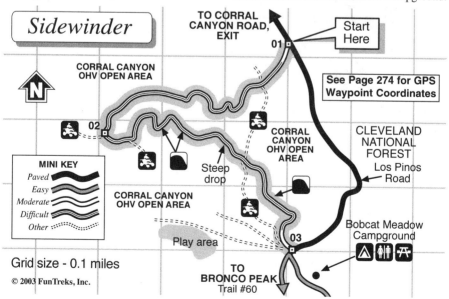

Sidewinder

TO CORRAL
CANYON ROAD,
EXIT

Start
Here

01

CORRAL CANYON
OHV OPEN AREA

N

See Page 274 for GPS
Waypoint Coordinates

02

CLEVELAND
NATIONAL
FOREST

CORRAL
CANYON
OHV OPEN
AREA

Los Pinos
Road

MINI KEY
Paved
Easy
Moderate
Difficult
Other

Steep
drop

CORRAL CANYON
OHV OPEN AREA

Bobcat Meadow
Campground

Play area

03

Grid size - 0.1 miles

© 2003 FunTreks, Inc.

TO
BRONCO PEAK
Trail #60

216

Sidewinder ◆61◆

Location: About 50 miles east of San Diego and south of Interstate 8 at Buckman Springs exit. Inside Corral Canyon OHV Area.

Difficulty: Difficult. Steep, unforgiving rock slabs and boulders. Lockers and high ground clearance a must. Tight, scratchy brush. Not for stock vehicles. Very hot in summer. Watch for snakes and poison oak.

Features: Although this trail is short, it's packed with obstacles from start to finish. Conveniently finishes at Bobcat Meadow Campground.

Time & Distance: Total length of trail is just one mile. Can be driven in about an hour if all goes well. Add time for large groups.

To Get There: Follow directions to Corral Canyon OHV Area as described in Los Pinos Lookout Trail #59. When you reach Four Corners parking area, bear left and go another 0.6 miles on a narrow paved road. The unmarked road on the right is start of trail.

Trail Description: Reset your odometer at the start (01). Head southwest on a single-lane dirt road. Watch for ATVs and dirt bikes crossing at 0.1. Trail weaves west through a long stretch of tight brush and rock slabs. Drop down into a shady area and bear left at 0.4 miles (02). A dirt bike trail goes right. From this point, Sidewinder circles around and heads back to the paved road. At 0.5 bear left uphill where another dirt bike trail goes right. Driver's choice at 0.6; left is more difficult. At 0.7 you must cross a large tilted rock. I went high to the left, then squared up as much as possible as I turned downhill to the right. A steep drop follows before crossing another trail at 0.8. Driver's choice on the last obstacle at 0.9. Both sides are difficult and will test your articulation to the maximum. Trail ends at 1.0 miles (03) near the entrance to Bobcat Meadow Campground.

Return Trip: Left on the paved road takes you back to Four Corners. From there, go out the way you came in.

Services: Vault toilets at campgrounds. Gas available north at Pine Valley, south at Campo and east on I-8 at the Crestwood/ Live Oak Springs exit.

Maps: Corral Canyon OHV Area map, Cleveland National Forest, USGS 7.5-minute map of Morena Reservoir, CA, DeLorme Atlas & Gazetteer.

Area restricted to vehicles 40 inches wide or less. Stay on established routes.

View from Carrizo Overlook.

Carrizo Overlook has a few picnic tables.

McCain Valley Road.

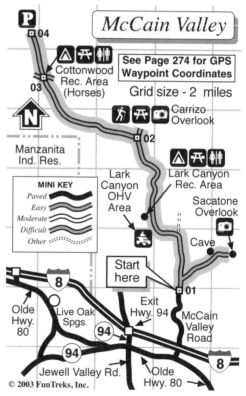

McCain Valley

See Page 274 for GPS Waypoint Coordinates

Grid size - 2 miles

P — 04

Cottonwood Rec. Area (Horses)
03

N

Carrizo Overlook
02

Manzanita Ind. Res.

MINI KEY
Paved
Easy
Moderate
Difficult
Other

Lark Canyon OHV Area

Lark Canyon Rec. Area

Sacatone Overlook

Cave

Start here

01

8

Olde Hwy. 80

Live Oak Spgs.

Exit Hwy. 94

94

McCain Valley Road

94

Jewell Valley Rd.

Olde Hwy. 80

8

© 2003 FunTreks, Inc.

218

McCain Valley 62

Location: About 65 miles east of San Diego, 20 miles west of Ocotillo.

Difficulty: Easy. Graded/washboard road suitable for all SUVs and many passenger cars. Side trip to Sacatone Overlook is slightly rougher. Terrain within boundary of OHV area provides trails at all difficulty levels.

Features: Scenic drive with side trips to several interesting overlooks. Accesses Lark Canyon Recreation Site for ATVs and dirt bikes.

Time & Distance: Dirt road portion measures 12.2 miles one way. Allow 2 to 3 hours to get out and back. Add time for side trips.

To Get There: Get off Interstate 8 at the Boulevard/Jewell Valley exit, Highway 94. Head south about a half mile and turn left on Olde Highway 80. Go 1.8 miles east and turn left on McCain Valley Road. Head north underneath freeway. Pavement ends in a couple of miles.

Trail Description: Reset odometer when pavement ends (01). Continue north on wide dirt road passing a restricted conservation camp. Sacatone Overlook on right at 0.4 miles (see description below). Lark Canyon OHV area on left at 2.6 miles followed by Lark Canyon Recreation Site. Carrizo Scenic Overlook on right at 6.4 miles (02) (see description below). Cottonwood Recreation Site is reached at 10.5 miles (03). McCain Valley Road ends uneventfully at 12.2 miles (04).

The side trip to *Sacatone Overlook* is about 2 miles one way. You'll pass an interesting but unidentified cave on the left after 1.6 miles. Side roads branch off before overlook which provides views of Carrizo Gorge.

The side trip to *Carrizo Scenic Overlook* is just 0.2 miles. An interpretive panel describes the incredible view of the Carrizo Corridor including Vallecito Valley and Carrizo Gorge.

Return Trip: Return the way you came.

Services: Self-pay campsites at Recreation Areas include vault toilets, picnic tables and fire rings. Cottonwood Recreation Site is for equestrians. Gas is available at the Golden Acorn Casino which is the next exit west on I-8.

Maps: USGS 250,000 scale map San Diego, CA, DeLorme Atlas & Gazetteer.

219

Valley flattens out north of Table Mountain.

Good camping at these boulders.

Hike to this view of Carrizo Gorge (looking north).

Looking south to Round Mountain.

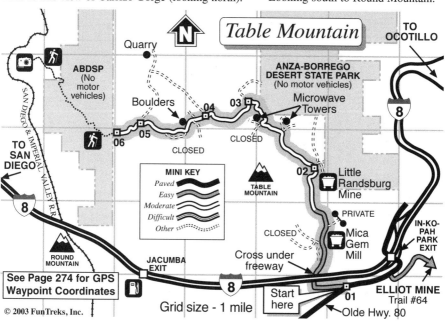

Table Mountain

TO OCOTILLO

Quarry

ABDSP
(No motor vehicles)

ANZA-BORREGO DESERT STATE PARK
(No motor vehicles)

Microwave Towers

8

Boulders

04

03

CLOSED

SAN DIEGO & IMPERIAL VALLEY R.R.

06 05

CLOSED

TO SAN DIEGO

8

MINI KEY
Paved
Easy
Moderate
Difficult
Other

TABLE MOUNTAIN

02

Little Randsburg Mine

PRIVATE

CLOSED

Mica Gem Mill

IN-KO-PAH PARK EXIT

ROUND MOUNTAIN

JACUMBA EXIT

Cross under freeway

See Page 274 for GPS Waypoint Coordinates

© 2003 FunTreks, Inc.

8

Grid size - 1 mile

Start here

01

Olde Hwy. 80

ELLIOT MINE
Trail #64

220

Table Mountain

Location: About 72 miles east of San Diego and 12 miles SW of Ocotillo.

Difficulty: Moderate. Mild rocky climbs and washes with soft sand. Suitable for aggressive stock 4x4 SUVs. Very hot in summer.

Features: Remote and scenic high desert drive. Hike from end of trail to ridge overlooking Carrizo Gorge with views of the historic San Diego and Imperial Valley Railroad, Table Mountain and Jacumba Valley.

Time & Distance: Trip is 6.2 miles one way. Allow 2 to 3 hours round trip. Hike is 2.2 miles one way but the last mile is very steep.

To Get There: Exit Interstate 8 at In-Ko-Pah Road. Follow Olde Hwy. 80 southwest along freeway 0.9 miles. Turn right onto a dirt road near the freeway brake-check station.

Trail Description: Reset your odometer as you turn off Olde Hwy. 80 (01). Head west and turn right under freeway at 0.5 miles. Head north avoiding roads that branch off to the left towards Table Mountain. After passing Mica Gem Mill, visible on the right, bear left at 1.3 miles where a private road goes right. At 2.3 miles (02), take the far left fork of three. The road gets rockier and begins to climb. Bear left as you approach a microwave tower at 3.1. Climb a ridge at 3.4 and bear right. The road to the left dead ends. Stay right of the second microwave tower.

At 3.9 miles (03), turn left and head downhill. The road begins to flatten out. Continue straight at 4.2 then bear left at 4.6 miles (04). Continue straight at 4.8 and 4.9. After passing a large group of boulders at 5.0, turn right into a sandy wash. Bear right out of the wash when it ends at 5.4. At 5.8 miles (05), a road goes right uphill. You turn left and drop into a wash. Once in the wash turn right and follow it. Turn right out of this wash at 6.0 and head uphill. Stop at 6.2 miles (06) where wilderness begins (not marked). Hiking trail follows closed 4WD road northwest over ridge, through another wash, then climbs steeply up switchbacks to high point above Carrizo Gorge.

Return Trip: Return the way you came.

Services: Closest gas at Jacumba exit, about 4 miles west on Interstate 8.

Maps: USGS 100K map El Cajon, CA, Sidekick Map, DeLorme Atlas & Gazetteer.

Coming down from Elliot Mine.   Smugglers Cave.

Valley of the Moon as seen from Elliot Mine.   One of several mine shafts.

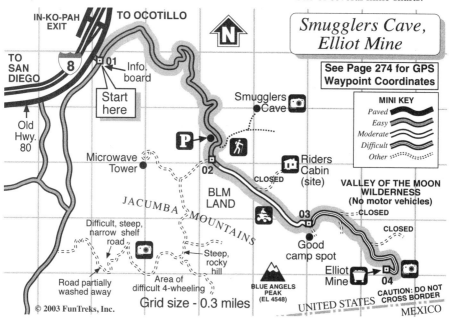

IN-KO-PAH EXIT

TO OCOTILLO

N

Smugglers Cave, Elliot Mine

TO SAN DIEGO

8

01 Info. board

See Page 274 for GPS Waypoint Coordinates

Start here

Old Hwy. 80

Smugglers Cave

MINI KEY
Paved
Easy
Moderate
Difficult
Other

P

Microwave Tower

02

Riders Cabin (site)

CLOSED

VALLEY OF THE MOON WILDERNESS (No motor vehicles)

JACUMBA

BLM LAND

MOUNTAINS

03

CLOSED

CLOSED

Difficult, steep, narrow shelf road

Good camp spot

Steep, rocky hill

Elliot Mine

04

Road partially washed away

Area of difficult 4-wheeling

BLUE ANGELS PEAK (EL 4548)

CAUTION: DO NOT CROSS BORDER

© 2003 FunTreks, Inc.

Grid size - 0.3 miles

UNITED STATES

MEXICO

222

Smugglers Cave/ Elliot Mine

64

Location: About 72 miles east of San Diego and 12 miles southwest of Ocotillo. South of Interstate 8 near the U.S./Mexico border.

Difficulty: Difficult. Most of trail is easy to moderate. Last portion nearing Elliot Mine is narrow, rocky shelf road. Aggressive, stock 4x4 SUVs with high ground clearance can make it. Ends only 1/4 mile from U.S. border.

Features: Captivating drive into unique mountainous area. Short hike to Smugglers Cave. Good rock-crawling to Elliot Mine where you can look down on dramatic Valley of the Moon Wilderness. Heavily patrolled by U.S. Border Patrol. Be careful not to wander over Mexican border or risk arrest and confiscation of vehicle. Watch for illegal immigrants.

Time & Distance: Just 3.2 miles to Elliot Mine. Allow about 2 hours for round trip. Add time to explore area.

To Get There: Exit Interstate 8 at In-Ko-Pah Road. From southeast side of freeway, follow Old Highway 80 south about 0.2 miles. Turn left at kiosk.

Trail Description: Reset your odometer at the information board (01). Follow dirt road northeast. Continue straight at 0.3. The road curves right and heads uphill. To hike to Smugglers Cave, park on right at 1.5 miles. Walk uphill, climb over ridge on left side of road and hike down old 4WD road 0.3 miles northeast to cave. After hike, continue uphill. Bear left when the road forks at 1.6 miles (02). Right goes to microwave towers and several difficult 4WD roads. Continue straight down first moderate challenge at 1.8 miles. Bear right at 2.0. Road to left is now closed. Bear left at 2.4 (03). Good camp spot on right. Continue straight at 2.6, then immediately bear left uphill ignoring closed road on right. Stay right uphill at 2.8. Road to left is now closed. Road becomes steep and difficult. Bear left at 2.9 and 3.1. One tight squeeze before you reach the top at 3.2 miles (04). Explore the area where you'll find several large open mine shafts. Be careful; watch the kids.

Return Trip: Return the way you came.

Services: Closest gas at Jacumba exit, about 4 miles west on Interstate 8.

Maps: USGS 7.5-min. map In-Ko-Pah Gorge, CA, Sidekick Map Smugglers Cave & Table Mountain, DeLorme Atlas & Gazetteer.

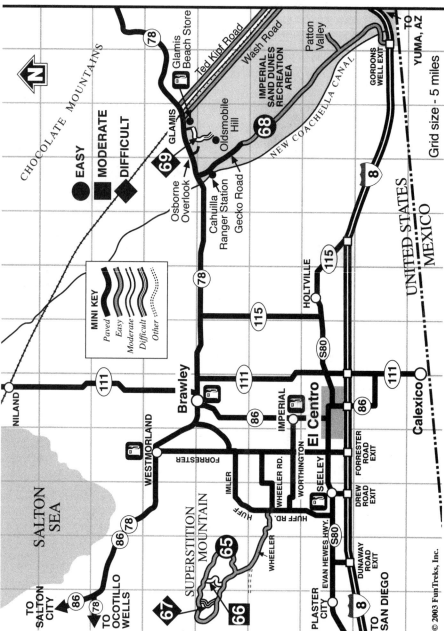

AREA 9

Superstition Mountain, Imperial Sand Dunes

65. Superstition Mountain Loop
66. Sand Dam Canyon
67. Knock-on-Wood
68. Sand Highway
69. Glamis/Oldsmobile Hill

MINI KEY
Paved
Easy
Moderate
Difficult
Other

EASY
MODERATE
DIFFICULT

CHOCOLATE MOUNTAINS

Glamis Beach Store
Ted Kipf Road
Wash Road
Patton Valley

IMPERIAL SAND DUNES RECREATION AREA

78

GLAMIS

69

Osborne Overlook
Cahuilla Ranger Station
Gecko Road
Oldsmobile Hill

68

NEW COACHELLA CANAL

GORDONS WELL EXIT

8

TO YUMA, AZ

Grid size - 5 miles

HOLTVILLE

115

115

S80

111

111

86

Brawley

86

IMPERIAL

El Centro

SEELEY

WESTMORLAND

FORRESTER

IMLER

WHEELER RD.

HUFF RD.

WORTHINGTON

WHEELER

HUFF

EVAN HEWES HWY.

S80

DREW ROAD EXIT

FORRESTER ROAD EXIT

DUNAWAY ROAD EXIT

PLASTER CITY

8

TO SAN DIEGO

SUPERSTITION MOUNTAIN

65

67

66

SALTON SEA

NILAND

111

78

86

78

86

78

TO SALTON CITY

TO OCOTILLO WELLS

Calexico

111

86

UNITED STATES
MEXICO

© 2003 FunTreks, Inc.

224

Superstition Mountain, Imperial Sand Dunes

Rising from barren desert on a forgotten parcel of land between Navy bombing ranges, Superstition Mountain offers a variety of offroad opportunities, perhaps unmatched anywhere in southern California. Drivers of all vehicle types are free to roam a special mountain replete with backcountry surprises. Find rock-crawling challenges as difficult as you like in remote canyons or cruise easy rolling sand dunes sized just right for Jeeps and SUVs. The mountain is best understood by the San Diego 4-Wheelers who have explored and charted the area for years. In mid January, the club sponsors a popular run attended by hundreds of excited four wheelers. Base camp is set up on the desert floor south of the mountain near the information board.

No four-wheel-drive book on southern California would be complete without some coverage of Glamis and the Imperial Dunes Recreation Area. Although this well-publicized area is most popular with dune-buggy, ATV and dirt bike riders, everyone should drive, at least once, this incredible creation of mother nature. Trails in this book were selected especially for SUV and Jeep owners looking to get a taste of the area.

Lucky Lady, optional shortcut described in *Superstition Mountain Loop, Trail #65.*

From information board, Lucky Lady is north through valley. Superstition Mtn. Loop is right.

Go around wall of sand that blocks Poleline Road.

Leaving Tower #1 on Lucky Lady Trail.

Optional Jamie's Obstacle.

Optional Wrangler Canyon.   Optional Sand Slide Canyon.   ATVs climb south side.

Superstition Mountain Loop 65

Location: Northwest of El Centro, south of the Salton Sea.

Difficulty: Easy. Winds through an area of shallow, deeply cut washes and small shifting sand dunes. In all cases, easy options are available. Lucky Lady Trail is a more interesting shortcut across the mountain. It's somewhat more challenging because of shifting sands and complex route-finding. Difficult Wrangler Canyon, Jamie's Obstacle and Sand Slide Canyon are optional side trips. (Route-finding tip: Use the three towers, blockhouse and paved roads for directional landmarks.)

Features: If you're not familiar with the mountain, it is suggested that you drive the loop trail first. All other trails eventually feed back to this route. Once you recognize the route, you can find your way home easier. Camp on the desert floor in a large flat area south of the information board. The ground is firm here and well-suited for motorhomes and large campers.

Time & Distance: The main loop is less than 17 miles and takes 2-3 hours. Lucky Lady shortens the trip by about 2 miles, but can take longer.

To Get There: (Refer to Area 9 map.) Get off Interstate 8 at Dunaway Road or Drew Road west of El Centro. Take S80 east or west to Huff Road. Follow Huff Road north about 6.3 miles. Turn left on Wheeler after you go by Wheeler Road on the right (*Reset odometer*). Stay on this wide dirt road as it heads west then northwest. After 4.6 miles, bear right heading almost north. You should see the information board near a fork at 6.8 miles.

From points north, head south on Forrester Road at Westmoreland from Highway 86. After about 8 miles, turn west on Imler Road. After it swings south (and becomes Huff Rd.), turn west on Wheeler after two dips.

Trail Description: Reset odometer at the fork near the information board (01). Bear right and follow the best traveled road. Stay straight at 1.2 miles where a fork goes left. The main road gradually curves around to the right. Drive away from the mountain before intersecting with Poleline Road at 2.5 miles (02). Turn left and follow the road along the power lines. I ran into a large wall of sand at 3.2 miles but circled around it on the right side. The road curves back and forth under the power lines as it cuts across washes and more sand obstructions. Cross the first paved road at 3.9. A wash at 6.2 miles (03) goes left to Wrangler Canyon. (See directions next page.)

Continue following power lines and cross second paved road at 6.4. At 7.4 miles (04), pass entrance to Sand Dam Canyon, Trail #66, at left. The turn for Jamie's Obstacle is on the left at 7.7 miles (05). (See directions next page.)

227

After 8.3 miles, you must stay on the road. The surrounding area is no longer open to cross-country travel. Continue to follow the poles where a road goes left at 8.4. You reach the third paved road at 8.6 miles. At this point, the power lines turn south and follow the paved road. Cross the paved road and continue west. A road to Knock-on-Wood, Trail #67, goes left at 9.7 miles (06).

Continue west. Bear right at 10.4 where a lesser road goes left. Turn south on a wide road at 10.9 miles (07). Roads begin to take off in all directions. From this point, use line-of-sight to guide you. At 12.1 miles (08), bear left a bit and head due east uphill to the mouth of Sand Slide Canyon reached at 12.8 miles (09). (See separate directions below.)

After Sand Slide Canyon, continue along the base of the mountain. You should see a defined road going uphill on the left at 13.6 miles (10). This road goes up to Tower #3 and Sand Dam. To get back to the information board where you started, continue along the base of the mountain about 3 miles. If you get lost at any time, head south to Powerline Road. Follow it left back to the area near the information board (see map).

Lucky Lady shortcut. (Note: At the time of this writing, the San Diego 4-Wheelers were planning to mark this route with closely spaced sign posts. Hopefully, this will be done by the time you read this.)

Reset odometer at information board (01). Head due north to a valley visible on the horizon (see top photo, page 226). At 1.2 miles (11), bear right and make your way east across the dunes. When you reach Tower #1 at 1.8 miles (12), go north around the left side of the tower downhill over sandy ridges. Zigzag west at 2.1 and north at 2.3. Head northeast at 2.6 miles (13) as it gets rockier. Turn left out of a canyon at 2.9. Turn out of a V-notch at 3.0. Bear right at cairn at 3.2 miles (14). Go right at 3.3 and left at a T at 3.4. Bear left at 3.6 miles (15) when you reach Poleline Road.

Wrangler Canyon: Go south in wash from Poleline Road (03). Stay right in the wash at 0.2. The narrow spot at 0.3 is Wrangler Canyon (16). Turn left to return to Poleline Road or continue on complex Rabbit's Foot Trail.

Jamie's Obstacles: Go south from Poleline Road (05) 0.1 miles bearing slightly left. Look for two nasty notches in a rock wall called Jamie's Obstacle I and II (17). Go up one and loop back down the other. This spot connects to other difficult trails in the area.

Sand Slide Canyon: The difficult way is to go left uphill beside the canyon and slide down a steep, sandy hill into the canyon. The easy way is to just drive up the canyon and turn around. This is a fun place for everyone.

Services: Nothing anywhere near the mountain. Gas and other services are available in Imperial, Seeley, Brawley and El Centro.

Maps: Only the mountain and tower service roads are shown on USGS 100,000 scale map El Centro, CA. I know of no other maps on this area.

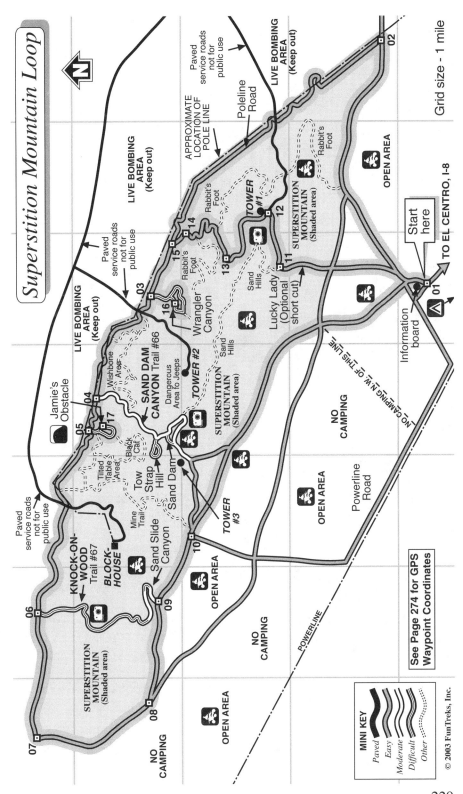

Superstition Mountain Loop

N

Grid size - 1 mile

LIVE BOMBING AREA (Keep out)

Paved service roads not for public use

LIVE BOMBING AREA (Keep out)

APPROXIMATE LOCATION OF POLE LINE

Poleline Road

02

Rabbit's Foot

TOWER #1

12

Rabbit's Foot

SUPERSTITION MOUNTAIN (Shaded area)

OPEN AREA

Start here

TO EL CENTRO, I-8

Information board

01

Sand Hills

11

Lucky Lady (Optional short cut)

14

15

Rabbit's Foot

13

Sand Hills

03

Wrangler Canyon

16

Sand Hills

NO CAMPING

LIVE BOMBING AREA (Keep out)

Paved service roads not for public use

Jamie's Obstacle

Wishbone Area

SAND DAM CANYON Trail #66

Dangerous Area fo Jeeps

TOWER #2

SUPERSTITION MOUNTAIN (Shaded area)

04

05

17

Tilted Table Area

Black Cat

Tow Strap Hill

Sand Dam

TOWER #3

OPEN AREA

Powerline Road

Paved service roads not for public use

KNOCK-ON-WOOD Trail #67

BLOCK-HOUSE

Mine Trail

Sand Slide Canyon

10

OPEN AREA

NO CAMPING

06

SUPERSTITION MOUNTAIN (Shaded area)

09

OPEN AREA

NO CAMPING

POWERLINE

07

NO CAMPING

08

OPEN AREA

NO CAMPING N.W. OF THIS LINE

See Page 274 for GPS Waypoint Coordinates

MINI KEY
Paved
Easy
Moderate
Difficult
Other

© 2003 FunTreks, Inc.

229

Sand Dam Canyon just below Sand Dam.

Steepest part of Sand Dam.

Sand Dam in background as seen from top of Tow Strap Hill.

Heading back to camp.

Alternate cross-country route to Lucky Lady.

Sand Dam Canyon

SUPER-
STITION
MTN. LOOP
Trail #65

TO
KNOCK-
ON-WOOD
Trail #67

Start here

01

Ramsey's Hill

Tow Strap Hill

02

MINI KEY
Paved
Easy
Moderate
Difficult
Other

Sand Dam

Tower #3

DANGEROUS
AREA FOR JEEPS

03

To Lucky Lady

Tower #2

TO
INFORMATION
BOARD

See Page 275 for GPS
Waypoint Coordinates

© 2003 FunTreks, Inc.

Grid size - 0.2 miles

230

Sand Dam Canyon 66

Location: Cuts through Superstition Mountain which is northwest of El Centro and south of the Salton Sea.

Difficulty: Moderate. Follows a narrow, flat-bottom canyon that exits up a steep mountain of sand. The difficult portion of the hill can be bypassed. Optional Tow Strap Hill is extremely steep with loose rock set in soft sand. A winch anchor point is provided. Optional Ramsey's Hill is extreme.

Features: This short trail takes you through the heart of Superstition Mountain to a fun play area. Optional obstacles in the area include Sand Dam, Tow Strap Hill and Ramsey's Hill. The trail is described here from north to south because it is the easiest way to find the trail. It can also be driven in the other direction once you know where it is.

Time & Distance: The trail itself is only 1.7 miles but you must drive 7.4 miles around Superstition Mountain Loop to reach the start. It's another 3 miles back to the information board. Allow about 2 hours driving time. You can spend several additional hours exploring the area.

To Get There: Follow directions for Superstion Mountain Loop, Trail #65. You reach the start of Sand Dam Canyon after 7.4 miles.

Trail Description: *Reset your odometer at the start* (01). Head south through a steep-walled canyon. Go by Ramsey's Hill on the left at 0.4 miles. Bear right at 0.9 miles (02) following a sign to Tow Strap Hill. Turn left uphill at 1.0 to a flat area below Sand Dam. (Straight goes to Tow Strap Hill then loops back.) You can attempt to drive straight up Sand Dam but it is very challenging. To continue, bear left uphill on a wide sandy ledge that's not as steep. You'll still need plenty of speed even with aired-down tires. Turn right as you come over the first ridge and continue uphill on a long, steep climb. You reach the top at 1.7 miles (03).

Return Trip: Work your way downhill to the left using line-of-sight to return to information board. It's another 3 miles along the base of mountain.

Services: Gas and food available in Imperial, Seeley, Brawley and El Centro.

Maps: USGS 7.5-minute map Superstition Mountain, CA, N3252.5-W11545.

A few boulders on the first part of the trail.

Closer to the top.

Everyone pitches in to help lead vehicle.

Attempts to drive up the Sand Slide failed.

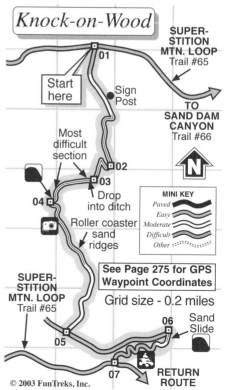

Knock-on-Wood

Start here

Sign Post

01

SUPER-STITION MTN. LOOP
Trail #65

TO
SAND DAM CANYON
Trail #66

Most difficult section

02

03

Drop into ditch

04

Roller coaster sand ridges

N

MINI KEY
Paved
Easy
Moderate
Difficult
Other

See Page 275 for GPS Waypoint Coordinates

SUPER-STITION MTN. LOOP
Trail #65

Grid size - 0.2 miles

06
Sand Slide

05

07

RETURN ROUTE

© 2003 FunTreks, Inc.

Knock-on-Wood ◀67▶

Location: Crosses western end of Superstition Mtn. northwest of El Centro.

Difficulty: Difficult. Climbs steeply up an extremely narrow drainage cut. Sharp boulders and narrow openings are barely passable. Long wheel-based vehicles will have great difficulty. Lockers recommended both front and rear. Body damage and mechanical breakage possible.

Features: A memorable hardcore challenge. Good views at the top. Sand Slide Canyon is a great play area.

Time & Distance: From start of trail to end of Sand Slide Canyon is 2.3 miles. Allow 2-4 hours depending upon capability and number of vehicles.

To Get There: Follow directions for Superstition Mountain Loop, Trail #65. Knock-on-Wood goes left at 9.7 miles. To shorten trip, cut through Sam Dam Canyon from south to north. The Mine Trail can also be used to cross the mountain if you have a friend who knows the way (see map for Trail #65).

Trail Description: Reset your odometer at the start (01). Head south to sign post marking Knock-on-Wood at 0.2 miles. Continue south climbing a rocky ridge. Blockhouse should be visible on left. Turn right down a switchback at 0.6 miles (02). At the bottom, turn left and follow valley south until you reach a rocky ditch at 0.7 miles (03). Drop into the ditch and follow it west then south uphill. Much time can be spent on this long and difficult climb. The worst spot is reached at 1.0 miles (04). Many vehicles high-center on a large, awkwardly positioned boulder. Turn left out of the ditch after this spot, then bear right (south). It flattens out at the top with good views of Salton Sea to the north. Bear slightly left as you descend the other side. Descend rolling ridges of sand, then turn left when you reach a T at 1.6 miles (05). Turn left uphill at 1.7 to reach top of Sand Slide Canyon at 2.0 miles (06). Bottom of Sand Slide Canyon is reached at 2.3 miles (07).

Return Trip: Work your way downhill heading east using line-of-sight to return to information board. It's about 3.7 miles along the base of mountain.

Services: Gas and food available in Imperial, Seeley, Brawley and El Centro.

Maps: USGS 7.5-minute map Superstition Mountain, CA, N3252.5-W11545.

RVs camp along paved Gecko Road.

East to Patton Valley.

Automated pay stations.

Sand Highway has gentle grades and is often well tracked.

Tall dunes at Patton Valley.

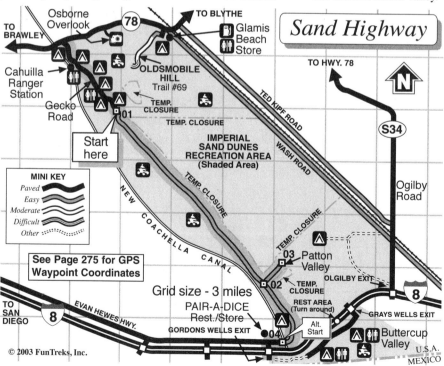

Sand Highway

TO BLYTHE

TO BRAWLEY

Osborne Overlook

78

Glamis Beach Store

Cahuilla Ranger Station

Gecko Road

OLDSMOBILE HILL
Trail #69

TEMP. CLOSURE

TEMP. CLOSURE

Start here

01

IMPERIAL SAND DUNES RECREATION AREA
(Shaded Area)

TEMP. CLOSURE

TO HWY. 78

N

S34

Ogilby Road

TED KIPF ROAD

WASH ROAD

MINI KEY

Paved
Easy
Moderate
Difficult
Other

See Page 275 for GPS
Waypoint Coordinates

NEW COACHELLA CANAL

TEMP. CLOSURE

TEMP. CLOSURE

03 Patton Valley

OLGILBY EXIT

02

TEMP. CLOSURE

Grid size - 3 miles

PAIR-A-DICE
Rest./Store

REST AREA
(Turn around)

GRAYS WELLS EXIT

TO SAN DIEGO

8

EVAN HEWES HWY.

GORDONS WELLS EXIT

04

Alt. Start

8

Buttercup Valley

U.S.A.
MEXICO

© 2003 FunTreks, Inc.

234

Sand Highway ⑥⑧

Location: Inside Imperial Sand Dunes Recreation Area east of El Centro.

Difficulty: Easy. Soft sand with gentle grades. Stay in existing tracks as much as possible and away from back sides of dunes. Air down if necessary. To avoid digging in, don't slam on your brakes or accelerate quickly.

Features: Relax as you cruise along miles of gently rolling sand dunes. Watch dune buggies climb amazingly steep grades at Patton Valley. Visit Buttercup Valley south of I-8. Camping fills up quickly on weekends. Before you go, learn and follow all park regulations. All vehicles must display a 6 inch by 12 inch red or orange flag at least 8 feet above ground. Best time mid-October through May. Fee required for primary vehicle only.

Time & Distance: About 18 miles of sand. Add 4 miles for Patton Valley. Allow 1 to 2 hours. Add time to explore other areas.

To Get There: From Brawley, go east on Hwy. 78 about 20 miles to Gecko Road. Drive 6 miles south until pavement ends. To start from I-8, get off on north side of Gordons Wells Exit. Go east on paved road 0.4 miles. Turn left on gravel road until it crosses canal then head north along sandy ridge.

Trail Description: *Reset odometer when pavement ends at Gecko Road* (01). Proceed southeast across sand. There are usually tracks to follow unless it's windy. Follow stakes to closed area (if still there). Otherwise, the sand falls away on the west side forming a ridge that's easy to follow. Canal and power lines are also visible. Turn left at 13.4 miles (02) for Patton Valley. You'll see the big dunes before 2 miles (03). Return to Sand Highway and continue south. Gradually move right heading for towers. Follow gravel road over canal. Turn right on paved road at 18.3 miles (04). Freeway exit just ahead.

Return Trip: Via Interstate 8. To return to Highway 78, take Ogilby Road to Wash Road or Ted Kipf Road. (Note: You can turn around at rest area in center of freeway just west of Grays Wells exit.)

Services: Vault toilets at Gecko Road and Buttercup Valley. Gas, restaurant and supplies at Glamis Store and Pair-a-Dice. Glamis Store has pay showers. Gas is expensive. Pair-a-Dice gas is sold in 5-gallon cans.

Maps: Automobile Club of Southern California map Imperial Sand Dunes, USGS 250,000 scale map El Centro, CA, DeLorme Atlas & Gazetteer.

Oldsmobile Hill ahead.

So many choices. Where to next?

Dune buggies line up on a busy weekend.

Oldsmobile Hill.

Back sides of dunes are soft. Be careful.

What a place!

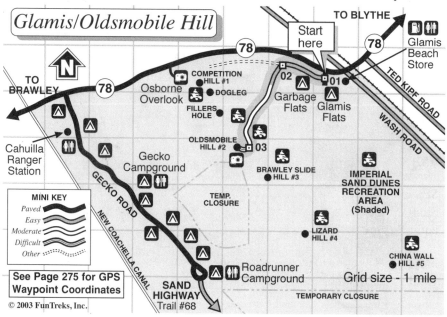

Glamis/Oldsmobile Hill

TO BLYTHE

Start here

Glamis Beach Store

TO BRAWLEY

78

78

78

TED KIPF ROAD

WASH ROAD

COMPETITION HILL #1

Osborne Overlook

DOGLEG

FILLERS HOLE

02

01

Garbage Flats

Glamis Flats

OLDSMOBILE HILL #2

03

Cahuilla Ranger Station

Gecko Campground

BRAWLEY SLIDE HILL #3

IMPERIAL SAND DUNES RECREATION AREA (Shaded)

GECKO ROAD

NEW COACHELLA CANAL

TEMP. CLOSURE

LIZARD HILL #4

CHINA WALL HILL #5

Grid size - 1 mile

MINI KEY
Paved
Easy
Moderate
Difficult
Other

SAND HIGHWAY
Trail #68

Roadrunner Campground

TEMPORARY CLOSURE

See Page 275 for GPS Waypoint Coordinates

© 2003 FunTreks, Inc.

236

Glamis/ Oldsmobile Hill ◆69◆

Location: North end of Imperial Sand Dunes Recreation Area, east of Brawley and northwest of Yuma, AZ.

Difficulty: Difficult. Rating applies only to Oldsmobile Hill, a good test for Jeep or SUV. Requires speed, momentum and a little practice to reach the top. Don't turn sideways on the hill. Back down slowly if you don't make it all the way. Use medium low gear to balance power and speed. Air down your tires as much as possible. To avoid digging in, don't slam on your brakes or accelerate quickly. Be careful going over the back side of any sand dune where the wind has dropped the softest sand. It's easy to get stuck or even roll over if the dune is large enough.

Features: Conquer a major sand hill and enjoy great views at the top. Experience Glamis first hand as you cruise awesome sand dunes. Limit yourself to dunes suitable for your vehicle. Before you go, learn and follow all park regulations. All vehicles must display a 6 inch by 12 inch red or orange flag at least 8 feet above ground. Best time mid-October through May. Fee required for primary vehicle only. Camping areas fill up quickly. If possible, avoid dangerously crowded winter holiday weekends.

Time & Distance: The 3 miles to Oldsmobile Hill take just a few minutes but allow plenty time to explore the area.

To Get There: Take highway 78 about 25 miles east of Brawley. Turn south on a paved side road about 1.5 miles before the Glamis Beach Store.

Trail Description: Reset your odometer at the start (01). Turn right off the paved side road and head west alongside Hwy. 78. After 0.7 miles (02), turn south and follow a small valley. Oldsmobile Hill is on right at 3.1 miles (03).

Return Trip: Return the way you came.

Services: Ranger station and vault toilets on Gecko Road. Glamis Beach Store has gas, a restaurant, a small grocery store, flush toilets for customers and pay showers. Gas is expensive.

Maps: Automobile Club of Southern California map Imperial Sand Dunes, USGS 250,000 scale map El Centro, CA, DeLorme Atlas & Gazetteer.

AREA 10
Other Trails

70. Last Chance Canyon
71. Trona Pinnacles
72. Dumont Dunes
73. Sperry Wash
74. Sledgehammer Canyon
75. Berdoo Canyon

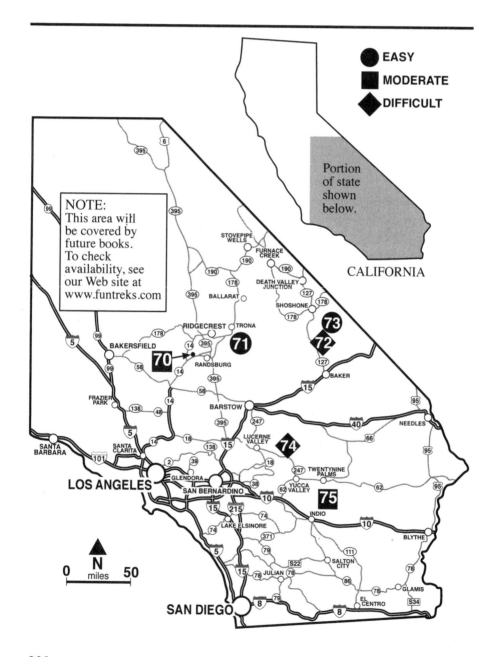

Other Trails

Each trail in Area 10 is presented independently. *Last Chance Canyon* offers a variety of easy and moderate terrain and includes a visit to unusual and historic Burro Schmidt Tunnel. The road through *Trona Pinnacles* does not require four-wheel drive; it's just an impressive backcountry experience that you shouldn't miss. *Dumont Dunes* is a smaller area than Imperial Sand Dunes and receives less publicity. If you like the sand dune experience, but hate big crowds, give this area a try. While there, drive nearby *Sperry Wash*. This geologically interesting route concludes at Tecopa Hot Springs which features therapeutic hot-spring baths. Some are maintained by the county for public use at no charge. *Sledgehammer Canyon* is one of the toughest and best-known trails in southern California. It represents one of a half dozen or more extreme trails clustered in well-known Johnson Valley. To learn about other trails in the area, contact the Victor Valley 4-Wheelers (see appendix). They've worked hard to build you some outstanding hardcore trails. *Berdoo Canyon* allows you to visit beautiful Joshua Tree National Park and, at the same time, enjoy some interesting four-wheeling. Save this trail for the end of your visit because it exits the park a long distance to the south. All six trails in Area 10 offer something unique and are worthy of your consideration.

Upper Johnson Valley as seen from top of *Sledgehammer Canyon, Trail #74.*

At this point you exit the wash and the trail gets easier.

Be careful on this steep hill.

Burro Schmidt's tool shack. Ask owners for a look inside.

Dugout near Cudahy Camp.

Randsburg General Store, around since 1904.

Schmidt Tunnel, nearly 2,000 feet long.

240

Last Chance Canyon 70

Location: East of Bakersfield, southwest of Ridgecrest and west of Randsburg.

Difficulty: Moderate. The first part of trip is the toughest. It winds through an eroded wash with moderate and difficult options. Heavy rains can move things around making conditions unpredictable. Pick your line carefully. The remainder of the trip is mostly easy except for one steep climb up a rocky hill. Poorly marked side roads make route-finding confusing.

Features: A scenic canyon surrounded by striking red and pink buttes. Many mines and dugouts in the area. Some are visible from the trail. The highlight of the trip is a visit to Burro Schmidt's Tunnel (see Historical Highlights). Excellent mountain views as you depart. If you are coming from Highway 395, be sure to stop at historic Randsburg. Their tiny general store is nearly 100 years old and still a very busy place.

Time & Distance: Allow about 4 hours for this 18.8-mile trip.

To Get There: Head north on Highway 14. Before you reach Redrock State Park, turn northeast on Redrock Randsburg Road. After 6.0 miles, turn left on a single-lane gravel road. A sign indicates you are entering Red Rock Canyon State Park. If you are coming from Ridgecrest or Randsburg, head southeast 6.1 miles on Redrock Randsburg Road from the intersection at Garlock Road. The turn is on the right 0.3 miles after Saltdale Road.

Trail Description: Reset your odometer at the start (01). Head north across desert terrain. Enter a wide wash at 0.8 miles. It gradually narrows and gets rockier. The road climbs in and out of the wash with different choices along the way. Scout ahead to avoid getting into trouble. Stay left in wash at 2.4 where a road goes right uphill. Wind back and forth in and out of the wash as it widens again. The wash is closed at 3.7 miles (02). Turn right out of the wash, then immediately turn left on a road that parallels the wash. (Easier Pleasant Valley Road goes straight.) Stay on the road at all times. It is lined with rocks and very easy to follow. A rough spot at 4.4 miles crosses the wash. Concrete foundations mark Cudahy Mining Camp site at 4.6. An impressive dugout can be seen across the canyon. Miners lived in these dugouts during hard times. The trail goes left up a steep rocky hill at 4.8 miles.

After the hill, bear right where a road goes left and drop back down into a sandy wash. At 5.3 miles, go by a dilapidated house trailer at a mine on the right. Stay on the main road ignoring side roads as the wash widens.

Several major roads converge at 7.8 miles (03). Left eventually goes back out to Highway 14. Stay right or straight in a wide wash. There was a small sign here for the Schmidt Tunnel. How long it lasts is anyone's guess. Bear slightly right at 8.2 out of the wash then right again at 8.7 miles (04). (This is a major intersection with confusing signs. Left bypasses Schmidt's Tunnel.) Bear left on EP15 at 8.8 where Pleasant Valley Road goes right.

Bear right at 10.2 miles (05). You'll come back to this spot. Bear left at 10.9 until you reach Burro Schmidt's cabin at 11.0. The property is privately owned and was occupied at the time of this writing (see Historical Highlights). Register and proceed uphill at no charge. The tunnel is reached at 11.1 miles (06). Return the way you came and turn right at 12.0 miles (05).

Continue straight at 13.6 miles then again at 13.8 miles (07). Roads that join here head back to Last Chance Canyon. Bear right at 14.5 miles (08) on EP100. Follow this road through Mesquite Canyon. Continue straight at 14.8 and 15.3. Redrock Randsburg road is reached at 18.8 miles (09).

Return Trip: Right takes you back to Highway 14 and Los Angeles. Left goes to Highway 395, Randsburg and Ridgecrest.

Services: Nothing on trail. Supplies at the Randsburg General Store open every day. Closest gas in Ridgecrest. Gas is also available in California City on Highway 14 heading back to Los Angeles. Gas may be available in Johannesburg just east of Randsburg.

Historical Highlights: William Henry (Burro) Schmidt started digging his tunnel the same year as the Great San Francisco Earthquake in 1906. His plan was to charge a toll to shortcut passage through the area. Long before he finished, a good road was built around Copper Mountain, rendering his tunnel obsolete. No one knows why he continued to dig, mostly by hand, a total of 38 years. He was dubbed the "Human Mole" when he was featured in "Ripley's Believe It or Not" and Time Magazine in the 1940s. The tunnel is almost 2,000 feet long with a great view on the other side. You can hike through it with a flashlight. Some say the tunnel will outlast the pyramids of Egypt. Schmidt operated the tunnel as a tourist attraction until his death at the age of 83 in 1954. At that time, a woman named Tonie Seger bought the property and continued to greet visitors. Although more than 90 years old, and no longer active, she still lived there when I stopped by on March 6, 2002. A younger man was taking care of her and the property. He took time to show me the nearby tool shack packed with Burro Schmidt's lifelong memorabilia. Although a fee is not charged to see the tunnel, donations are appreciated.

Maps: Hileman's Gem, Mineral and 4-Wheel Drive Map #1, USGS 100,000-scale map Cuddeback Lake, CA, DeLorme Atlas & Gazetteer.

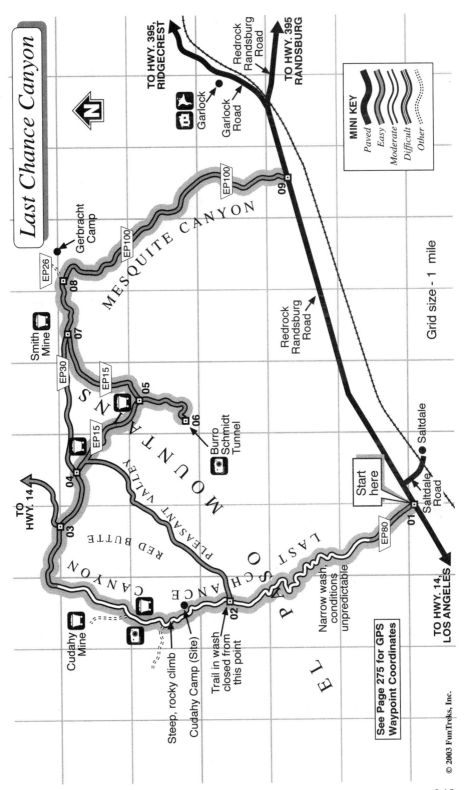

Last Chance Canyon

TO HWY. 395, RIDGECREST

TO HWY. 395 RANDSBURG

Redrock Randsburg Road

Garlock
Garlock Road

MINI KEY
Paved
Easy
Moderate
Difficult
Other

N

EP100
09

MESQUITE CANYON

Gerbracht Camp
EP26
EP100
08
07
Smith Mine
EP30
EP15
05
06
Burro Schmidt Tunnel
EP15
04
03
TO HWY. 14

MOUNTAINS

PLEASANT VALLEY
RED BUTTE

LAST CHANCE CANYON

Cudahy Mine
Cudahy Camp (Site)
Steep, rocky climb
Trail in wash closed from this point
02
Narrow wash, conditions unpredictable

EL PASO

Redrock Randsburg Road

Saltdale
Start here
Saltdale Road
01
EP80

TO HWY. 14, LOS ANGELES

Grid size - 1 mile

See Page 275 for GPS Waypoint Coordinates

© 2003 FunTreks, Inc.

243

The first cluster of pinnacles is 5 miles from Highway 178. Always stay on existing roads.

Many miles of roads can be explored in the area.

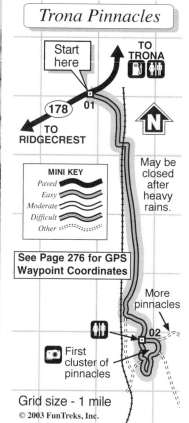

Trona Pinnacles

Start here

TO TRONA

178 01

TO RIDGECREST

N

May be closed after heavy rains.

MINI KEY
Paved
Easy
Moderate
Difficult
Other

See Page 276 for GPS Waypoint Coordinates

More pinnacles

02

First cluster of pinnacles

Grid size - 1 mile

© 2003 FunTreks, Inc.

244

Trona Pinnacles (71)

Location: South of Trona, east of Ridgecrest.

Difficulty: Easy. Suitable for passenger cars when dry. When wet, four-wheel drive is needed; however, the area is usually closed after heavy rains. Four-wheel drive is recommended to cross the sand washes between the two main pinnacle groups. Too hot during the summer.

Features: Explore a network of roads that connects over 500 tufa pinnacles, some as high as 140 feet. Hike, picnic and camp overnight at this designated National Natural Landmark. Stay on existing roads at all times.

Time & Distance: The largest cluster of pinnacles is just 5 miles from Highway 178. You can spend an hour or a weekend exploring the area.

To Get There: From Ridgecrest, head east on Highway 178. Turn right on a dirt road 7.7 miles east of the intersection of 178 and Trona-Red Mountain Road. Watch for Trona Pinnacles sign. From Trona, head south on Hwy. 178 and watch for sign on left when 178 turns southwest for the last time. The start is about 20 miles from Ridgecrest and 8 miles from Trona.

Trail Description: *Reset odometer as you turn off Highway 178* (01). Head east 0.5 miles then turn south. You'll be on dirt road RM143. The road curves left and crosses tracks at 1.3 then continues south. Turn left at 4.3 miles. Go east then drop downhill towards the pinnacles. Interpretive sign and vault toilet reached at 5.0 miles (02).

Return Trip: Return the way you came.

Services: One vault toilet at pinnacles site. Gas and food in Trona. Full services in Ridgecrest. Primitive camping only. Pack out all trash.

Historical Highlights: Between 10,000 and 100,000 years ago this area was entirely under water and part of a chain of lakes stretching from Mono Lake to Death Valley. Fresh ground water bubbled up from springs on the bottom of the lake and reacted with the high chemical content of the lake water. Calcium carbonate deposits, called tufa, accumulated around the mouth of the springs and built up over time. After the water receded, tall spires were left standing for all to enjoy.

Maps: USGS 100,000 scale map Ridgecrest, CA, DeLorme Atlas & Gazetteer.

Some dunes are 450 feet high. Jeeps and SUVs should stay on lower slopes.

Campground is flat and suitable for motor homes.

Stay on firm sand.

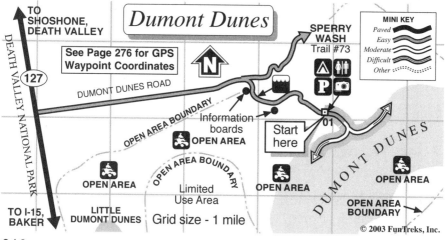

TO SHOSHONE, DEATH VALLEY

Dumont Dunes

See Page 276 for GPS Waypoint Coordinates

SPERRY WASH
Trail #73

MINI KEY
Paved
Easy
Moderate
Difficult
Other

127

DUMONT DUNES ROAD

DEATH VALLEY NATIONAL PARK

OPEN AREA BOUNDARY

Information boards

OPEN AREA

Start here

01

DUNES

DUMONT

OPEN AREA

OPEN AREA BOUNDARY

OPEN AREA

OPEN AREA

Limited Use Area

OPEN AREA BOUNDARY

TO I-15, BAKER

LITTLE DUMONT DUNES

Grid size - 1 mile

© 2003 FunTreks, Inc.

246

Dumont Dunes ◆72◆

Location: Between Baker and Shoshone, east of Highway 127.

Difficulty: Difficult. Many dunes are beyond the capability of Jeeps and SUVs so choose your route carefully. Air down tires as much as possible for maximum traction. Don't slam on your brakes or accelerate quickly. Always travel with another vehicle in case you get stuck. Carry plenty of water and avoid this area during the summer.

Features: SUVs and Jeeps can cruise along lower slopes as they explore the area. ATVs, dirt bikes and dune buggies can be more aggressive. Make sure you stay within marked boundary where open travel is permitted. Areas beyond the OHV area are extremely sensitive. All vehicles must be licensed or display green sticker. All vehicles must have whip mast at least 8 ft. above ground with red or orange flag. This was a non-fee area at the time of this writing, but that could change.

Time & Distance: The campground is 4.2 miles from Highway 127. Distance driven and time spent exploring dunes is up to you.

To Get There: Take Highway 127 north from Baker 33.8 miles. *Reset odometer* and turn right on wide Dumont Dunes Road. Bear right at 2.8 miles where Sperry Wash, Trail #73, goes straight. Head south and cross Amargosa River, usually just a trickle. A concrete pad makes this crossing easy for motor homes. The road goes uphill through a wide valley past an information board at 3.4 miles. Stop here to review regulations. A good climb remains before you reach a broad plateau and camping area at 4.2 miles (01). The area is large enough for hundreds of campers and motor homes. Dry camping only. Pack out all trash.

Trail Description: Head south from camping area (01) and go wherever you like within the OHV area. Watch for boundary markers.

Return Trip: Return the way you came or go out via Sperry Wash, Trail #73.

Services: Two vault toilets at the campground. Gas and food in Baker and Shoshone. Commercial campgrounds in Tecopa Hot Springs.

Maps: BLM pamphlet of Dumont Dunes OHV Area, USGS 100,000 scale map Owlshead Mountains, CA, Sidekick Map, DeLorme Atlas & Gazetteer.

Amargosa River is crossed several times.

Outstanding scenery along the way.

One of several old mine buildings (Lower Noonday Camp).

Public bath houses at Tecopa Hot Springs are free.

Nearing Sperry Townsite.

Unique cairns mark trail.

Boulder on pedestal.

248

Sperry Wash 🄷

Location: Between Baker and Shoshone. South of Tecopa Hot Springs.

Difficulty: Easy. Shallow stream crossings, sandy washes and mild rocky canyons. Suitable for high-clearance 4x4 SUVs.

Features: Enjoy nearby Dumont Dunes, Trail #72, then follow Amargosa River to Sperry Townsite. From there, cross Kingston Range Wilderness through a designated non-wilderness corridor. Pass through an area of large talc mines and conclude with a visit to Tecopa Hot Springs. This small town is known for its hot-spring baths. Most are located in commercial camp-grounds, but one is maintained by the county and open to the public at no charge. Green-sticker vehicles are allowed on this route until Western Talc Road. You must stay on the main route at all times.

Time & Distance: From the start, you'll travel about 29 miles until you're back on Highway 127 west of Tecopa Hot Springs. Allow about 4 hours.

To Get There: Take Highway 127 north from Baker 33.8 miles and turn right on Dumont Dunes Road. The trail is on the left after 2.8 miles before you reach the information board.

Trail Description: Reset you odometer at the start (01). Pass through a ranch-style entry with an overhead sign for Sperry Wash. Head east on a well-defined road. At 0.3 miles, cross Amargosa River for the first time. The river may be dry but several inches of water is more likely. From this point the road winds back and forth across the river bed many times. The route is marked with large cairns which are sometimes hard to spot. Just stay in the river valley heading generally north/northeast. The left side of the trail is the boundary for the open area of Dumont Dunes. Bear left at 0.9 miles where a road joins on the right. The trail goes left at 1.3 miles.

A large sign indicates you are entering a non-wilderness corridor (through Kingston Range Wilderness) at 3.4 miles. At 4.1 miles (02), a sign for Amargosa Canyon ACEC marks the location of Sperry Townsite. Only a few foundations remain. The road leaves the Amargosa River Valley at 4.5 miles (03) and turns east into Sperry Wash. Conditions worsen slightly from this point. Watch for cairns marked with interesting animal footprints (sand-blasted in the rock by the BLM). The canyon walls gradually close in as the trail gets rougher. Curious pedestals can be seen clinging to canyon walls as you proceed. The canyon widens again after 8 miles. Bear right at a fork at 11.0 miles then quickly bear left at 11.1. A road to the right is marked closed. Bear left again at 11.4 and 11.7.

At 11.8 miles (04) another ranch-style sign marks the end of Sperry Wash. Green Sticker vehicles must turn back here. Continue straight downhill on a rough paved road following power lines. After passing a large mine, bear right downhill at 12.0. Stay right again at 12.3 and pass a large mine. The road improves as you continue downhill. You'll pass an interesting mine building and water tank before reaching paved Furnace Creek Road at 15.6 miles (05).

Turn left on Furnace Creek Road and begin a gradual descent from Tecopa Pass. The road switches back and forth from pavement to gravel. Continue straight at 21.4 miles where China Ranch Road goes left. Bear left on Spanish Trail Highway at Tecopa at 23.1 miles. Turn right at 24.6 miles (06) on Tecopa Hot Springs Road. (Left goes directly to Hwy. 127.) As you pass through Tecopa Hot Springs, you'll see the county-maintained public bath houses on the right at 26.5 miles. Continue northwest on Tecopa Hot Springs road until you reach Highway 127 at 29.1 miles (07).

Return Trip: Shoshone is 5 miles to the right on Highway 127 and Baker is 51 miles to the left.

Services: Nothing anywhere along the trail, although nearby Dumont Dunes has a vault toilet. Shoshone is the closest place for gas at the end of the trip.

Historical Highlights: As you pass through Amargosa Canyon, look for remains of the old T&T (Tonopah & Tidewater) Railroad that was built in 1905. It continued up Amargosa Canyon and serviced many important mining operations in Death Valley. The town of Sperry serviced the railroad during that time.

Maps: USGS 250,000 scale map Trona, CA, DeLorme Atlas & Gazetteer.

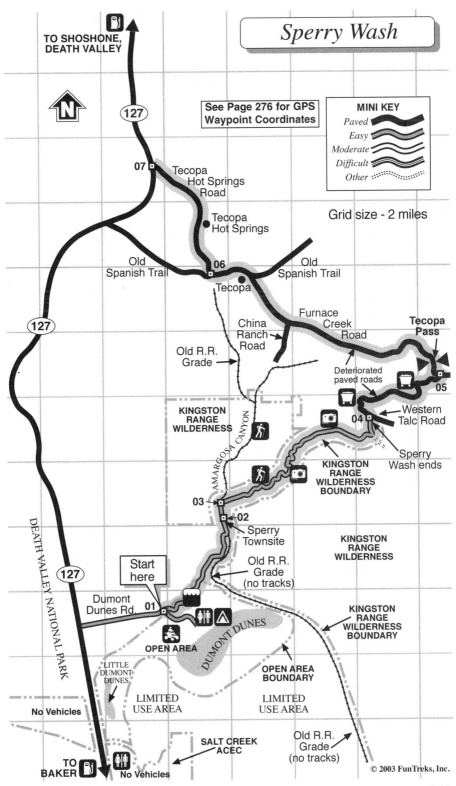

Sperry Wash

TO SHOSHONE,
DEATH VALLEY

127

N

See Page 276 for GPS
Waypoint Coordinates

07

Tecopa
Hot Springs
Road

Tecopa
Hot Springs

Old
Spanish Trail

06

Tecopa

Old
Spanish Trail

127

China
Ranch
Road

Furnace
Creek
Road

Tecopa
Pass

Old R.R.
Grade

Deteriorated
paved roads

05

KINGSTON
RANGE
WILDERNESS

AMARGOSA CANYON

Western
Talc Road

04

Sperry
Wash ends

KINGSTON
RANGE
WILDERNESS
BOUNDARY

03

02

Sperry
Townsite

KINGSTON
RANGE
WILDERNESS

Start
here

Old R.R.
Grade
(no tracks)

Dumont
Dunes Rd.

01

127

DEATH VALLEY NATIONAL PARK

KINGSTON
RANGE
WILDERNESS
BOUNDARY

DUMONT DUNES

OPEN AREA

LITTLE
DUMONT
DUNES

OPEN AREA
BOUNDARY

LIMITED
USE AREA

LIMITED
USE AREA

No Vehicles

SALT CREEK
ACEC

Old R.R.
Grade
(no tracks)

TO
BAKER

No Vehicles

© 2003 FunTreks, Inc.

251

Heading east from dry lake, Sledgehammer goes up canyon seen at left.

Trail dedication.

The fun starts here.

Looking down on Upper Johnson Valley.

Expert spotter at work.

Future 4-wheeler helps guide his dad.

Leave message at Mail Box.

Nearing the top and still in one piece.

252

Sledgehammer Canyon ◆74◆

Location: East of Lucerne Valley, southeast of Barstow and north of Yucca Valley.

Difficulty: Extremely difficult. Climbs a steep, narrow, boulder-strewn canyon. Lockers required front and rear. Recommend 35-inch tires or larger. (I got through with 33s, an expert spotter, a few well-placed rocks and a good winch.) Mechanical and body damage likely. Route-finding is complex and challenging.

Features: Sledgehammer, Jackhammer, Clawhammer, After Shock, Outer Limits and Wrecking Ball make up a cluster of nationally recognized extreme trails called the *Hammers*. Sledgehammer is described here in detail. The *Hammers* are located on a treacherous mountain in the southeast corner of Johnson Valley OHV Area. This area extends more than 20 miles west to Camp Rock Road and is open to cross-country travel to all vehicles including green-sticker ATVs and dirt bikes. You are allowed to camp up to 14 days anywhere in the area; just don't block any roads. Pack out all trash. To learn more about the other trails, contact the Victor Valley Four Wheelers or attend their annual *Fun in the Sun Rocktoberfest* held in early October (see appendix). Learn about new trails under construction.

Time & Distance: The complete loop, as described here, is 22 miles. Allow 6 to 7 hours minimum. The extreme portion of this route measures only 1.1 miles but can still take many hours depending upon the number and capability of your vehicles. I did not drive the escape route, but was told it is was very steep and tippy.

To Get There: Take Highway 247 east from Lucerne Valley about 24 miles. Turn north on Boone Road just east of mile post 21.

Trail Description: *Reset odometer as you turn off Highway 247* (01). Head north on Boone Road. It turns northeast and intersects with Barnes Road at 2.1 miles. Turn left, then bear northeast at 2.6 miles. You reach Means Dry Lake at 3.9 miles (02). Head east across the north end of the lake until you see a well-defined road heading towards the mountains. As you get closer to the mountains, you'll see three roads going uphill across a sandy area. The road to Sledgehammer goes up a canyon to the left of these three roads. (See photo opposite page.) The road is less defined as you proceed; just keep heading east. You'll cross a dry wash at 5.5 miles. A lesser road goes uphill to the right at 5.7 miles. You bear slightly left uphill. As you come around a hill on your right at 5.9, the road splits 3 ways. Bear slightly right on the center fork even though the main road seems to go left. Roads go in all directions. Follow pink ribbons that may be left on trees. Bear left when the road forks at 6.0 miles. (The road dead ahead is the exit point of the escape route.) Continue uphill across a sandy area as you join a better road. Turn left and drop down into a wash at 6.3 miles. (Right takes you to a spectator parking area.) At 6.4 miles (03), bear right at a large white sign (pictured on previous page).

Reset your odometer at the sign (03). Stay to the right as you start up the canyon. The action starts immediately. If you stack rocks, make sure you remove them afterwards. At 0.3 miles, pass through the V-Notch.* More work remains before you reach the mail box at 0.6 miles. Jackhammer joins the trail on the left at this point. Sledgehammer now turns south. The very difficult Waterfall is reached at 0.8 miles. This obstacle has a bypass. A sandy spot at 0.9 miles (04) is a good place for lunch. The first escape route goes right at this point. Many people think this is the end of the trail but more challenges remain. Continue uphill through one last section of difficult rock climbs. The difficult section finally ends at 1.1 miles. You can still escape to the right but you'll miss some spectacular scenery.

As you continue on the trail, bear left downhill at 1.3 miles. Driver's choice at 1.6. We took the easier way to the left. Continue straight through Alien Flats, a saddle at 2.1 miles (05). Bear left uphill at 2.3. Great views of Upper Johnson Valley at 2.4 miles. Continue straight at 3.3 miles (06) as you cross a fault line from a 1976 earthquake. The trail narrows to a single track in places. Continue straight when a trail joins on the left at 3.8. Descend one last difficult hill at 4.2. Watch for red ribbons. Bear left on a better trail at 4.5. After dropping into a wash briefly at 4.7, immediately bear left out of the wash. Bear left as you join a larger road at 5.1 miles (07). Continue straight at 5.3 as Clawhammer joins on the left. The road passes through a wide valley and swings west. Bear left at 7.9 miles (08). You'll soon be heading south. At 10.0 miles (09) bear right on a better road. Make a hard left at 11.0 miles (10) and return to the dry lake.

Return Trip: Go out the same way you entered.

Services: None. Primitive camping only. Full services in Lucerne Valley.

Maps: USGS 100,000 scale map Big Bear Lake, CA, DeLorme Atlas & Gazetteer. (Reference only; Sledgehammer does not appear on these maps.)

---

*Shortly after the V-Notch, you'll pass a dedication plaque to Donna Jean Shaner, a past member of the Victor Valley 4-Wheelers and wife of Chuck Shaner, considered "father" of the Hammers. Chuck was my spotter on this trip and got me through without a scratch.

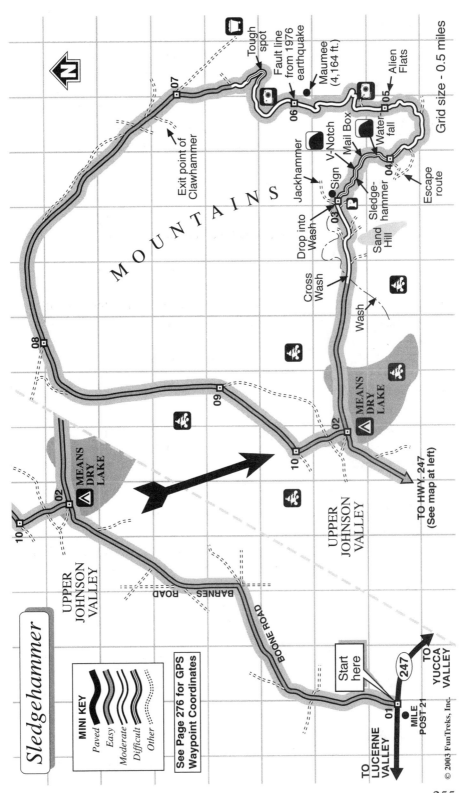

Sledgehammer

MINI KEY

Paved
Easy
Moderate
Difficult
Other

See Page 276 for GPS Waypoint Coordinates

© 2003 FunTreks, Inc.

Grid size - 0.5 miles

N

MOUNTAINS

Tough spot
Fault line from 1976 earthquake
Maumee (4,164 ft.)
Alien Flats
07
06
05
Exit point of Clawhammer
V-Notch
Mail Box
Water fall
Jackhammer
Sign
Sledge-hammer
04
Escape route
Drop into Wash
Sand Hill
03
Cross Wash
Wash
08
09
10
02
MEANS DRY LAKE
MEANS DRY LAKE
02
10
UPPER JOHNSON VALLEY
UPPER JOHNSON VALLEY
TO HWY. 247
(See map at left)

BARNES ROAD
BOONE ROAD

Start here
247
01
MILE POST 21
TO YUCCA VALLEY
TO LUCERNE VALLEY

255

Check at visitor center on conditions in Berdoo Canyon before you start.

Joshua trees along Geology Tour Road.

Early 1900s concrete dam at Squaw Tank.

Just a few rough spots in Berdoo Canyon.

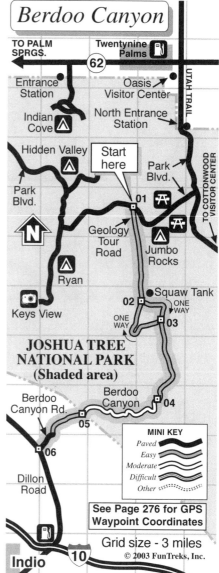

Berdoo Canyon

TO PALM SPRGS.

Twentynine Palms

62

Entrance Station

Oasis Visitor Center

North Entrance Station

UTAH TRAIL

Indian Cove

Hidden Valley

Start here

Park Blvd.

Park Blvd.

01

TO COTTONWOOD VISITOR CENTER

Geology Tour Road

Jumbo Rocks

Ryan

Squaw Tank

02

ONE WAY

ONE WAY

03

Keys View

JOSHUA TREE NATIONAL PARK (Shaded area)

Berdoo Canyon

04

Berdoo Canyon Rd.

05

06

Dillon Road

MINI KEY

Paved
Easy
Moderate
Difficult
Other

See Page 276 for GPS Waypoint Coordinates

Grid size - 3 miles

Indio

10

© 2003 FunTreks, Inc.

Berdoo Canyon 75

Location: South of Twentynine Palms inside Joshua Tree National Park

Difficulty: Moderate. Only the last part through Berdoo Canyon is moderate. Flash floods can quickly increase difficulty. Check at the visitor center for latest conditions. Suitable for stock, high-clearance, 4x4 SUVs.

Features: See beautiful Joshua Tree National Park then exit the park on an interesting four-wheel-drive road. Ask at visitor center for the *Geology Tour Road Guide* that describes, in detail, the first part of this route. Stay on designated roads at all times. Street-legal vehicles only.

Time & Distance: Allow 2 to 4 hours for this 23.4-mile trip. The Geology Tour, by itself, is 18 miles.

To Get There: From Interstate 10 north of Palm Springs, take Highway 62 north then east about 43 miles to Twentynine Palms. Follow signs south to the Oasis Visitor Center. Continue south into the park through the North Entrance Station. Follow signs to Jumbo Rocks Campground then go another 1.6 miles west. Turn left on a marked road for the Geology Tour.

Trail Description: Reset your odometer as you leave paved road (01). Follow a graded dirt road south. Stop, see wind caves and dam at Squaw Tank on left at 5.4 miles. At 5.6 miles (02), bear left and begin a one-way loop. Head east along base of ridge then follow road south. Turn left at 8.0 miles (03) at sign for Berdoo Canyon. Follow a sandy two-track road south. Bear right at 13.2 miles (04) where biking trail goes left. Head west through Berdoo Canyon as conditions gradually worsen. Shift into low range when necessary. Note earlier damage from flash flooding. Exit park at 19.5 miles (05). Follow a wide wash out of the canyon through an ugly area of junk and washed up debris. You can drive on parts of a destroyed paved road. Stay left at 20.2 miles. Exit wash on paved road at 20.3. Pavement is finally unbroken after 22.2 miles. Dillon Road is reached at 23.4 miles (06).

Return Trip: Turn left on Dillon Road and follow it 6.3 miles south to I-10.

Services: Full services in Twentynine Palms and Indio. Gas at Interstate 10. Porta-potty at Squaw Tank.

Maps: Joshua Tree National Park Official Map, DeLorme Atlas & Gazetteer.

Ballarat Ghost Town below Pleasant Canyon/South Park (Trail #6).

APPENDIX

Extremely difficult obstacle at the start of Doran Loop (Trail #19).

GPS Basics

Frequently asked Questions:

What is GPS? GPS stands for Global Positioning System. Satellites circle the earth and broadcast signals to receiving units below. These signals allow you to determine your position on the earth. Five to 12 satellites can be picked up at any one time. A GPS unit with 12-satellite capability has the best chance of determining your position quickly.

Is GPS necessary? No. Some people prefer to rely on instinct, orienteering and map-reading skills. In many areas roads are well defined and easy to follow. You may travel with people who are familiar with the trail or you may prefer hiring a guide. Most of the trails in this book can be driven without the use of GPS.

Then why should I buy a GPS unit? It's the fastest and easiest way to determine your position. Like any new device, you'll wonder how you got along without it.

What kind of GPS unit do I need? There are many brands and models in all price ranges. It depends on your needs. Don't get one with less than 12 parallel satellite channels. It's handy to be able to download and upload data to a computer, but this is not required. Many GPS units have built-in maps. The amount of detail in the maps is usually a function of price.

How complicated is it to use a GPS unit? My GPS unit came with a small 100-page user's manual. It took a little time to read but it was simple and easy to understand. After a little practice, using the unit becomes second nature. Basic units are much simpler.

What are waypoints and trackpoints? Waypoints are important locations you choose to mark along your route, like where you start, key intersections along the way, and your final destination. Waypoints are recorded when you consciously hit a button. Trackpoints are automatically recorded as you move along. They're often referred to as a breadcrumb trail.

How accurate is GPS? It's gotten much better since the government reduced the *Selective Availability* error. Prior to that they scrambled the signal, allowing a worst-case error of about a 300-ft. radius. Clinton's announcement on May 1, 2000, says that error is now down to 20 meters or about 60 ft. Subsequent tests of the new system are showing even better accuracy. Future supplemental projects, like the FAA's Wide Area Augmentation System (WAAS), promise even more accuracy.

Do I need a computer to use a GPS unit? No, but if you have a computer, you'll be able to do a lot more. You can download waypoints and trackpoints to your home computer onto digital maps and see exactly where you went. You can print maps showing your exact route. You can save a large number of routes to upload to your GPS unit anytime you want. You can exchange routes and maps with friends. You can store many detailed maps in the computer at a very low cost per map. You can see a much bigger picture of a map than what you see on your tiny GPS screen. You can use maps with more detail.

If you use a laptop, you can take it with you and follow your progress on the screen. You can download hundreds of waypoints and trackpoints instantly into your GPS unit and avoid the tedious task of entering them by hand. Most GPS units don't have a keypad, so entering numerical data takes a long time without a computer.

Is a laptop easy to use in the field? No. It's hard to find a good place to set it up. The screen is hard to see in the sun. It's exposed to damage from dust and vibration. I keep mine in its case much of the time and pull it out when I need it. Despite these drawbacks, it has been indispensable at times and saved me many hours of wandering around aimlessly. I know I'll never get lost when I have it with me.

I already have paper maps. Will a GPS unit help me? Yes. You can plot your GPS location on any map that has tick marks along the edge for latitude/longitude or UTM coordinates. You can get a general idea where you are by sighting across the map. To determine your exact position, you'll need to draw lines. (A template is needed with UTM.) Large fold-out maps can be awkward in the car. I like the handy booklet-style format of an atlas like the DeLorme *Atlas & Gazetteer* or Benchmark's *Road & Recreation Atlas.*

What's UTM (Universal Transverse Mercator)? It's an alternative to using Latitude/Longitude coordinates. Many people prefer it because it's easier to plot on a map. Most topo maps have ruled UTM grid lines. Others argue that UTM is not as accurate as Lat./Long. Some maps may have only one set of coordinates. Most GPS units give coordinates both ways. Both are given in this book.

What maps do I need? Again it depends on your needs. The greatest amount of detail is shown on USGS 7.5 minute maps, but many maps are needed to cover a large area. Forest Service maps are practical when you're on forest land but don't help in other areas. The BLM also has maps but they vary in quality. Your best buy is an atlas-style map that covers an entire state. If you're using a computer, several companies now offer statewide map packages with the same detail as 7.5 minute maps. A state the size of

California requires about 12 CDs for these rasterized maps. The packages also include the software to manipulate the data. Vector quality maps have less detail but cover more area.

What's the difference between rasterized and vector maps? A rasterized image looks like a photograph of the original map. It takes a lot of computer space. When you zoom out you lose detail. Up close, however, it has the best detail. A vector map is a line conversion and looks more like a drawing in flat color. It lacks detail, but looks the same as you zoom in and out. It doesn't require as much computer space and can be downloaded directly into some new GPS units.

What's mapping software do? Among other things, it allows you to manipulate maps on the screen, download and upload your waypoints and trackpoints, save map images and print them out. It finds the next map as you run off the page and switches automatically to the next map when you're moving in your vehicle with your GPS on.

What specific equipment and maps do you use, Mr. Wells? I use a Garmin II Plus GPS receiver. I bought two additional accessories— a dash mount and a computer cord. The computer cord is split with one part that goes to my cigarette lighter which powers the GPS unit. I've never needed an outside antenna.

I have a Dell Inspiron 7000 laptop with a 14.5″ screen, 4 gig HD, 64 MB ram, and 300 MHz. It has two 4-hour batteries, but since I don't leave the computer on all the time, I've never needed the second battery.

I've been using this equipment for over three years, which means it is not state-of-the-art; however, for my needs it works perfectly. Make sure you compare brands and check out the latest equipment before you buy.

I use a CD map package called All Topo Maps by iGage. The California set includes 2,850 USGS 7.5 minute maps, 121 USGS 1:100,000-scale maps and 38 USGS 1:250,000-scale maps. Because of what I do, I have special needs that the average person doesn't. The maps are complete with collars and are as close as you can get to using a real USGS map. The software has an excellent search tool with a large data base. When I have questions, I have no problem getting through on their toll-free tech support number.

What other mapping software is available? The three best-known brands of mapping software are National Geographic, DeLorme and Maptech. National Geographic maps are rasterized and usually cover one state at a time. DeLorme and Maptech are vector maps which cover the entire United States. They are all excellent packages and offer many high-tech features. Each has advantages and disadvantages depending upon your specific needs. Before you buy, shop around and compare all brands. Go to a store that has them installed on a computer so you can try them out. Not all stores carry all brands. Maptech is harder to find than the other two. You may have to go to several stores.

How much did you spend on your GPS equipment? My equipment is about three years old now, so take that into consideration. The Garmin II Plus was about $250 plus a little more for the accessories. My Dell laptop was about $3,000. I recently checked the cost of the iGage mapping package; it still sells for about $120. I also carry many folding maps that would be expensive to replace.

I don't want to spend that much but would still like to have a GPS unit. What can I do? The most important thing a GPS unit does is tell you where you are. A simple unit will do that. You can buy a quality GPS unit with basic features for about $100. If you don't have any maps, invest in a DeLorme *Southern and Central California Atlas and Gazetteer,* which costs about $20. With this you can plot your general position quickly and easily. Simply look along the edge of the map for longitude and latitude. I use this method about 95% of the time.

If you have a home PC, I'd definitely spend a little more for a GPS unit that can download and upload data to your computer. The first time you try to key waypoints into your GPS unit, you'll know why a computer is important.

How can I learn more about GPS? The first thing I did was buy and read a book called *GPS Made Easy* by Lawrence Letham (see references and reading section). It explained GPS in easy-to-understand terms. Finding information about GPS units, different brands, etc., is more difficult.

You can find excellent information on the Internet. Check out 4x4books.com, which sells GPS equipment and mapping products. They show and compare most GPS products and have the latest information on new products. You can also contact the manufacturers directly. (See addresses and phone number section that follows.)

GPS Waypoint Coordinates

The following table lists waypoints for each trail. Waypoints are shown in Latitude/Longitude (degrees/minutes/seconds) and UTM coordinates. No coordinate should be in error by more than a radius of 20 meters or approximately 60 feet. All coordinates were compiled using All Topo Maps (iGage) software (DATUM=NAD27). Only significant intersections or special features were assigned waypoints.

Wpt.	Mile	Latitude North	Longitude West	UTM Easting	UTM Northing	Zone
1. TITUS CANYON						
01	0	36 51 33.4	116 50 42.3	513811E	4079070N	11
02	15.7	36 50 54.4	117 03 29.7	494807E	4077859N	11
03	26.8	36 47 16.4	117 11 26.0	482997E	4071158N	11
2. CHLORIDE CITY						
01	0	36 45 01.8	116 56 09.1	505726E	4066998N	11
02	2.2	36 44 12.4	116 54 42.2	507883E	4065475N	11
03	5.3	36 43 03.8	116 53 03.8	510325E	4063362N	11
04	6.6	36 42 17.7	116 52 54.7	510552E	4061943N	11
3. COTTONWOOD/ MARBLE CANYON						
01	0	36 36 21.6	117 08 48.2	486877E	4050975N	11
02	8.5	36 38 33.2	117 16 10.6	475898E	4055052N	11
03	10.8	36 37 53.9	117 17 40.8	473654E	4053849N	11
04	19.5	36 32 25.4	117 20 38.4	469208E	4043741N	11
05	2.7	36 36 59.1	117 19 56.9	470270E	4052172N	11
4. ECHO PASS/ INYO MINE						
01	0	36 26 15.4	116 49 23.9	515834E	4032302N	11
02	9.1	36 29 46.8	116 42 35.3	525989E	4038839N	11
03	9.6	36 29 36.4	116 42 10.8	526602E	4038520N	11
04	5.2	36 31 48.1	116 40 17.3	529410E	4042586N	11
5. JAIL CANYON						
01	0	36 08 41.5	117 13 58.3	479050E	3999841N	11
02	2.0	36 10 18.6	117 13 37.3	479583E	4002830N	11
03	3.1	36 11 07.5	117 13 09.7	480276E	4004336N	11
04	5.6	36 11 36.4	117 10 48.9	483794E	4005219N	11
6. PLEASANT CANYON/ SOUTH PARK						
01	0	36 02 52.5	117 13 23.7	479891E	3989085N	11
02	6.0	36 01 58.3	117 08 02.4	487927E	3987401N	11
03	10.7	36 01 08.3	117 04 24.9	493370E	3985854N	11

Wpt.	Mile	Latitude North	Longitude West	UTM Easting	UTM Northing	Zone
04	12.9	36 00 02.1	117 05 50.8	491218E	3983818N	11
05	13.9	35 59 31.8	117 05 25.3	491855E	3982882N	11
06	17.8	35 59 36.4	117 09 24.6	485863E	3983031N	11
07	23.3	36 00 00.1	117 13 09.6	480231E	3983773N	11

7. GOLER WASH/ MENGEL PASS

Wpt.	Mile	Latitude North	Longitude West	UTM Easting	UTM Northing	Zone
01	0	35 51 33.3	117 10 44.5	483835E	3968152N	11
02	3.8	35 51 42.3	117 07 37.7	488521E	3968423N	11
03	6.0	35 51 38.1	117 05 45.4	491338E	3968291N	11
04	6.6	35 51 34.6	117 05 15.4	492090E	3968182N	11
05	3.3	35 53 59.9	117 04 52.9	492658E	3972655N	11
06	4.7	35 54 51.9	117 04 54.4	492621E	3974258N	11
07	5.4	35 55 24.0	117 05 01.0	492457E	3975249N	11

8. BUTTE VALLEY

Wpt.	Mile	Latitude North	Longitude West	UTM Easting	UTM Northing	Zone
01	0	35 57 14.5	116 44 44.5	522933E	3978679N	11
02	10.9	35 58 09.1	116 55 34.3	506654E	3980334N	11
03	11.9	35 55 25.0	117 04 54.2	492628E	3975279N	11

9. FISH CANYON ESCAPE TRAIL

Wpt.	Mile	Latitude North	Longitude West	UTM Easting	UTM Northing	Zone
01	0	35 50 44.4	117 18 05.7	472766E	3966673N	11
02	2.7	35 51 30.6	117 16 05.3	475790E	3968088N	11
03	5.9	35 53 26.4	117 15 02.4	477376E	3971651N	11
04	8.3	35 53 54.0	117 13 02.6	480382E	3972492N	11
05	12.4	35 51 30.7	117 10 44.5	483836E	3968071N	11

10. SANTA YNEZ PEAK

Wpt.	Mile	Latitude North	Longitude West	UTM Easting	UTM Northing	Zone
01	0	34 30 15.9	119 48 42.1	241848E	3821483N	11
02	13.2	34 31 41.1	119 58 53.1	226332E	3824556N	11
03	19.3	34 32 01.0	120 03 40.2	219034E	3825386N	11

11. AGUA CALIENTE SPRINGS

Wpt.	Mile	Latitude North	Longitude West	UTM Easting	UTM Northing	Zone
01	0	34 29 28.9	119 47 40.6	243379E	3819989N	11
02	12.3	34 29 28.0	119 41 20.6	253072E	3819699N	11
03	30.1	34 32 21.3	119 33 48.9	264731E	3824740N	11
04	6.7	34 26 44.4	119 41 12.9	253134E	3814651N	11

12. LOCKWOOD/ MILLER JEEP TRAIL

Wpt.	Mile	Latitude North	Longitude West	UTM Easting	UTM Northing	Zone
01	0	34 44 07.3	119 02 16.4	313425E	3845391N	11
02	2.1	34 43 18.6	119 03 18.7	311809E	3843921N	11
03	4.9	34 42 21.9	119 01 54.7	313910E	3842131N	11
04	9.1	34 41 59.7	118 59 58.2	316861E	3841387N	11
05	2.8	34 40 33.8	118 58 39.6	318811E	3838704N	11
06	-	34 40 34.6	118 58 36.8	318882E	3838727N	11
07	-	34 43 52.4	118 52 20.5	328573E	3844635N	11

Wpt.	Mile	Latitude North	Longitude West	UTM Easting	UTM Northing	Zone
13. ALAMO MOUNTAIN LOOP						
01	0	34 43 52.7	118 52 21.1	328557E	3844645N	11
02	12.5	34 40 10.9	118 56 52.3	321527E	3837945N	11
03	15.8	34 39 02.8	118 57 20.5	320769E	3835858N	11
04	19.7	34 38 18.8	118 55 08.0	324115E	3834438N	11
05	3.3	34 40 34.0	118 58 36.1	318899E	3838706N	11
14. PRONGHORN TRAIL						
01	0	34 43 07.0	118 50 13.8	331769E	3843180N	11
02	1.3	34 43 06.2	118 49 18.9	333166E	3843128N	11
03	02.9	34 43 55.8	118 49 12.9	333346E	3844654N	11
04	6.0	34 45 43.8	118 48 39.2	334264E	3847965N	11
05	6.7	34 46 44.7	118 52 49.1	327944E	3849958N	11
15. LIEBRE MOUNTAIN						
01	0	34 42 56.2	118 42 35.4	343425E	3842641N	11
02	3.2	34 42 46.4	118 37 49.9	350684E	3842219N	11
03	9.5	34 41 29.9	118 33 13.3	357684E	3839752N	11
04	12.6	34 42 11.8	118 31 38.1	360126E	3841002N	11
16. ROWHER TRAIL						
01	0	34 34 33.7	118 22 23.9	374034E	3826688N	1
02	1.6	34 33 50.0	118 21 31.2	375358E	3825325N	11
03	2.6	34 33 38.8	118 20 47.1	376477E	3824965N	11
04	3.0	34 33 17.9	118 20 40.5	376638E	3824317N	11
05	3.8	34 32 42.2	118 21 04.1	376020E	3823225N	11
06	5.2	34 31 54.0	118 21 56.1	374674E	3821759N	11
07	1.9	34 31 34.4	118 22 54.1	373188E	3821176N	11
08	4.7	34 29 59.3	118 22 52.7	373184E	3818245N	11
17. SIERRA PELONA ROAD						
01	0	34 29 59.3	118 22 52.7	373184E	3818245N	11
02	2.8	34 31 37.8	118 22 53.6	373203E	3821279N	11
03	1.9	34 30 52.4	118 24 27.5	370789E	3819915N	11
04	5.5	34 32 52.1	118 24 02.7	371473E	3823592N	11
05	10.0	34 33 44.7	118 20 41.5	376623E	3825143N	11
06	14.8	34 34 48.1	118 22 04.3	374541E	3827125N	11
18. WALL STREET CANYON OVERLOOK						
01	0	34 55 16.1	116 50 52.6	513889E	3864109N	11
02	1.6	34 56 23.8	116 50 18.6	514755E	3866211N	11
03	4.3	34 57 20.8	116 48 29.5	517512E	3867958N	11
04	2.8	34 58 17.8	116 50 46.0	514048E	3869707N	11
05	3.0	34 58 09.1	116 50 49.8	513953E	3869439N	11
06	4.0	34 57 58.8	116 51 29.3	512950E	3869122N	11
07	4.4	34 58 07.1	116 51 48.6	512462E	3869377N	11

Wpt.	Mile	Latitude North	Longitude West	UTM Easting	UTM Northing	Zone
08	4.9	34 57 53.0	116 52 10.1	511917E	3868940N	11
09	5.1	34 57 45.2	116 52 11.9	511871E	3868701N	11
10	0.7	34 58 13.1	116 52 12.6	511853E	3869559N	11
11	4.5	35 00 10.2	116 54 45.5	507973E	3873163N	11

19. DORAN LOOP

Wpt.	Mile	Latitude North	Longitude West	UTM Easting	UTM Northing	Zone
01	0	34 56 23.6	116 51 28.5	512976E	3866188N	11
02	0.6	34 56 47.9	116 51 07.2	513515E	3866938N	11
03	0.7	34 56 54.7	116 51 11.5	513406E	3867146N	11
04	1.5	34 57 55.2	116 51 36.2	512776E	3869010N	11
05	1.7	34 57 58.7	116 51 29.6	512943E	3869117N	11
06	0.5	34 58 20.4	116 51 14.8	513318E	3869788N	11
07	1.0	34 58 08.7	116 50 49.9	513947E	3869428N	11
08	0.6	34 57 44.9	116 50 59.9	513698E	3868695N	11

20. ODESSA CANYON

Wpt.	Mile	Latitude North	Longitude West	UTM Easting	UTM Northing	Zone
01	0	34 56 23.6	116 51 28.5	512976E	3866188N	11
02	0.6	34 56 47.9	116 51 07.2	513515E	3866938N	11
03	2.1	34 57 44.9	116 50 59.9	513698E	3868695N	11
04	2.7	34 58 08.7	116 50 50.0	513947E	3869428N	11
05	0.5	34 58 20.4	116 51 14.8	513317E	3869788N	11
06	0.9	34 57 58.7	116 51 29.6	512943E	3869117N	11
07	0.2	34 57 55.2	116 51 36.2	512776E	3869010N	11
08	1.6	34 56 58.6	116 51.09.6	513452E	3867266N	11

21. PHILLIPS LOOP

Wpt.	Mile	Latitude North	Longitude West	UTM Easting	UTM Northing	Zone
01	0	34 56 24.1	116 50 18.6	514748E	3866205N	11
02	0.4	34 56 37.9	116 50 37.2	514277E	3866630N	11
03	0.9	34 56 59.9	116 50 37.3	514272E	3867311N	11
04	1.6	34 57 25.4	116 50 39.8	514206E	3868095N	11
05	2.7	34 56 44.2	116 50 23.4	514627E	3866827N	11
06	0.4	34 56 43.5	116 51 17.6	513251E	3866803N	11

22. MULE CANYON ROAD

Wpt.	Mile	Latitude North	Longitude West	UTM Easting	UTM Northing	Zone
01	0	34 55 16.1	116 50 52.6	513889E	3864109N	11
02	1.6	34 56 44.3	116 50 23.4	514627E	3866827N	11
03	4.3	34 57 20.5	116 48 29.4	517515E	3867949N	11
04	6.0	34 57 08.8	116 47 05.6	519641E	3867591N	11
05	8.2	34 55 21.4	116 46 32.8	520480E	3864286N	11

23. ACHY-BREAKY

Wpt.	Mile	Latitude North	Longitude West	UTM Easting	UTM Northing	Zone
01	0	34 46 49.5	117 03 16.9	494996E	3848495N	11
02	0.6	34 47 07.3	117 02 55.3	495545E	3849045N	11
03	0.8	34 47 13.3	117 02 59.4	495441E	3849231N	11
04	1.0	34 47 23.5	117 02 53.4	495594E	3849543N	11
05	1.3	34 47 30.4	117 02 50.5	495666E	3849757N	11

Wpt.	Mile	Latitude North	Longitude West	UTM Easting	UTM Northing	Zone
06	1.6	34 47 36.4	117 02 38.2	495980E	3849941N	11
07	1.7	34 47 35.3	117 02 30.3	496180E	3849907N	11
08	1.8	34 47 30.5	117 02 27.8	496244E	3849760N	11
09	1.9	34 47 29.7	117 02 20.9	496418E	3849733N	11
10	2.3	34 47 19.9	117 02 15.2	496564E	3849435N	11
11	2.5	34 47 27.0	117 02 11.0	496671E	3849652N	11
12	3.0	34 47 11.8	117 02 08.2	496742E	3849182N	11
13	3.1	34 47 16.1	117 02 06.4	496787E	3849317N	11
14	3.2	34 47 12.0	117 02 00.1	496949E	3849190N	11
15	3.4	34 47 05.9	117 01 56.9	497028E	3849000N	11
16	3.9	34 46 45.8	117 01 55.7	497060E	3848383N	11
17	4.2	34 46 36.7	117 02 07.9	496750E	3848103N	11
18	4.4	34 46 42.8	117 02 17.2	496512E	3848291N	11
19	4.8	34 46 54.9	117 02 21.9	496394E	3848664N	11
20	5.0	34 46 47.6	117 02 29.0	496213E	3848437N	11
21	5.6	34 47 01.1	117 02 51.2	495648E	3848853N	11
22	6.2	34 47 03.9	117 03 14.4	495060E	3848939N	11

24. MOJAVE ROAD EAST

Wpt.	Mile	Latitude North	Longitude West	UTM Easting	UTM Northing	Zone
01	0	35 03 07.5	114 40 31.6	712009E	3881093N	11
02	1.5	35 03 34.7	114 42 06.1	709597E	3881874N	11
03	7.9	35 06 52.0	114 46 19.5	703040E	3887810N	11
04	11.3	35 06 46.2	114 49 41.8	697921E	3887515N	11
05	18.6	35 06 43.7	114 57 12.2	686521E	3887199N	11
06	24.0	35 05 28.3	114 57 15.5	686484E	3884871N	11
07	28.5	35 05 59.8	115 00 46.6	681117E	3885734N	11
08	31.2	35 06 20.8	115 02 53.4	677894E	3886319N	11
09	36.0	35 07 20.8	115 07 42.5	670539E	3888025N	11
10	37.3	35 07 35.7	115 08 43.0	668999E	3888457N	11
11	39.8	35 08 18.9	115 11 10.1	665252E	3889721N	11

25. MOJAVE ROAD CENTRAL

Wpt.	Mile	Latitude North	Longitude West	UTM Easting	UTM Northing	Zone
01	0	35 08 18.9	115 11 09.9	665255E	3889719N	11
02	3.9	35 08 23.8	115 15 17.9	658977E	3889757N	11
03	8.4	35 09 12.5	115 19 37.7	652376E	3891145N	11
04	10.5	35 08 50.6	115 21 30.3	649541E	3890424N	11
05	20.6	35 10 34.2	115 30 30.1	635831E	3893399N	11
06	25.9	35 11 19.7	115 35 57.8	627520E	3894681N	11
07	29.0	35 10 08.7	115 38 50.3	623187E	3892433N	11
08	32.4	35 11 07.2	115 41 31.2	619093E	3894182N	11
09	37.5	35 10 22.9	115 46 36.3	611693E	3892719N	11
10	44.0	35 11 56.2	115 52 17.1	602740E	3895490N	11

26. MOJAVE ROAD WEST

Wpt.	Mile	Latitude North	Longitude West	UTM Easting	UTM Northing	Zone
01	0	35 11 56.2	115 52 17.1	602740E	3895490N	11
02	6.3	35 11 12.1	115 57 10.8	595327E	3894052N	11

Wpt.	Mile	Latitude North	Longitude West	UTM Easting	UTM Northing	Zone
03	10.2	35 09 41.6	116 00 43.7	589970E	3891208N	11
04	19.0	35 06 31.7	116 08 31.5	578186E	3885249N	11
05	21.6	35 05 25.8	116 10 52.1	574644E	3883188N	11
06	31.2	35 02 34.1	116 18 30.3	563077E	3877811N	11
07	34.8	35 01 32.4	116 21 33.0	558460E	3875879N	11
08	36.6	35 02 30.1	116 23 34.1	555381E	3877636N	11
09	40.2	35 04 15.4	116 24 41.6	553652E	3880871N	11

27. RINCON-SHORTCUT ROAD

Wpt.	Mile	Latitude North	Longitude West	UTM Easting	UTM Northing	Zone
01	0	34 14 16.2	117 51 45.2	420564E	3788669N	11
02	13.3	34 12 54.9	117 58 52.9	409600E	3786262N	11
03	17.2	34 14 05.9	118 00 47.6	406685E	3788479N	11
04	26.2	34 16 24.2	118 01 57.8	404934E	3792754N	11

28. CUCAMONGA BIG TREE TRAIL

Wpt.	Mile	Latitude North	Longitude West	UTM Easting	UTM Northing	Zone
01	0	34 10 22.2	117 37 43.4	442056E	3781304N	11
02	3.7	34 11 10.3	117 36 14.0	444352E	3782772N	11
03	6.1	34 11 53.3	117 35 18.6	445777E	3784086N	11
04	12.1	34 13 07.3	117 33 07.2	449154E	3786347N	11
05	16.6	34 12 28.6	117 29 53.6	454102E	3785129N	11
06	23.7	34 12 05.5	117 26 54.0	458695E	3784398N	11

29. CLEGHORN RIDGE

Wpt.	Mile	Latitude North	Longitude West	UTM Easting	UTM Northing	Zone
01	0	34 17 53.9	117 27 22.0	458026E	3795133N	11
02	7.0	34 17 45.5	117 25 17.4	461210E	3794859N	11
03	11.0	34 17 45.0	117 22 36.3	465327E	3794827N	11
04	15.0	34 18 01.7	117 20 10.3	469062E	3795329N	11

30. PILOT ROCK ROAD

Wpt.	Mile	Latitude North	Longitude West	UTM Easting	UTM Northing	Zone
01	0	34 16 15.9	117 17 22.0	473355E	3792057N	11
02	0.7	34 16 14.7	117 16 41.8	474383E	3792018N	11
03	2.6	34 16 52.6	117 17 17.8	473466E	3793186N	11
04	8.8	34 18 18.5	117 18 32.0	471575E	3795839N	11

31. SANTIAGO PEAK

Wpt.	Mile	Latitude North	Longitude West	UTM Easting	UTM Northing	Zone
01	0	33 38 14.9	117 25 17.2	460914E	3721848N	11
02	3.4	33 39 43.8	117 26 49.9	458538E	3724595N	11
03	7.5	33 42 28.4	117 30 01.5	453629E	3729686N	11
04	15.5	33 42 41.2	117 31 54.4	450726E	3730094N	11
05	7.6	33 44 54.5	117 27 06.8	458144E	3734166N	11

32. GRAPEVINE CANYON

Wpt.	Mile	Latitude North	Longitude West	UTM Easting	UTM Northing	Zone
01	0	34 16 10.1	116 56 47.2	504931E	3791842N	11
02	6.8	34 19 11.5	117 00 33.5	499145E	3797428N	11
03	12.3	34 20 34.9	117 03 48.0	494174E	3799998N	11
04	15.6	34 22 56.7	117 03 14.1	495042E	3804365N	11

Wpt.	Mile	Latitude North	Longitude West	UTM Easting	UTM Northing	Zone
05	20.3	34 24 51.8	117 01 57.0	497012E	3807908N	11
06	22.8	34 27 01.3	117 01 57.0	497015E	3811896N	11

33. WILLOW CREEK ROAD

01	0	34 16 10.6	117 08 12.8	487398E	3791864N	11
02	3.3	34 17 35.3	117 09 24.6	485567E	3794475N	11
03	5.2	34 18 02.2	117 10 58.3	483173E	3795306N	11
04	7.4	34 17 50.8	117 12 28.3	480871E	3794962N	11

34. DISHPAN SPRINGS

01	0	34 16 10.3	117 08 13.4	487383E	3791854N	11
02	2.4	34 15 53.4	117 06 58.0	489309E	3791331N	11
03	3.5	34 15 40.6	117 06 04.1	490688E	3790937N	11
04	4.8	34 15 38.7	117 05 01.1	492299E	3790875N	11

35. HOLCOMB CREEK

01	0	34 16 30.8	117 03 00.8	495377E	3792477N	11
02	3.9	34 16 56.4	117 00 09.5	499758E	3793266N	11
03	5.9	34 18 01.2	116 58 54.2	501683E	3795263N	11

36. BUTLER PEAK

01	0	34 16 46.8	116 57 38.9	503607E	3792972N	11
02	2.2	34 16 02.8	116 59 17.9	501076E	3791616N	11
03	4.8	34 15 25.7	117 00 25.1	499358E	3790471N	11
04	1.3	34 16 37.4	116 58 36.9	502124E	3792681N	11

37. JOHN BULL TRAIL

01	0	34 18 17.9	116 50 47.3	514127E	3795788N	11
02	1.1	34 19 08.7	116 51 13.1	513467E	3797351N	11
03	2.7	34 19 03.3	116 52 23.4	511669E	3797181N	11
04	3.0	34 19 06.4	116 54 14.0	508842E	3797275N	11
05	4.0	34 18 22.9	116 54 40.4	508170E	3795933N	11

38. JACOBY CANYON

01	0	34 18 16.9	116 49 44.3	515739E	3795757N	11
02	0.4	34 18 11.4	116 50 07.0	515157E	3795589N	11
03	2.9	34 19 02.1	116 48 51.4	517087E	3797154N	11

39. GOLD MOUNTAIN

01	0	34 16 35.7	116 48 59.7	516700E	3792402N	11
02	2.5	34 17 05.4	116 50 21.4	514792E	3793555N	11
03	2.9	34 17 15.5	116 50 23.3	514744E	3793866N	11
04	4.5	34 17 57.2	116 50 11.1	515055E	3795146N	11

40. CLARKS SUMMIT

01	0	34 10 14.7	116 49 31.7	516085E	3780908N	11

Wpt.	Mile	Latitude North	Longitude West	UTM Easting	UTM Northing	Zone
02	6.2	34 11 40.5	116 54 39.3	508209E	3783540N	11
03	12.0	34 13 02.6	116 52 43.7	511163E	3786071N	11
04	17.1	34 12 34.1	116 56 37.5	505182E	3785190N	11
05	5.8	34 11 00.2	116 58 12.4	502755E	3782297N	11
06	7.8	34 10 22.6	116 56 57.0	504685E	3781137N	11
07	13.0	34 10 08.4	116 53 32.2	509929E	3780705N	11

41. SKYLINE DRIVE

Wpt.	Mile	Latitude North	Longitude West	UTM Easting	UTM Northing	Zone
01	0	34 13 38.3	116 51 59.0	512307E	3787173N	11
02	1.2	34 12 54.4	116 55 18.0	507216E	3785816N	11
03	6.4	34 12 34.3	116 56 37.6	505178E	3785195N	11
04	11.8	34 13 43.7	116 55 58.7	506172E	3787332N	11
05	13.0	34 14 18.7	116 55 19.9	507166E	3788411N	11

42. HEARTBREAK RIDGE

Wpt.	Mile	Latitude North	Longitude West	UTM Easting	UTM Northing	Zone
01	0	34 12 26.7	116 44 13.3	524224E	3784990N	11
02	6.3	34 14 37.1	116 42 21.7	527070E	3789013N	11
03	8.3	34 13 26.0	116 41 40.0	528148E	3786827N	11
04	9.2	34 12 56.7	116 42 05.2	527501E	3785922N	11
05	13.3	34 13 38.2	116 40 15.1	530316E	3787211N	11
06	15.1	34 14 09.6	116 41 14.0	528806E	3788174N	11
07	16.4	34 14 46.7	116 42 07.4	527435E	3789309N	11

43. RATTLESNAKE CANYON

Wpt.	Mile	Latitude North	Longitude West	UTM Easting	UTM Northing	Zone
01	0	34 22 12.0	116 38 59.6	532192E	3803042N	11
02	3.8	34 20 38.4	116 41 52.1	527794E	3800146N	11
03	16.1	34 14 00.7	116 38 36.8	532828E	3787913N	11
04	8.7	34 10 53.8	116 32 06.3	542843E	3782196N	11
05	16.2	34 07 11.1	116 26 42.5	551169E	3775376N	11

44. LOWER COYOTE CANYON

Wpt.	Mile	Latitude North	Longitude West	UTM Easting	UTM Northing	Zone
01	0	33 19 31.5	116 22 00.6	558932E	3687349N	11
02	4.0	33 21 55.7	116 24 53.7	554431E	3691765N	11
03	7.3	33 22 26.5	116 26 54.3	551310E	3692696N	11
04	9.5	33 21 58.1	116 28 49.7	548332E	3691807N	11

45. CALCITE MINE

Wpt.	Mile	Latitude North	Longitude West	UTM Easting	UTM Northing	Zone
01	0	33 16 52.2	116 05 44.4	584214E	3682629N	11
02	0.6	33 17 15.0	116 06 11.1	583517E	3683326N	11
03	1.9	33 17 56.5	116 06 34.7	582897E	3684600N	11

46. TRUCKHAVEN

Wpt.	Mile	Latitude North	Longitude West	UTM Easting	UTM Northing	Zone
01	0	33 18 10.2	115 58 51.8	594863E	3685131N	11
02	1.6	33 17 16.7	116 00 12.7	592786E	3683463N	11
03	2.2	33 17 20.8	116 01 41.9	590478E	3683567N	11
04	2.0	33 17 38.8	116 03 00.0	588452E	3684102N	11

Wpt.	Mile	Latitude North	Longitude West	UTM Easting	UTM Northing	Zone
05	3.1	33 17 46.6	116 03 17.5	587999E	3684338N	11
06	0.8	33 18 08.0	116 03 05.3	588308E	3685001N	11
07	5.2	33 19 26.3	115 59 50.6	593321E	3687460N	11

47. FONTS POINT

Wpt.	Mile	Latitude North	Longitude West	UTM Easting	UTM Northing	Zone
01	0	33 18 11.9	116 14 17.5	570922E	3684980E	11
02	3.9	33 15 27.8	116 13 57.6	571476E	3679928E	11

48. THE SLOT

Wpt.	Mile	Latitude North	Longitude West	UTM Easting	UTM Northing	Zone
01	0	33 09 32.5	116 13 04.5	572931E	3668998N	11
02	0.9	33 10 16.3	116 12 44.7	573432E	3670349N	11
03	3.5	33 11 11.0	116 13 13.5	572673E	3672029N	11
04	2.3	33 12 43.5	116 12 44.0	573417E	3674885N	11
05	4.1	33 11 54.3	116 11 17.1	575679E	3673385N	11

49. OCOTILLO WELLS SVRA

Wpt.	Mile	Latitude North	Longitude West	UTM Easting	UTM Northing	Zone
01	0	33 09 04.5	116 09 59.0	577742E	3668172N	11
02	5.7	33 11 04.2	116 05 08.0	585249E	3671923N	11
03	7.8	33 11 19.6	116 03 03.8	588462E	3672425N	11
04	8.9	33 10 58.4	116 02 03.2	590035E	3671787N	11
05	11.5	33 10 44.5	115 59 39.1	593773E	3671393N	11
06	16.1	33 09 59.7	115 56 36.1	598525E	3670060N	11
07	18.3	33 10 33.3	115 58 38.9	595334E	3671064N	11
08	21.8	33 07 33.9	115 58 34.6	595489E	3665544N	11

50. PUMPKIN PATCH

Wpt.	Mile	Latitude North	Longitude West	UTM Easting	UTM Northing	Zone
01	0	33 11 03.9	116 05 07.7	585256E	3671911N	11
02	0.9	33 11 44.9	116 05 32.8	584595E	3673168N	11
03	1.9	33 12 15.8	116 05 18.1	584967E	3674126N	11
04	2.2	33 12 29.0	116 05 18.8	584947E	3674530N	11
05	2.4	33 12 39.0	116 05 09.6	585183E	3674841N	11
06	4.4	33 13 22.6	116 04 03.7	586877E	3676199N	11

51. CROSS OVER TRAIL

Wpt.	Mile	Latitude North	Longitude West	UTM Easting	UTM Northing	Zone
01	0	33 11 19.6	116 03 03.5	588469E	3672426N	11
02	2.8	33.13 00.9	116 01 54.4	590229E	3675561N	11
03	4.3	33 14 13.6	116 01 49.8	590327E	3677801N	11
04	5.4	33 15 03.8	116 01 27.7	590885E	3679353N	11
05	6.7	33 15 57.7	116 01 04.9	591460E	3681019N	11

52. ORIFLAMME CANYON

Wpt.	Mile	Latitude North	Longitude West	UTM Easting	UTM Northing	Zone
01	0	33 00 27.4	116 27 19.6	550867E	3652071N	11
02	1.8	33 01 06.0	116 28 44.4	548661E	3653248N	11
03	4.1	33 00 38.3	116 31 05.9	544994E	3652379N	11
04	5.5	33 03 14.0	116 32 29.4	542807E	3657163N	11
05	3.2	33 04 03.0	116 32 48.5	542305E	3658671N	11

Wpt.	Mile	Latitude North	Longitude West	UTM Easting	UTM Northing	Zone
53. BLAIR VALLEY						
01	0	33 02 48.2	116 24 46.4	554819E	3656429N	11
02	2.0	33 02 11.9	116 23 21.1	557036E	3655323N	11
03	5.7	33 00 34.3	116 22 38.1	558170E	3652323N	11
04	9.8	33 00 20.5	116 23 11.0	557318E	3651893N	11
05	11.1	33 02 13.7	116 24 35.1	555117E	3655367N	11
54. PINYON MOUNTAIN ROAD						
01	0	33 03 24.6	116 25 14.6	554082E	3657547N	11
02	7.6	33 03 03.3	116 18 10.3	565089E	3656957N	11
03	8.9	33 03 15.4	116 17 12.2	566593E	3657340N	11
04	18.0	32 58 46.9	116 12 49.7	573462E	3649119N	11
05	20.9	32 57 38.0	116 10 40.0	576849E	3647023N	11
06	0.9	32 58 12.8	116 10 18.0	577408E	3648101N	11
07	5.4	32 59 35.1	116 07 03.5	582437E	3650674N	11
08	9.6	33 02 22.9	116 05 45.9	584406E	3655858N	11
55. SANDSTONE CANYON						
01	0	33 02 23.9	116 05 45.0	584429E	3655891N	11
02	4.3	32 59 34.8	116 07 03.8	582428E	3650666N	11
03	6.9	32 58 52.8	116 08 57.9	579477E	3649346N	11
04	8.7	32 58 14.8	116 10 17.7	577415E	3648165N	11
05	12.5	32 58 45.8	116 12 49.3	573474E	3649086N	11
06	15.0	32 59 37.3	116 14 31.5	570808E	3650653N	11
56. CANYON SIN NOMBRE						
01	0	32 49 47.9	116 10 10.1	577735E	3632554N	11
02	4.3	32 52 22.8	116 08 36.8	580123E	3637341N	11
03	5.5	32 52 56.9	116 09 30.0	578733E	3638380N	11
04	7.1	32 53 41.7	116 10 41.8	576854E	3639747N	11
57. MUD CAVES/ DIABLO DROPOFF						
01	0	32 53 41.7	116 10 41.8	576854E	3639747N	11
02	1.2	32 54 36.0	116 10 58.8	576400E	3641415N	11
03	2.3	32 55 18.5	116 11 00.1	576357E	3642723N	11
04	6.4	32 57 10.6	116 12 53.4	573389E	3646153N	11
05	8.9	32 56 20.3	116 11 21.1	575796E	3644623N	11
06	10.3	32 57 17.5	116 11 14.1	575965E	3646384N	11
07	11.3	32 57 37.9	116 10 40.7	576826E	3647022N	11
08	6.3	32 52 56.9	116 09 30.0	578733E	3638380N	11
58. MORTERO WASH						
01	0	32 47 34.1	116 06 24.6	583633E	3628480N	11
02	4.1	32 44 46.5	116 08 19.5	580686E	3623295N	11
03	6.4	32 45 55.6	116 09 56.8	578138E	3625401N	11
04	1.0	32 43 05.8	116 08 24.2	580589E	3620193N	11

Wpt.	Mile	Latitude North	Longitude West	UTM Easting	UTM Northing	Zone
05	3.5	32 42 56.6	116 06 17.5	583891E	3619935N	11
06	6.2	32 44 34.7	116 05 07.3	585692E	3622972N	11
07	8.0	32 45 28.8	116 03 43.8	587850E	3624657N	11

59. LOS PINOS LOOKOUT

Wpt.	Mile	Latitude North	Longitude West	UTM Easting	UTM Northing	Zone
01	0	32 43 30.1	116 33 30.1	541385E	3620699N	11
02	4.6	32 44 50.8	116 34 28.4	539857E	3623180N	11
03	7.7	32 45 14.7	116 37 07.8	535705E	3623899N	11
04	10.1	32 43 38.9	116 37 13.0	535581E	3620947N	11
05	11.8	32 42 54.8	116 36 52.3	536125E	3619593N	11
06	13.7	32 42 13.0	116 35 46.4	537846E	3618312N	11

60. BRONCO PEAK

Wpt.	Mile	Latitude North	Longitude West	UTM Easting	UTM Northing	Zone
01	0	32 42 17.3	116 32 58.7	542211E	3618462N	11
02	1.1	32 42 19.7	116 33 42.4	541072E	3618532N	11
03	1.9	32 42 19.0	116 34 13.4	540267E	3618507N	11
04	2.7	32 41 44.9	116 33 55.1	540746E	3617458N	11

61. SIDEWINDER

Wpt.	Mile	Latitude North	Longitude West	UTM Easting	UTM Northing	Zone
01	0	32 43 03.0	116 33 27.1	541465E	3619865N	11
02	0.4	32 42 55.5	116 33 45.5	540988E	3619633N	11
03	1.0	32 42 46.1	116 33 27.3	541464E	3619346N	11

62. MCCAIN VALLEY

Wpt.	Mile	Latitude North	Longitude West	UTM Easting	UTM Northing	Zone
01	0	32 41 45.0	116 15 31.4	569487E	3617620N	11
02	6.4	32 46 16.2	116 16 58.5	567161E	3625955N	11
03	10.5	32 48 00.7	116 20 14.7	562037E	3629140N	11
04	12.2	32 49 24.4	116 20 40.3	561356E	3631713N	11

63. TABLE MOUNTAIN

Wpt.	Mile	Latitude North	Longitude West	UTM Easting	UTM Northing	Zone
01	0	32 38 09.7	116 07 00.6	582841E	3611092N	11
02	2.3	32 39 27.4	116 07 30.0	582057E	3613480N	11
03	3.9	32 40 15.7	116 08 26.5	580572E	3614954N	11
04	4.6	32 40 07.1	116 09 00.2	579696E	3614683N	11
05	5.8	32 39 60.0	116 10 00.9	578119E	3614448N	11
06	6.2	32 39 53.3	116 10 23.6	577528E	3614239N	11

64. SMUGGLERS CAVE/ ELLIOT MINE

Wpt.	Mile	Latitude North	Longitude West	UTM Easting	UTM Northing	Zone
01	0	32 38 23.4	116 06 22.8	583825E	3611524N	11
02	1.6	32 37 57.5	116 05 45.1	584812E	3610733N	11
03	2.4	32 37 36.1	116 05 12.4	585671E	3610082N	11
04	3.2	32 37 23.6	116 04 44.8	586393E	3609704N	11

65. SUPERSTITION MOUNTAIN LOOP

Wpt.	Mile	Latitude North	Longitude West	UTM Easting	UTM Northing	Zone
01	0	32 55 33.3	115 48 35.8	611267E	3643512N	11
02	2.5	32 55 44.4	115 46 22.6	614723E	3643892N	11

274

Wpt.	Mile	Latitude North	Longitude West	UTM Easting	UTM Northing	Zone
03	6.2	32 57 38.2	115 48 42.0	611065E	3647355N	11
04	7.4	32 58 04.2	115 49 37.8	609606E	3648140N	11
05	7.7	32 58 08.0	115 49 53.6	609197E	3648254N	11
06	9.7	32 58 34.7	115 51 36.1	606527E	3649045N	11
07	10.9	32 58 34.1	115 52 44.3	604755E	3649009N	11
08	12.1	32 57 40.0	115 52 20.4	605391E	3647343N	11
09	12.8	32 57 36.8	115 51 34.5	606585E	3647264N	11
10	13.6	32 57 19.2	115 50 53.3	607662E	3646733N	11
11	1.2	32 56 32.8	115 48 29.5	611411E	3645346N	11
12	1.8	32 56 40.7	115 47 57.2	612248E	3645597N	11
13	2.6	32.57 01.3	115 48 22.2	611591E	3646225N	11
14	3.2	32 57 14.9	115 48 08.7	611938E	3646648N	11
15	3.6	32 57 27.2	115 48 14.8	611774E	3647024N	11
16	0.3	32 57 25.9	115 48 45.3	610984E	3646975N	11
17	0.1	32 58 02.1	115 49 53.1	609210E	3648070N	11

66. SAND DAM CANYON

Wpt.	Mile	Latitude North	Longitude West	UTM Easting	UTM Northing	Zone
01	0	32 58 04.3	115 49 37.4	609616E	3648144N	11
02	0.9	32 57 38.3	115 49 56.5	609131E	3647336N	11
03	1.7	32 57 22.0	115 50 10.0	608787E	3646831N	11

67. KNOCK-ON-WOOD

Wpt.	Mile	Latitude North	Longitude West	UTM Easting	UTM Northing	Zone
01	0	32 58 34.7	115 51 36.1	606526E	3649045N	11
02	0.6	32 58 12.5	115 51 33.5	606601E	3648362N	11
03	0.7	32 58 09.3	115 51 37.9	606487E	3648263N	11
04	1.0	32 58 05.5	115 51 44.9	606307E	3648144N	11
05	1.6	32 57 42.3	115 51 43.1	606360E	3647431N	11
06	2.0	32 57 41.0	115 51 20.5	606949E	3647397N	11
07	2.3	32 57 36.8	115 51 34.7	606581E	3647263N	11

68. SAND HIGHWAY

Wpt.	Mile	Latitude North	Longitude West	UTM Easting	UTM Northing	Zone
01	0	32 54 32.2	115 06 54.6	676270E	3642577N	11
02	13.4	32 45 58.1	114 57 55.0	690596E	3627002N	11
03	2.0	32 47 00.3	114 56 40.2	692507E	3628954N	11
04	18.3	32 42 46.6	114 56 31.8	692876E	3621147N	11

69. GLAMIS/ OLDSMOBILE HILL

Wpt.	Mile	Latitude North	Longitude West	UTM Easting	UTM Northing	Zone
01	0	32 59 34.6	115 04 44.7	679475E	3651953N	11
02	0.7	32 59 36.5	115 05 22.8	678485E	3651992N	11
03	3.1	32 57 49.4	115 05 51.7	677795E	3648681N	11

70. LAST CHANCE CANYON

Wpt.	Mile	Latitude North	Longitude West	UTM Easting	UTM Northing	Zone
01	0	35 21 42.4	117 53 51.7	418444E	3913336N	11
02	3.7	35 23 59.2	117 55 20.5	416243E	3917569N	11
03	7.8	35 26 13.4	117 54 10.6	418043E	3921688N	11
04	8.7	35 25 60.0	117 53 24.8	419194E	3921254N	11

Wpt.	Mile	Latitude North	Longitude West	UTM Easting	UTM Northing	Zone
05	10.2	35 25 13.8	117 52 18.5	420852E	3919828N	11
06	11.1	35 24 38.2	117 52 30.9	420530E	3918732N	11
07	13.8	35 26 07.7	117 51 12.4	422533E	3921472N	11
08	14.5	35 26 11.7	117 50 31.9	423557E	3921587N	11
09	18.8	35 23 19.1	117 48 57.7	425888E	3916249N	11

71. TRONA PINNACLES

Wpt.	Mile	Latitude North	Longitude West	UTM Easting	UTM Northing	Zone
01	0	35 40 53.3	117 23 26.1	464656E	3948492N	11
02	5.0	35 37 06.8	117 22 21.3	466257E	3941506N	11

72. DUMONT DUNES

Wpt.	Mile	Latitude North	Longitude West	UTM Easting	UTM Northing	Zone
01	4.2	35 41 33.7	116 14 05.1	569238E	3949935N	11

73. SPERRY WASH

Wpt.	Mile	Latitude North	Longitude West	UTM Easting	UTM Northing	Zone
01	0	35 41 55.8	116 15 05.6	567714E	3950605N	11
02	4.1	35 44 27.8	116 13 14.3	570473E	3955308N	11
03	4.5	35 44 46.8	116 13 12.7	570510E	3955896N	11
04	11.8	35 47 06.1	116 08 19.9	577826E	3960246N	11
05	15.6	35 48 03.7	116 05 50.8	581551E	3962056N	11
06	24.6	35 50 54.3	116 13 28.9	570013E	3967213N	11
07	29.1	35 53 57.8	116 15 26.9	567010E	3972845N	11

74. SLEDGEHAMMER

Wpt.	Mile	Latitude North	Longitude West	UTM Easting	UTM Northing	Zone
01	0	34 22 07.5	116 32 41.2	541857E	3802942N	11
02	3.9	34 24 47.7	116 30 50.0	544676E	3807889N	11
03	6.4	34 24 52.5	116 28 24.8	548381E	3808056N	11
04	0.9	34 24 28.2	116 28 03.2	548936E	3807310N	11
05	2.1	34 24 31.0	116 27 33.5	549694E	3807389N	11
06	3.3	34 25 13.2	116 27 30.0	549785E	3808701N	11
07	5.1	34 26 13.2	116 27 23.3	549938E	3810549N	11
08	7.9	34 27 19.9	116 29 45.6	546295E	3812588N	11
09	10.0	34 25 52.8	116 30 13.7	545593E	3809898N	11
10	11.0	34 25 14.6	116 30 51.8	544625E	3808718N	11

75. BERDOO CANYON

Wpt.	Mile	Latitude North	Longitude West	UTM Easting	UTM Northing	Zone
01	0	34 00 21.9	116 05 02.5	584586E	3763014N	11
02	5.6	33 55 38.9	116 04 33.3	585414E	3754304N	11
03	8.0	33 54 37.8	116 03 23.9	587211E	3752437N	11
04	13.2	33 50 35.8	116 03 27.8	587182E	3744983N	11
05	19.5	33 49 50.2	116 08 14.7	579818E	3743515N	11
06	23.4	33 47 59.2	116 11 05.2	575463E	3740061N	11

Glossary

A.C.E.C. Area of Critical Environmental Concern

Adventure Pass - A special permit required if you stop to recreate along a route in Angeles, Los Padres, Cleveland and San Bernardino National Forests. No permit required if you are just passing through.

Airing down - Letting air out of your tires to improve traction.

Articulation - Flexibility of your suspension system. Greater articulation keeps your wheels on the ground on undulating terrain. Also referred to as *wheel-travel*.

ATV - All-terrain vehicle. Also called a *quad*.

BLM - Bureau of Land Management.

Cairn - A stack of rocks that marks an obscure trail.

Clevis - A U-shaped device with a pin at one end that is used to connect tow straps.

Come-along - A hand-operated ratchet that functions as a winch.

Dispersed camping - Free camping on public lands away from developed recreation facilities. Usually limited to 14 days or less depending upon area. Camp near existing roads and use existing sites whenever possible. Pack out your trash.

Dry camping -Camping where no water is provided.

Dual-purpose motorcycle - A street-legal dirt bike.

Green Sticker - A special license for vehicles not equipped for highway use. Includes ATVs, dirt bikes, sand rails, dune buggies and snowmobiles.

High centered - When your undercarriage gets stuck on a rock, mound, log, or ridge. Usually requires you to jack up your vehicle to get free.

High-lift jack - A tool that allows you to quickly lift your vehicle high off the ground. Considered a necessity on hard-core trails. Also substitutes for a winch.

Lift - A vehicle modification that raises the suspension or body of a vehicle to provide greater ground clearance.

Locker - Optional gearing installed inside your differential that equalizes power to wheels on both sides of an axle. Eliminates loss of power when climbing steep undulating hills. Not the same as locking-in your hubs.

Low range - A second range of gears that increases the power of your vehicle. Used for climbing steep grades, especially at higher altitude.

Mortero - Indian grinding hole. Depressions in rock formed by pounding grain or seeds with an elongated rock or pestle.

OHV - Off Highway Vehicle.

Petroglyphs - Native American motifs abraded into rock surfaces.

Red Sticker - Same as Green Sticker except riding days are limited. Check with each specific OHV area for specific dates when riding is not permitted.

Skid plates - Plates that protect vulnerable parts of your undercarriage.

Snatch block - A pulley that opens so it can be slipped over your winch cable.

Street legal vehicle - Any vehicle equipped and licensed to drive on the highway.

SVRA - State Vehicular Recreation Area.

Switchback - A tight turn on a zigzag road that climbs a steep grade.

Tow point, tow hook - A point on your vehicle that enables you to quickly and safely attach a tow strap. Considered a basic necessity for four-wheeling.

References & Reading

4-Wheeler's Guide, Trails of the San Bernardino Mountains, by William C. Teie, Deer Valley Press, Rescue, CA. Includes color maps, photos and illustrations of 20 4WD trails in the San Bernardino Mountains. (ISBN 0-9640709-6-0, 1999)

Afoot & Afield in San Diego County, by Jerry Schad, Wilderness Press, Berkeley, CA. Comprehensive hiking guide with maps and photos. Includes 220 hiking trails in San Diego County. (ISBN 0-89997-229-2, revised 1998)

Anza-Borrego A to Z, by Diana Lindsay, Sunbelt Publications, San Diego, CA. Comprehensive directory of place names and history of the Anza-Borrego Desert. Companion to *Anza-Borrego Desert Region.* (ISBN 0-932653-38-3, 2001)

(The) Anza-Borrego Desert Region, by Lowell & Diana Lindsay, Wilderness Press, Berkeley, CA. Comprehensive guide to Anza-Borrego Desert State Park and surrounding region. Includes maps and photos of hiking trails and backroads. (ISBN 0-89997-187-3, revised 1998)

California Coastal Byways, By Tony Huegel, The Post Company, Idaho Falls, ID. Covers 50 SUV backroads near California's coast. Guidebook includes maps and photos. (ISBN 0-9636560-5-8, revised 1996)

California Desert Byways, By Tony Huegel, The Post Company, Idaho Falls, ID. Covers 50 SUV backroads in California desert regions. Guidebook includes maps and photos. (ISBN 0-9636560-3-1, revised 1996)

Death Valley In '49, by William Lewis Manly, Heyday Books, Berkeley, CA. Fascinating first person account of wagon trip across the western U.S. in 1849. Includes harrowing stories of life and death situations that occurred while crossing Death Valley. (ISBN 1-890771-47-3, latest printing in 2001)

Death Valley SUV Trails, by Roger Mitchell, Track & Trail Publications, Oakhurst, CA. Covers 46 SUV backroads in Death Valley. Guidebook includes maps and photos. (ISBN 0-9707115-0-6, 2001).

Desert Survival Handbook, by Charles A. Lehman, Primer Publishers, Phoenix, AZ. A basic guide to desert survival. (ISBN 0-935810-34-X, 1996)

Glovebox Guide to Unpaved Southern California, by Harry Lewellyn, Glovebox Publications, Santa Ana, CA. Four-wheel-drive roads of southern California as they were in 1987. Includes maps and 101 unrated roads. (Out of print)

GPS Made Easy by Lawrence Letham, published by the Mountaineers, Seattle, WA. Hundred-page handbook covers the basics of GPS. (1998)

(A) Guide to California Off-Road Adventures, California State Parks, Sacramento, CA. Full-color, fold-out map of all OHV areas in California. (Revised annually)

Mojave Road Guide, An Adventure Through Time, by Dennis G. Casebier, Tales of the Mojave Road Publishing Company, Essex, CA. A comprehensive guide to the Mojave Road with detailed maps, photos and history. (ISBN 0-914224-29-8, 1999)

Road Guide to Joshua Tree National Park, by Barbara and Robert Decker, Double Decker Press, Mariposa, CA. Small guide to all roads inside Joshua Tree National Park. Includes photos and a few maps. (ISBN 1-888898-05-4, 1999)

Sidekick Off-Road Maps, by Rick Russell, Sidekick, Chino, CA. Individual folded maps include directions and photos of specific areas including: Arrowhead, Big Bear Lake, Calico Mountains, Panamint Mountains and more. (Dates vary)

Addresses & Phone Numbers

(Note: All information correct as of Jan. 1, 2003.)

Bureau of Land Management
Web site: www.blm.gov

California State Office
2800 Cottage Way, Suite W1834
Sacramento, CA 95825-1886
(916) 978-4400

Bakersfield Field Office
3801 Pegasus Drive
Bakersfield, CA 93308
(661) 391-6000

Barstow Field Office
2601 Barstow Road
Barstow, CA 92311
(760) 252-6000

El Centro Field Office
1661 South Fourth Street
El Centro, CA 92243
(760) 337-4400

Needles Field Office
101 W. Spikes Road
Needles, CA 92363
(760) 326-7000

Palm Springs, South Coast Field Office
690 W. Garnet, P.O. Box 581260
North Palm Springs, CA 92258-1260
(760) 251-4800

Ridgecrest Field Office
300 South Richmond Road
Ridgecrest, CA 93555
(760) 384-5400

Chambers of Commerce
Azusa - (626) 334-1507
Bakersfield - (661) 327-4421
Barstow - (760) 256-8617
Big Bear - (909) 866-4607
Brawley - (760) 344-3160
Death Valley - (760) 852-4524
El Centro - (760) 352-3681
Glendora - (626)-963-4128
Hesperia - (760) 244-2135
Indio - (760) 347-0676
Lake Arrowhead - (909) 337-3715
Lake Elsinore - (909) 245-8848

Los Angeles - (213) 580-7500
Palm Springs - (760) 325-1577
Pasadena - (626) 795-3355
Ramona - (760) 789-1311
Redlands - (909) 793-2546
Ridgecrest - (760) 375-8331
San Bernardino - (909) 885-7515
San Diego - (619) 544-1300
Santa Barbara - (805) 965-3023
Twentynine Palms - (760) 367-3445
Victorville - (760) 245-6506
Yucca Valley - (760) 365-6323

Maps, Books & GPS Sources

4X4*BOOKS*.com
(308) 381-4410
Fax: (877) 787-2993

All Topo Maps (iGage Map Corp.)
P.O. Box 58596
Salt Lake City, UT 84158
(888) 450-4922, www.igage.com

DeLorme Mapping
P. O. Box 298
Yarmouth, ME 04096
(207) 846-7000, www.delorme.com

Garmin International
1200 E. 151st Street
Olathe, KS 66062
(800) 800-1020, www.garmin.com

Lowrance Electronics, Inc.
12000 E. Skelly Drive
Tulsa, OK 74128-1703
(800) 324-1356, www.lowrance.com

Magellan Corporation
960 Overland Court
San Dimas, CA 91773
(909) 394-5000, www.magellangps.com

Maptech
10 Industrial Way.
Amesbury, MA 01913
(888) 839-5551, www.maptech.com

National Geographic Maps
P.O. 4357
Evergreen, CO 80437 1-800-962-1643
www.nationalgeographic.com/maps

OziExplorer
www.oziexplorer.com
oziexp.html (in Australia)

Wide World of Maps, Inc.
2626 West Indian School Road
Phoenix, AZ 85017-4397   (602) 279-2323

National Parks/ Preserves
Web site: www.nps.gov
Death Valley National Park
P.O. Box 579
Death Valley, CA 92328-0579
(760) 786-2331

Joshua Tree National Park
74485 National Park Drive
Twentynine Palms, CA 92277
(760) 367-5500

Mojave National Preserve
222 E. Main Street, Suite 202
Barstow, CA 92311
(760) 255-8801

Off-Highway Vehicle Areas
Corral Canyon OHV Area
Cleveland National Forest
Descanso Ranger District
(619) 445-6235

Dumont Dunes OHV Area
BLM Barstow Field Office
(760) 252-6000

Imperial Sand Dunes Recreation Area
BLM El Centro Field Office
(760) 337-4400
    Cahuilla Ranger Station (760) 344-3919
    Glamis Beach Store (760) 344-9090
    Pair-A-Dice Store (760) 572-5332

Johnson Valley OHV Area
BLM Barstow Field Office
(760) 252-6000

Lark Canyon OHV Area (McCain Valley)
BLM El Centro Field Office
(760) 337-4400

Rasor OHV Area
BLM Barstow Field Office
(760) 252-6000

Rowher Flat OHV Area
Angeles National Forest
Santa Clara/ Mojave River Ranger District
(661) 296-9710

Stoddard Valley OHV Area
BLM Barstow Field Office
(760) 252-6000

Superstition Mountain OHV Area
BLM El Centro Field Office
(760) 337-4400

State Parks/ SVRAs
Web site: www.parks.ca.gov

California Department of Parks & Recreation
Off-Highway Motor Vehicle Recreation Division
(OHMVR)
P.O. Box 942896
Sacramento, CA 94296-0001
(916) 324-4442

Anza-Borrego Desert State Park
200 Palm Canyon Drive
Borrego Springs, CA 92004
(760) 767-5311

Hungry Valley State Vehicle Recreation Area
P.O. Box 1360
Lebec, CA 93243
(661) 248-7007

Ocotillo Wells State Vehicle Recreation Area
P.O. Box 360
Borrego Springs, CA 92004
(760) 767-5391

Red Rock Canyon State Park
(Mojave Desert Information Center)
43779 15th Street West
Lancaster, CA 93534
(661) 942-0662 (Menu selection #3)

Refugio State Beach
10 Refugio Beach Road
Goleta,CA 93117 (805) 968-1033

Silverwood Lake State Recreation Area
14651 Cedar Circle
Hesperia, CA 92345
(760) 389-2281

U.S. Forest Service
Web site: www.fs.fed.us
Angeles National Forest Supervisors Office
701 N. Santa Anita Avenue
Arcadia, CA 91006
(626) 574-1613
Adventure Pass (626) 574-5200

San Gabriel River Ranger District
110 N. Wabash Avenue
Glendora, CA 91741, (626) 335-1251

Saugus Ranger District
30800 Bouquet Canyon Road
Saugus,CA 91350, (661) 296-9710

Cleveland National Forest Supervisors Office
10845 Rancho Bernardo Road, Suite 200
San Diego, CA 92127-2107
(858) 674-2901
Adventure Pass (858) 673-6180

Descanso Ranger District
3348 Alpine Road
Alpine, CA 91901
(619) 445-6235

Palomar Ranger District
1634 Black Canyon Road
Ramona, CA 92065
(760) 788-0250

Trabuco Ranger District
1147 E. 6th Street
Corona,CA 92879
(909) 736-1811

Los Padres National Forest Supervisors Office
6755 Hollister Avenue, Suite 150
Goleta, CA 93117
(805) 968-6640, (Adventure Pass same number)

Mt. Pinos Ranger District
34580 Lockwood Valley Road
Frazier Park, CA 93225
(661) 245-3731

Santa Barbara Ranger District
3505 Paradise Road
Santa Barbara, CA 93105
(805) 967-3481

San Bernardino Nat. Forest Supervisors Office
1824 S. Commercenter Circle
San Bernardino, CA 92408-3430
(909) 383-5588, (Adventure Pass same number)

Arrowhead Ranger District
28104 Highway 18, P.O. Box 350
Skyforest, CA 92385
(909) 337-2444

Big Bear Ranger District
41397 North Shore Drive, Highway 38
P.O. Box 290
Fawnskin, CA 92333
(909) 866-3437

Cajon Ranger District (Lytle Creek)
1209 Lytle Creek Road
Lytle Creek, CA 92358
(909) 887-2576

4-Wheel-Drive Associations

Blue Ribbon Coalition
www.sharetrails.org
(208) 237-1008

California Association of 4-Wheel Drive Clubs
www.cal4wheel.com
(800) 494-3866

California Off-Road Vehicle Association
(CORVA)
www.corva.org

National Off-Highway Vehicle Conservation Council
www.nohvcc.org
(800) 348-6487

San Diego Off-Road Coalition
www.sdorc.org
(619) 562-2528

Tread Lightly
www.treadlightly.org
(800) 966-9900

4-Wheel-Drive Clubs

(For a complete listing of over 140 clubs in California, go to **www.cal4wheel.com**)

Riverside 4-Wheelers
www.riverside4wheelers.org
E-mail - stevecj846@aol.com

San Diego 4-Wheelers
www.sd4wheel.com
Email: webmaster@sd4wheel.com

Tierra Del Sol 4-Wheel Drive Club
P.O.Box 4371
San Diego, CA 92164
www.tds4x4.com
E-mail: webmaster@tds4x4.com

Victor Valley 4-Wheelers
See state web site www.cal4wheel.com
(760) 948-1424 (Leave message)

4-Wheel-Drive Guide Service

Western Adventures
4 x 4 Driving School and Guide Service
P.O. Box 2451
Ramona, CA 92065
(760) 789-1563
www.4westernadventures.com

Index

A

Achy-Breaky 82, 83, 100-103
Adopt-a-Cabin 33, 44, 46, 47, 48, 51, 52, 54, 55
Adopt-a-Trail 133
Adventure Pass 14, 16, 277, 280, 281
Afton Canyon 114-117
Agua Caliente Springs 59, 62, 63
Aha Macav Parkway 107, 109
Airing Down 27, 28, 277
Alamo Mountain Loop 59, 66-69
Amargosa 41
Amargosa Canyon 250, 251
Anvil Spring 52, 53
Anza-Borrego Desert State Park 16, 164, 165, 186, 187, 278, 280
Archaeological Sites 22
Arrastras 158, 159
Articulation 13,140,170,277
Aspen Glen Picnic Area 156, 157
ATVs (All Terrain Vehicles) 13, 14, 76, 133, 184, 226, 277
Automobile Club of Southern California 17, 112, 116, 235
Avi Casino 107, 109
Azusa 120, 121

B

Badwater Road 54, 55
Ballarat 32, 33, 48, 49, 258
Banner 188, 189
Barker Ranch 50-53
Barstow 82, 83
Beatty, NV 35, 42
Berdoo Canyon 238, 239, 256, 257
Bert Smith Cabin 110, 111, 113
Big Bear 16, 132, 133, 144, 279, 281
Big Pine Flat Campground 134, 135
Bismarck Mine 84, 86, 87
Blair Valley 190-193
Blow Sand Hill 179, 181
Blue Canyon 62
Blu-In Park 177, 180
Bobcat Meadow Campground 214-217
Borrego Badlands 165, 174, 175
Borrego Springs 164
Bouquet Reservoir 77, 78
Briggs Cabin 46-49

Briggs Mine 51, 56
Broadcast Peak 60, 61
Bronco Peak 187, 214, 215
Burro Schmidt Tunnel 240-243
Butler Peak 144, 145
Butte Valley 54, 55
Buttercup Valley 15, 234, 235
Butterfield Stage Route 191-193, 201
Buttes Pass 176, 177

C

Cairn 105, 248, 277
Cajon Junction 126, 127
Calamity Canyon 122-125
Calcite Mine 168, 169
Calico Ghost Town 82, 83
Calico Mountains 82, 83
Calico Peak 98
California Association of 4-Wheel Drive Clubs 101, 281
Camp Rock 85, 99
Campfires 22
Canyon Sin Nombre 200, 201
Carl Mengel 52
Carrizo Badlands 200, 201
Carrizo Gorge 206, 207, 209, 218, 219, 220, 221
Caruthers Canyon 111, 113
CB Radio 19, 21, 286
Cedar Canyon Road 111-113
Cellphones 19
Charles Manson 50-53
Checklist 20
Chloride City 36, 37
Chloride Cliff 36, 37
Clair Camp 47
Clarks Grade 154, 155
Clarks Summit 152-155
Cleghorn Ridge 119, 126, 127
Colter Spring 48, 49
Competition Hill 236
Cooper Mine 48, 49
Corona Mine 44, 45
Corral Canyon 15, 186, 187, 210-217
Cottonwood Canyon 38, 39
Cottonwood Recreation Site 218, 219
Crab Flats Campground 138, 139, 141, 143
Cross Over Trail 184, 185

Crossing Streams 26
Cucamonga Big Tree Trail 119, 122-125

D

Death Valley National Park 15, 32, 33, 280
Deep Creek 138, 139
Dehydration 20
DeLorme Atlas & Gazetteer 17, 263
Dennis G. Casebier 105, 278
Desert Garden 166, 167
Desert Magazine 192
Desert Survival 18, 278
Desert Tortoise 22, 83
Devil's Slide 179, 181
Diablo Dropoff 202-205
Dishpan Springs 132, 133, 138, 139
Divide Peak OHV Area 62, 63
Doran Loop 82, 83, 88-91, 259
Dos Cabezas 206-209
Dumont Dunes 15, 239, 246, 247, 280
Dutchman Campground 66, 67

E

Early Man Archaeological Site 98, 99
Echo Pass 40-43
Elk Ridge 66
Elliot Mine 187, 222, 223
Espinosa Trail 210, 211, 213
Eye of the Needle 40, 41

F

Fawnskin 141-145
Fireplug (The) 170-173
Fish Canyon Escape Trail 56, 57
Fish Creek Wash 195-197, 198, 199, 204
Flash Floods 18, 162, 199
Fonts Point 174, 175
Fort Irwin Road 86, 87
Fort Piute 106-109
Frazier Park 65-67
Furnace Creek 16, 32, 33
Furnace Creek Ranch 42, 43

G

Gecko Road 234-237
Geologist's Cabin 52-55
Geology Tour 256, 257
Ghost Mountain 192
Gibraltar Road 62, 63
Glamis 224, 225, 236, 237
Glamis Beach Store 234, 237
Glendora 121
Goat Canyon Trestle 206-209
Goffs 108, 109
Gold Hill Mine 54, 55

Gold Mountain 150, 151
Goler Wash 50-53
Gorman 70, 71
Government Holes 110-113
GPS 12, 17, 260-276
Grand View Loop 156, 157
Grand View Point 156, 157
Granites (The) 116, 117
Grapevine Canyon 134, 135
Green Sticker 13, 277
Green Valley (Lake Arrowhead) 141, 143
Green Valley (North of L.A.) 75-77

H

Hammers (The) 252-255
Hanna Flat Campground 134, 142, 143
Hantavirus 51
Heart Attack Hill 194-197
Heartbreak Ridge 158-161
Hells Gate 32, 37
Hidden Valley 84, 85, 93, 98
High Centered 24
High Desert Roundup 88, 100, 101
Holcomb Creek 132, 133, 140-143
Hungry Valley SVRA 15, 59, 67, 70, 280
Hyperthermia 19, 20
Hypothermia 20

I

Imperial Sand Dunes 14, 15, 17, 224, 225,
234-237, 280
Impossible Railroad (The) 208
Indian Truck Trail 130, 131
Inyo Mine 40-43
Irwin Turkey Farm 107, 109
Ivanpah Road 107-111

J

Jackass Canyon Road 115, 117
Jackhammer 252-255
Jackpot Canyon 47, 49
Jacoby Canyon 148, 149
Jail Canyon 44, 45
Joe Elliot Campground 122-125
John Bull 132, 133, 146, 147
Johnson Valley 15, 239, 252-255, 280, 286
Joshua Tree National Park 16, 239, 256,
257, 278, 280
Julian 186, 187

K

Kabob Hill 66, 67
Kelbaker Road 111, 113
Kelso Sand Dunes 111
Kelso-Cima Road 112, 113

Kinevan Road 60, 61
Knock-on-Wood 232, 233
Kramer Arch 96, 97

L

Lake Arrowhead 132, 133, 136, 137
Lake Cachuma 60
Lake Elizabeth 73
Lake Elsinore 118, 119, 130, 131
Lake Hughes 73
Lanfair Valley 106, 108, 109
Lark Canyon 218, 219, 280
Last Chance Canyon 238, 239, 240-243
Leadfield 34, 35
Liebre Mountain 72, 73
Lightning 18, 124
Locker (differential locker) 13, 277, 286
Lockwood/ Miller Jeep Trail 58, 59, 64-67
Lookout Towers 144, 187, 210
Los Pinos Lookout 187, 210-213
Lotus Mine 4, 50, 51-53
Lower Coyote Canyon 166, 167
Lower Largo Flats 141, 143
Lucerne Valley 134, 135
Lucky Baldwin (Doble) Mine 148, 149
Lytle Creek Road 123-125

M

Mail Box (Mojave Road) 110, 112, 113
Mail Box (Sledgehammer) 252, 254, 255
Maintenance of Vehicle 21
Marble Canyon 38, 39
Marl Springs 110-113
Marshal South Home 191-193
McCain Valley 218, 219
MDA Offroad for Hope 179
Means Dry Lake 253, 255
Mechanical Problems 19
Mengel Pass 50-53
Middle Park 48, 49
Miller Jeep Trail 64-67
Mojave National Preserve 16, 17, 104, 280
Mojave Road 17, 104-117
Mojave Road Guide 105, 278
Monarch Canyon 36, 37
Mortero Wash 206-209
Morteros 122, 124, 191, 192, 208, 277
Mud Caves 202-205
Mud Pots 178-181
Mule Canyon Cut-Across 96, 97
Mule Canyon Road 82, 83, 98, 99
Myers Ranch 52, 53

N

Nature Calls 22
Needles Highway 107, 109
Newman Cabin 51, 53

O

Ocotillo Wells 164, 165
Ocotillo Wells SVRA 15, 178-181
Odessa Canyon 82, 83, 92-95
OHV 6, 13, 14, 15, 59, 277
Old Ridge Route 72, 73
Oriflamme Canyon 188, 189

P

Pacific Crest Trail 73, 127, 189
Painted Cave 63
Pair-a-Dice 234, 235
Palm Wash 169, 172, 173
Panamint Mountains 16, 33, 36
Panamint Valley 56, 57
Panamint Valley Days 33
Patton Valley 234, 235
Peace Valley Road 70, 71
Penny Can Tree 106-109
Petroglyphs 35, 107, 277
Phillips Loop 82, 83, 96, 97
Pictograph Hiking Trail 190-193
Pictographs 190, 191, 207, 208
Pilot Rock Road 128, 129
Pinnacles OHV Area 136, 137
Pinyon Dropoff 194-197
Pinyon Mountain Road 187, 194-197
Pioneertown 162, 163
Pleasant Canyon 46-49
Pronghorn Trail 59, 70, 71
Pumpkin Patch 182, 183

Q

Quail Lake 72, 73

R

Radford Truck Trail 155
Rancho del Cielo 61
Rancho Dos Vista 60, 61
Randsburg 240-243
Rasor OHV Area 16, 115, 117, 280
Rattlesnake Canyon 62, 63, 162, 163
Red Sticker 14, 277
Redlands Canyon 54, 55
Refugio Pass 60, 61
Rhyolite 42
Ridgecrest 241-243
Rincon-Shortcut Road 119, 120, 121
Rock Garden (Achy-Breaky) 102, 103
Rock Garden (Holcomb Creek) 140, 141

Rock Springs 110-113
Rodriguez Canyon 188, 189
Ronald Reagan's Ranch 60, 61
Rowher Flat 15, 74-81, 280
Russel Camp 33, 51-55

S

Salton City 171-173, 181
San Bernardino Nat. Forest 16, 132, 133
San Gabriel Canyon OHV Area 120, 121
Sand Dam Canyon 230, 231
Sand Dunes (Driving on) 27
Sand Highway 234, 235
Sand Slide Canyon 226-229, 232, 233
Sandstone Canyon 198, 199
Santa Barbara 58-63
Santa Ynez Peak 59-61
Santiago Peak 119, 130, 131
Sawmill Mountain Road 73
Schwaub Townsite 42, 43
Scissors Crossing 195, 197
Seldom Seen Sam 48
Seward Mountain 68, 69
Shaw Pass 114, 115
Sheep Canyon 166, 167
Shell Reef 180-182
Sidekick Maps 278
Sidewinder 187, 216, 217
Sierra Pelona Road 78-81
Silverwood Lake State Recreation Area
126-129
Skyline Drive 156, 157
Sledgehammer Canyon 238, 239, 252-255
Slot (The) 176, 177
Smugglers Cave 187, 222, 223
Soda Dry Lake 105, 114, 115
South Park 46-49
Sperry Wash 238, 239, 248-251
Split Mountain 195-197, 198, 199
Spotter (Using a) 23
Squaw Tank 256, 257
Squeeze (Heartbreak Ridge) 158, 159
Squeeze (Pinyon Mtn.) 31, 187, 194-196
Staircase (The) 102, 103
Stoddard Valley OHV Area 82, 83, 100-103, 280
Stoddard Wells 15, 100-103
Stovepipe Wells 16, 33, 39
Street Legal 13, 187, 277
Striped Butte 54, 55
Sunset Campground 66, 67
Superstition Mountain 15, 224-229

Superstition Mountain Loop 226-229
SVRA (State Vehicular Recreation Area)
15, 179, 277, 280
Sweetwater Spring 86, 87

T

Table Mountain 220, 221
Tecopa Hot Springs 248-251
Thorndike Mine 48, 49
Tierra Del Sol Desert Safari 165, 170, 171
Tin Can Alley 85, 87, 98, 99
Tippy Situations 25, 70, 139, 253
Titus Canyon 34, 35
Tow Strap Hill 230, 231
Trail Etiquette 23
Traveler's Monument 115-117
Tread Lightly 21, 281
Trona Pinnacles 239, 244, 245
Truckhaven 165, 170, 171
Twentynine Palms 256, 257

U

U.S. Border Patrol 187
UTM (Universal Transverse Mercator) 261

V

Vallecito Mountains 194
Valley of the Moon 222, 223
Victorville 7, 279
Volunteer Gate 150

W

Wall Street Canyon 84-87
Walter Knott 86
Warm Springs Camp 54, 55
Washboard Roads 28
Watson Wash 110, 111, 113
West Camino Cielo Road 60, 61
William Manly 57
Willow Creek Road 136, 137
Winching 28
Wind Caves 198, 199
Wingate Road 47-49, 57
World Beater Mine 47, 49

Y

Yaquitepec 192, 193
Yellowjacket Trail 65, 67
Yermo 85-87, 98, 99
Yucca Valley 162, 163

285

The Author & His Vehicles

Charles A. Wells graduated from Ohio State University in 1969 with a degree in graphic design. After practicing design in Ohio, he moved to Colorado Springs, CO, in 1980 and worked 18 years in the printing business. Over the years, he and his family enjoyed a wide array of recreational activities including hiking, biking, rafting, and skiing. He bought his first SUV in 1994 and immediately got hooked exploring Colorado's remote backcountry. He later joined a four-wheel-drive club, did more traveling and learned about hard-core four-wheeling. This book follows four successful backroad guidebooks—two on Colorado, one on Arizona and one on Moab, Utah.

The author drives all the trails himself, writes the directions, shoots the photos and draws the maps. As a result, his guidebooks include meaningful detail and are extraordinarily accurate. The vehicles he used to drive the trails, over the years, are shown below.

Author with 1994 Jeep Grand Cherokee, Engineer's Pass, CO. Factory equipped with automatic transmission, skid plates and tow points. Author added CB radio and LT235-75R15 BFG all-terrain tires. (Note: Author has replaced this vehicle with a new stock Grand Cherokee you'll see in future books.)

1995 Jeep Cherokee on Soldiers Pass, Sedona, AZ. Equipped with Tomken 5″ lift, bumpers, rocker skids, tire carrier, and brush guard; 8,000 lb. Warn winch; Dana 44 rear axle; 410 gears; ARBs front & rear; Tera Low 4/1 transfer case; skid plates; stock 4-liter engine; K&N air filter; interior roll cage; 33 x 10.50 BFG A/T tires; tow points; fold-in mirrors; and CB radio.

2001 Jeep Wrangler on Sledgehammer, Johnson Valley, CA. Equipped with TeraFlex 3″ lift with long-arm kit, 9,000 lb. Warn winch, Dana 44 rear axle; 410 gears, Tera Low 4/1 transfer case, ARB lockers front and rear, skid plates with Predator high-clearance transmission cross member, High-Country rocker panel guards, Curry bumpers, Alumiflex tie rod, Xenon extended flairs, stock 4-liter engine, 33 x 12.50 BFG A/T tires and CB radio. (Author's note: I finally wore out my much-loved Cherokee at left and replaced it with the smaller Wrangler for easier towing behind my motorhome.)

286